A BANTAM PATHFINDER EDITION

THE GREAT GERMAN ACE AND THE FIGHTING CANADIAN

On April 20, 1918, the "Flying Baron" celebrated his eightieth personal victory with a luxurious champagne dinner. The next morning, as usual, he led his dreaded German Fokkers out on patrol. Almost immediately they fell upon a small group of Allied observation planes.

Two miles above, hidden by the clouds, Roy Brown, a young Canadian flight commander in the newly formed Royal Air Force, saw the unequal battle below.

Roy Brown and his men were outnumbered. The German planes were faster and better, the pilots more experienced. But Brown waggled his wings, peeled off, and began his two-mile dive, roaring down out of the sun, on to the tail of the famous red fighting plane of Baron von Richthofen, himself . . .

BANTAM PATHFINDER EDITIONS

Bantam Pathfinder Editions provide the best in fiction and nonfiction in a wide variety of subject areas. They include novels by classic and contemporary writers; vivid, accurate histories and biographies; authoritative works in the sciences; collections of short stories, plays and poetry.

Bantam Pathfinder Editions are carefully selected and approved. They are durably bound, printed on specially selected high-quality paper, and presented in a new and handsome format.

THE RED KNIGHT OF GERMANY

THE STORY OF BARON VON RICHTHOFEN
GERMANY'S GREAT WAR BIRD

BY FLOYD GIBBONS

New Illustrated Abridgment

BANTAM PATHFINDER EDITIONS
NEW YORK / TORONTO / LONDON

RLI: $\frac{\text{VLM 8.0}}{\text{IL 7.12}}$

THE RED KNIGHT OF GERMANY

A Bantam Book / published by arrangement with Doubleday and Company, Inc.

PRINTING HISTORY

Doubleday edition published November 1927

2nd printing ......January 1928
3rd printing ....July 1928
4th printing ......January 1929
5th printing ....February 1929
6th printing ......March 1929
7th printing ....May 1929
8th printing ......August 1929
9th printing ...September 1929
10th printing ....October 1929
11th printing ..November 1929
12th printing ....April 1930
13th printing ....May 1930
14th printing ..September 1930
15th printing ..November 1930
16th printing ...February 1931
17th printing ....April 1931
18th printing.......March 1932

New Doubleday edition published January 1937
2nd printing ......January 1937
3rd printing ....November 1939
4th printing ....April 1940

Sun Dial Press edition published January 1937

Serialized in CHICAGO TRIBUNE *January 1928*

Bantam edition published February 1959
Bantam Pathfinder edition published September 1964
3rd printing
4th printing
5th printing
6th printing

Library of Congress Catalog Card Number: 59-5358.

For information address: Doubleday and Company, Inc., 575 Madison Avenue, New York 22, N. Y.
Published simultaneously in the United States and Canada.

Bantam Books are published by Bantam Books, Inc. Its trade-mark, consisting of the words "Bantam Books" and the portrayal of a bantam, is registered in the United States Patent Office and in other countries. Marca Registrada. Printed in the United States of America. Bantam Books, Inc., 271 Madison Ave., New York 16, N. Y.

The Red Knight of Germany

Chapter I

To kill and kill and kill was the cry. To burn, to destroy, to devastate, to lay waste. Men heard the madness and knew it for madness and embraced it, some with fear and some with joy. Kill or be killed. Survive or perish.

Pink, yellow, and green patches on maps personified themselves. The personifications glared at one another, then snarled, then cursed. Millions of hearts heard and beat faster. Males strutted; females loved them for it.

It was the march beat of tramping feet. It was the sharp staccato of steel-shod hoofs. It was the whir and growl of speeding motors. It was the shriek and roar of troop trains frontward bound.

His mother had not raised him to be a soldier.

She had made him wear curls and dressed him in white pretties. He had looked like a girl, and hated it.

Then came killing time—war.

He killed a hundred men in individual combat: shot them, burned them, crushed them, hurled their bodies down to earth.

He became the terror of the battle fronts. He grinned at grim death in a hundred duels above the clouds. He fought fair, hard, and to kill, and the better his foeman fought to kill him, the better he liked him for it.

He shot down eighty fighting planes. He matched his life against that of any man. He fought, not with hate, but with love for fighting. It was his joy, his sport, his passion. To him, to dare and to die was to live. He had the courage to kill and be killed, and war was his hunting licence. On home leave from man-killing at the front, he hunted and killed deer, elk, boar, bison, and birds, and brought their heads to his mother's home.

He was courageous and knew it, gloried in it, flaunted it with his challenge to the world of his enemies. He made them know him—he put his name on their lips—his name that was unknown, unheard of, when he started the war as a second "looie."

Wounded and decorated, he became the guest of kings and queens. Boys and the youth of a nation made him their idol, cheered him, followed him on the street.

He was young and blond, shy and handsome, proud and serious. Girls by the thousands worshipped his picture and filled his mail with letters by the sackful. One of them he loved. He wanted to make her his wife, but he did not want to make her his widow. He knew he was going to be killed.

He won the admiration and respect of his enemies. His instinct and duty it was to kill them; he did. Their duty and instinct it was to kill him; they did.

In one of the greatest air battles in the history of the world, he went down, still fighting, still killing. He died a national hero at the head of his fighting men in the service of his country. He was buried by his enemies with respect and military honours in unstinted recognition of his great courage, his sportsmanship, and his tireless, relentless spirit.

His name was Manfred von Richthofen.

Into the grisly story of World War I there came a refreshing gleam of the chivalry of old, when the pick of the flower of youth on both sides carried the conflict into the skies. Into that Knighthood of the Blue, Richthofen has been given a place of highest merit by those he fought with and against.

His life and death, his victories and his defeat, his loves, his hopes, his fears bring a new record to the halls of that same Valhalla in which rest the spirits of Guynemer, Hawker, Ball, McCudden, Immelmann, Lufberry, Quentin Roosevelt, and many others who fought aloft and died below with hearts that held emotions other than hate.

Young blood, hot and daring, raced through their veins, even as the wingèd steeds they rode raced on the wind to conquest or disaster. With keen young eyes, glinting along the barrels of their jibbering machine guns, they looked at close range into one another's souls as they pressed the triggers that sent one another tumbling down to death.

Some went down like flaming comets, burned beyond recognition before the charred remains struck the earth thousands of feet below. Some plunged earthward through the blue in drunken staggers as their bullet-riddled bodies slumped forward lifelessly on the controls. Some fell free from shattered planes at fearsome heights, poured out like the contents of a burst paper bag, and some, hurtling down in formless wrecks, buried themselves in the ground.

This was the death that Richthofen dealt out to his adversaries in the air—it was the same death they dealt to him. As he had given to many, so he received. As he fought, he died.

How many did he kill? The list is long and appalling. It is a string of victories, a chaplet in which the beads of glory and tragedy succeed one another to defeat and the grave. It has never before been compiled, and only after great research through the musty files and papers of the German archives in Potsdam is it possible to set forth the date of each one of these combats and to identify to some extent the airmen that fell before the German ace of aces.

On the day after his eightieth victory—April 21, 1918—he died as he dove upon the British flyer selected for his eighty-first victim. Strapped to the pilot's seat, his body sown with lead, the Uhlan of the sky came down between the blazing lines before Amiens. With only a dead man's hands on the flying controls, the bright red Fokker triplane of the ace of German aces landed on an even keel in front of Australian trenches. He was twenty-five years old.

To his country and the cause it was soon to lose, the loss of Richthofen was great. Ludendorff, when he heard the news, said, "He was worth as much to us as three divisions." His mother had not raised him to be a soldier, but in the military estimation of his fighting worth he was placed in the balance against thirty thousand bayonets.

The mother lived in the little town of Schweidnitz in German Silesia—lived in the large, cold, silent rooms and hall of the big white house that once reëchoed to the shouts of the boy who wore curls and looked like a girl. Dearer to this sad-faced, gray-haired woman than Ludendorff's high valuation of her son; dearer than the rows of ribbons and decorations and the acknowledgments of comrades and former foes, were three golden ringlets of fine-spun hair in a plain white pasteboard box and a mother's memories of the cherubic head that bore them.

Although Prussian junkers from a fighting stock that won its title of baron far back in the Seventeenth Century, the Richthofen family took little part in subsequent wars. They were landowners, squires of county seats who worked their estates with thrift and efficiency and found their sports in hunting and riding. Some held small government posts, but they always returned to the fields and forests and the country houses they loved.

And in the family of Schickfuss, from which came the mother of the famous ace, it was the same. Conservatives to the bone, it was their aim to work hard, respect order, and find their fun in hard riding and hard hunting. Old Uncle Alexander Schickfuss, after shooting the feathers and horns off all kinds of Silesian fauna, packed up his guns and sought the huntsman's joy in the wilds of Africa, in Ceylon, and in Hungary.

In the saddle and on the hunt, it was the same with Richthofen's father, with the exception that he became the first of the line to enter active service in the army. As an officer of a Uhlan regiment, he evidenced a high sense of duty as a soldier, but the greatest record he has left is on the walls of the Schweidnitz home in the shape of four hundred mounted deer heads and stuffed birds, all brought down afield by his gun. He served through the war as a major of reserve, but died shortly after the Armistice.

From this line of modern primitives came Manfred von Richthofen, born May 2, 1892, in Breslau. Organization, reputed to be the forte of his country, was not inborn with him. He was essentially an individualist. The spirit of the hunter, the stalker, was strong within him, and with it ran pride of conquest, the natural outgrowth of strong competitive and combative senses.

He felt strongly the same urge that drives the city-bred man to the wilds for relief from the pressure of organized life, to feel once more the discipline of nature instead of that of steel and asphalt and traffic regulations. The hunt was his life and the trophy was his prize. Richthofen was like his father and, no doubt, like all his forbears in the matter of trophies. The hunter must show the prey he ran to earth.

Since Stone Age days, man's abode, whether a cave or a tree nest, has been littered with the bones of those he slew in hunt or combat. Armorial halls festooned with captured standards, or walls studded with antlered or feathered heads, are expressions of the same strain. And so were the tons of German helmets that two million A. E. F.'ers brought back from France.

It was no different with the individual air fighters of World War I—the man-birds who hunted in the clouds. The boyhood bedroom of Richthofen in Schweidnitz remains to-day, with the exception of its owner's portraits, just as the victorious ace arranged and decorated it his last trip home before his death.

Its walls are covered with the linen scalps of fallen foes. They are the gaily painted red, white, and blue numbers and symbols cut from fighting planes that went down in defeat under the guns of Richthofen's red Fokker. To anyone who knew the war, the bedchamber is a "room of dead men's numbers," but it was not that to Mother Richthofen, whose son told her that the stripes of fabric placed on the walls were taken only from vanquished planes whose occupants survived the fight that forced them to earth behind the German lines.

The chandelier hanging from the ceiling over the centre table is the rotary motor of a French plane which the ace brought down near Verdun. Richthofen had it remade with electric bulbs on each cylinder head, and, in order to support the unusual weight, he had to reinforce the rafters in the ceiling, from which it is suspended on chains. The table itself is made from parts of broken propeller blades of all kinds. The night lamp on the bed table is formed from the metal hub of an airplane's undercarriage wheel. The centrepiece on the table is a flying compass, and the wall table under the large portrait is loaded down with silver cups commemorating battles in the sky.

Among all these gruesome trophies, each representing a death struggle in midair, one holds the position of honour over the bedroom door. It is the machine gun from an English plane that sent many German flyers to their death. It is the weapon of the first English ace, Major Lanoe Hawker. Hawker was one of the best flyers in the Allied ranks. He had received the Victoria Cross and many decorations, and had a long string of air victories to his credit. Richthofen himself had been decorated and had brought down ten enemy planes. It was a meeting of champions of the air. It was a battle of eagles, each determined upon the other's death, and it took place high over the battle lines between Bapaume and Albert, in full view of thousands of mud-grimed soldiers who watched the combat from their trenches.

Richthofen wrote the account of that fight for publication in Germany during the war:

I must confess that it was a matter of great pride to me to learn that the Englishman I shot down on November 23 [1916] was the English equivalent of our great Immelmann. Of course, I did not know who he was during the fight, but I did know from the masterly manner in which he handled his plane and the pluck with which he flew, that he was a wonderful fellow.

It was fine weather when I flew away from our airdrome that day. I was in the best of spirits and keen for the hunt. Flying at an altitude of about ten thousand feet, I observed three English planes. I saw that they saw me, and from their manœuvres I gathered that our hopes for the day's fun were mutual. They were hunting bent, the same as I. I was spoiling for a fight, and they impressed me much the same. They were above me, but I accepted the challenge. Being underneath and in no position to attack, I had to wait till the fellow dived on me. It was not long to wait. Soon he started down in a steep gliding dive, trying to catch me from behind.

He opens fire with his machine gun. Five shots rip out, and I change my course quickly by a sharp turn to the left. He follows, and the mad circle starts. He is trying to get behind me, and I am trying to get behind him. Round and round we go in circles, like two madmen, playing ring-around-a-rosie almost two miles above the earth. Both of our motors are speeded to the utmost; still neither of us seems to gain on the other. We are exactly opposite each other on the circumference of the circle, and in this position neither one of us can train our single forward shooting machine guns on the other.

First, we would go twenty times around to the right, and then swing into another circle going round twenty times to the left. We continued the mad race, neither gaining an advantage. I knew at once that I was dealing with no beginner, because he didn't appear to dream of trying to break off the fight and get out of the circling. His plane was excellent for manœuvring and speed, but my machine gave me an advantage by being able to climb better and faster. This enabled me at last to break the circle and manœuvre into a position behind and above him.

But in the circling light, both of us had lost height. We must have come down at least six thousand feet because now we were little more than three thousand feet above the ground. The wind was in my favour. Throughout the fight, at the same time we kept getting lower, the wind was gradually drifting us back across the German lines. I saw that now we were even behind the German lines in front of Bapaume, and my opponent should have noticed that it was time for him to back out of the fight, because he was getting farther into my territory.

But he was a plucky devil. With me behind and above him, he even turned round and waved his arm at me, as though to say, *"Wie gehts?"* We went into circles again—fast and furious and as small as we could drive them. Sometimes I estimated the diameters of the circles at between eighty and a hundred yards. But always I kept above him and at times I could look down almost vertically into his cockpit and watch each movement of his head. If it had not been for his helmet and goggles, I could have seen what sort of face he had.

He was a fine sportsman, but I knew that in time my close presence behind and above him would be too much for him, particularly as all the time we were getting lower and lower and farther behind my lines. We were getting so close to the ground that he would soon have to decide whether he would have to land behind our lines or whether he would break the circle and try to get back to his own side.

Apparently, the idea of landing and surrender never occurred to this sportsman, because suddenly he revealed his plans to escape by going into several loops and other manœuvres of equal folly. As he came out of them, headed back for his lines, my first bullets began whistling around his ears, because up to now, with the exception of his opening shots, neither one of us had been able to range on the other.

The battle is now close to the ground. He is not a hundred yards above the earth. Our speed is terrific. He starts back for his front. He knows I am right behind him and close on his tail. He knows my gun barrel is trained on him. He starts to zigzag, making sudden darts right and left—right and left—confusing my aim and making it difficult to train my gun on him. But the moment is coming. I am fifty yards behind him. My machine gun is firing incessantly. We are hardly fifty yards above the ground —just skimming it.

Now I am within thirty yards of him. He must fall. The gun pours out its stream of lead. Then it jams. Then it reopens fire. That jam almost saved his life. One bullet goes home. He is struck through the back of the head. His plane jumps and crashes down. It strikes the ground just as I swoop over. His machine gun rammed itself into the earth, and now it decorates the entrance over my door. He was a brave man, a sportsman, and a fighter.

Hawker's silent gun over her dead son's door was not the prize that his mother liked to look upon. She did not like to think of Mother Hawker somewhere, and she did not like to think that her son's gun rested in a similar place over the bedroom door of some English airman. But in Richthofen's bedroom is one trophy which she loved and which brought moisture to her eyes as she touched it tenderly.

It is a square piece of brown pasteboard on which are three duck feathers, held there by a gob of red sealing wax; it was the first trophy of the boy that wore the curls. It is the proud symbol of his first "kill."

"We passed our vacations in the country with Grandmother," Mrs. von Richthofen told me. "One day, Manfred could not suppress his fast-developing passion for hunting. He had his first air rifle, and with it he killed three or four of Grandmother's tame ducks that he found swimming on a little pond near the house.

"He proudly related his exploit to his grandmother, and I started to reprimand him. His good old grandmother stopped me from scolding him because, as she said, he had been right in confessing his misdeed. To-day, when I see those three duck feathers in his old room with all his trophies of war, I cannot keep back my tears."

That hunting passion that stood him so well in the air marked all of his early life. He hunted for prey and he hunted for the thrill of the hunt. To him, it was the expression of living. He had a splendid physique and the keenest vision. His agility became a matter of comment at an early age, when he mastered the trick of turning somersaults without using his hands.

His first exploits in the air were made by way of a large apple tree at the age of eight. He reached some difficult fruit on the uppermost branches and returned to the ground not by way of the trunk but by swinging and bending on the ends of the lowest branches.

"An easily terrified mother is a great obstacle to the physical development of her children," Mrs. von Richthofen said.

"When Manfred was a little boy, I believe many of my friends considered me rather a careless mother because I did not forbid the two boys to engage in some of the feats they liked, but I was then, and am still, convinced children can only become agile if they are allowed such freedom as will enable them to judge what they can safely demand of their bodies."

The future ace knew the tingle that all humans feel on high places. At the age of ten, when a schoolboy, he climbed the highest church tower in Wahlstatt, made a terrifying ascent over the eaves, and even mounted the uppermost lightning rod, to which he tied his pocket handkerchief. He said, in after life, that flying at dizzy heights like twenty thousand feet above the earth never reproduced the thrill that he had as a boy when he looked down on the town of Wahlstatt from the top of the steeple.

His daring extended even into the realms of the unknown, as, for instance, that time in his twelfth year when he had the temerity to hunt a ghost. There had long been a story to the effect that the Richthofen house had been haunted since the time that a man had hung himself from the rafters in the attic. The boy, with serious, questioning eyes, made the old caretaker of the house show him the exact spot from which the body had dangled.

He and his brother Lothar moved their bed to the attic and placed it under the spot. They arranged to spend the night there and trap the spectre. His mother, together with his sister, decided to impersonate the ghost. During the night, they crept to the attic and started rolling chestnuts across the floor. Manfred, who was asleep, was aroused by his young brother calling his attention to the unusual noise. The mother recounts that the elder boy was out of bed in an instant, brandishing a stick, and that she and her daughter only saved themselves from blows by hurriedly switching on the lights.

Young Richthofen had no special inclinations toward the life of a soldier. Concerning the decision that sent him away to a cadet school and marked him for a military career, he once wrote: "I was not particularly fond of being a cadet, but father desired it, and so I wasn't asked about it." Parental authority in the Richthofen home was supreme. Although the future ace had the natural hatred of discipline, his home life developed in him a great respect for superiors, an unquestioned obedience to authority, and a keen sense of duty. He despised dishonesty because he considered it cowardly.

As a student, he never distinguished himself. He disliked classes and worked only to the extent required to assure him passing marks, a tendency which did not increase his popularity with his teachers. But in the gymnasium and on the sports field he found his chief interest in athletic feats and contest. He suffered an early injury to one knee while performing on the bars, and for some time walked with a limp, but never permitted this handicap to interfere with his continued participation in sports. Boxing was not considered the manly sport in Germany in those days, so Richthofen never had a glove on, and his youth barred him from the duelling field.

After eight years in the cadet corps, he became Herr Lieutenant in the fall of 1912, and being assigned to the First Uhlan Regiment, named after the Russian emperor, Alexander I, came first to know and feel the pride of superiority that the man on horseback feels over the man on foot. Richthofen said it was his proudest moment, and that for the first time he began to love his duty and his life as a soldier. He liked to ride and to ride hard.

In the saddle, he was ever willing to dare much, but it does not appear that the young Uhlan officer's horsemanship quite equalled his intrepidity, because there are many stories of his frequent falls and mishaps. Once he was thrown and netted a cracked collar bone, and again, at a horse show, his mount took the water jump in full view of a packed gallery, but left the rider head foremost in the mud. In one of these early incidents, he displayed a Spartan endurance that won him the admiration of his fellow officers and commanders. It was in the cross-country ride for the Emperor's prize in 1913, and Richthofen, true to form, was pitched on his head in the first two miles. Again the collar bone snapped. Painful as it was, however, the rider remounted and rode on forty-five miles, reaching the finishing point on time and winning the prize.

Within ten months of this date, the young Uhlan for the first time was riding at the head of his men to war. His thoughts of flying were confined to the saddle, toward taking fences and hedges and charging across fields, when the great disaster broke out. Quartered with his regiment in a little Silesian town, six miles from the German-Russian frontier, he refused to believe the rumblings and threats of strife that began to appear in the newspapers.

He and his fellow officers did not believe it. So many times before, the orders had come to be in readiness to move, and as many times, nothing had happened. The cavalrymen, proud of their designation as the eyes of the army, followed orders but ignored the growing clamour. It would not happen. The day before the last order was received—the order to be in readiness to move at any minute—the Uhlan mess spent the evening playing cards, eating oysters, and drinking champagne. All were gay, and no one present had the thought that the world was on the verge of a spasm that was to last more than four years and from which but few of those happy ones present that night would emerge alive. Richthofen was twenty-two years old at the time.

The mother of a fellow officer had hastened to visit them, and they had laughingly assured her that there would be no war, and she in happiness had invited the entire mess to a special dinner. In the midst of the celebration a ranking officer from Army Headquarters opened the door and stood silently. He gazed on the merriment with a stern and serious face. It was August 1, 1914.

He was on a hastily ordered frontier inspection. Through him they learned that all the bridges in the surrounding country had been placed under heavy guard that night and fortifying work was progressing that minute on important places in the area. The news stopped the festivities only for a minute. It was only another false alarm. War could not be. Life was too good. Peace was too sweet. Why war?

On the following day, war was declared. That night, the officers that had attended the celebration rode across the frontier and invaded Russia. The declaration brought an end to all rumours.

Here was something final, and to uniformed youth it brought joy and the prospect of showing what mettle they had as a result of the long years of training. They knew their task and felt keenly its importance. They were the eyes of the army.

The High Command depended upon their reconnoitring their mounted raids behind the enemy lines, their dashing charges on enemy advance posts, their disruption of enemy communications—all these they thought of in the old terms of war and with the old pride of the cavalry.

Richthofen stood beside his horse in the courtyard of the barracks a few minutes before midnight. He had just made a final inspection of his troop of men and horses standing there in the darkness. In his pockets he carried orders which he knew by heart. He had studied them daily for more than a year. He was six miles from the frontier across which he was to ride on the great adventure.

A sharp command, the rattle of equipment as the troops mounted, the sound of iron-shod hoofs on the cobbles, and they rode off into the night—to war.

Chapter II

On the morning of August 3, 1914, the inhabitants of the little Russian village of Kielce, located just a few miles east of the German frontier, awoke to find a troop of German Uhlans patrolling the main street and occupying points of vantage on the road leading in and out of the village.

A twenty-two-year-old second lieutenant swung from his horse in front of a low building of weather-stained clapboards. His hair was blond; his cheeks were pink, his uniform was natty. With the handle of his riding crop he rapped on the wooden door, which was opened by the village priest, a tall man in black robes, whose pallid face was framed above by long black hair and below by a full red beard.

"Father," said the boy officer with heels together as though on parade, "it is my painful duty to inform you that war has been declared between Germany and your country and that your village is now occupied and surrounded by my men. I must notify you that you are my prisoner. My name is Manfred von Richthofen, Second Lieutenant of the First Regiment of Uhlans."

The formal speech didn't even sound real to the youngster who spoke it. Even less real it seemed to the cleric, who received it with a smile and folded hands, quite after the fashion he always employed in receiving visitors to the village. What nonsense was the boy talking? War? Troops? Prisoners? What sort of fun-making was this?

Two normally peacefully inclined humans, neither of whom had ever seriously thought of harming each other, much less of war, faced each other with smiles of equal strangeness on the opening day of a struggle that was to last through four long years, spread ruin among hundreds of millions, bring a continent to the brink of destruction, devastate thousands of square miles of peaceful countryside, wipe out millions of lives, and rock civilization.

The prisoner priest fades into the background, but the boy who took him captive captured the undefended town without firing a shot, and then found difficulty in convincing the villagers that they were prisoners—that boy became the national hero of his country and the greatest air fighter that the German war machine ever sent aloft. The incident, now lost in the reek and wallow of all that followed, was the first hostile act of the youth who became the ace of German aces in the air. In the act itself the boy became the man of war.

To make the peaceful villagers realize that they were prisoners, young Richthofen wrapped himself in sternness and locked the priest in the tower of the church.

"At the first sign of hostility from your villagers, you will be executed," Richthofen assured him, in a properly forbidding manner. "And I shall take such other measures as are necessary for the protection of the men under my command and the proper pacification of the inhabitants."

To insure against the priest's escape, Richthofen next removed the ladder leading to the belfry, and placed a sentry there, both to guard the priest and to watch the approaches to the town.

Then he reported in ponderous peacetime military fashion, writing long accounts of his mission and sending off couriers to either flank and to the rear. The frontier was a small river, and he, at the head of his patrol, had crossed it stealthily in the darkness. The young lieutenant and his men, all keyed up to the high pitch of the moment, expected to encounter resistance on the international line; and their surprise was beyond words when they passed over the little rustic bridge and found themselves on Russian soil without the firing of a shot. They had thought there was something funny about this war, after all. Maybe the order for hostilities had been recalled, maybe it was all a mistake, but there was nothing for them to do but to carry out orders until other instructions were received.

In five quiet, uneventful days young Richthofen's little patrol had dwindled to himself and two men; the rest had been sent off as dispatch carriers and as yet had not found their way back. It was quiet in the captured village—so quiet that the lieutenant released the priest with apologies from his belfry confinement and told him to return to his house. The villagers were not only peaceful and docile—they appeared to be helpful to the invaders. To Richthofen's primitive instincts of the hunt, transferred and made applicable to war, it didn't seem according to the rules of the game. How could a huntsman show his prowess when no one questioned or resisted him?

Puzzled, he went to sleep on the fifth night of the occupation and was awakened shortly after midnight by a tug at his shoulder. It was the sentry he had left posted on the belfry.

"The Cossacks are here," he whispered in a husky voice. He also was young. He had seen the enemy for the first time. His voice betrayed not fear but the thrill which comes with quickened heartbeats when fighting males approach contact with their adversaries.

Jumping out from his blankets, Richthofen became the hunter—or the quarry—he knew not which. Senses alert and keen, he stepped out into the night. There was a fine mist of rain falling and the darkness was complete. Under this covering he and his men led their three horses through a break in the churchyard wall and into an open field.

Trailing a carbine beside him, Richthofen returned through the churchyard and, keeping under cover of the wall, came to the village street. It was filled with men and horses. He recognized them immediately as Cossacks. He estimated their number at thirty. Some of them carried lanterns. They were noisy and raucous as they questioned the villagers. Seeing the leader of the newcomers in conversation with the priest, the young Uhlan doubled his caution.

He crossed the churchyard, leaped the opposite wall, and joined his two men with the horses in the field. They led the animals in silence across the open field and took to the shelter of the near-by woods. In the gray light of early morning, they saw the Cossacks ride out of the village, but they did not return to their old quarters, realizing that an outpost had been left to receive them. Funny war! No shooting—no hunting; just a schoolboy game of "robbers and policemen."

Unshaven, mud-splashed, and wrinkled from a week without removing their clothes, the trio returned to the garrison town on the seventh day after their departure, and were received as ghosts. Richthofen had been reported dead in a brush with Cossacks, and his mother had received condolences from friends far and near. An unmerited obituary is the best of jokes to vibrant youth at twenty-two.

His "return from the dead" netted him an ovation in the little garrison town, but this first sample of hero worship was short-lived, because, within twenty-four hours, the regiment had entrained and was off for destination unknown but guessed to be France. Day and night the troop train sped westward across Silesia and Saxony in the general direction of Metz.

Richthofen and four young second lieutenants, with all of their bags and equipment, were quartered in one second-class compartment. They had a table between them, and it was loaded down with bottles—bottles that were replenished at every stop, where cheering crowds awaited them.

The regiment was known. The First Uhlans and the One Hundred and Fifty-fifth Regiment of Infantry had been mentioned in the first official German communiqué as having taken the Russian town of Kalisch. They were greeted as heroes, and this greeting was not hard to take when accompanied by the flashing eyes and admiring glances of girls who offered them kisses and flowers and wine.

As neither Richthofen nor the three other officers had been in the Kalisch engagement, the celebration galled a bit at first, but as it was repeated at every place where the train stopped, they soon became used to it and liked it. It felt good to be taken as heroes. Why deny it? They stopped explanations.

Further than that, they invented wild tales of their encounters with the ferocious Russians, and one of the party, who had brought with him the sword of a Russian policeman, exhibited the weapon as first-hand evidence of the fierce combat in which it had been wrested from the grasp of a Cossack, and then sheathed in his own blood. Certain rust stains on the blade further bore out this tale.

The officers' compartment was crowded and hot, and blue with tobacco smoke. Fresh bottles succeeded the empty ones, which were sent out of the window at convenient targets. They sang and joked and laughed and made up more tales for the next enthusiastic throng that was to receive them.

Once the revelry was brought to an end with an incident which might have proved tragic. The train stopped suddenly in a long dark tunnel, and those on board were not aware of the reason. Bombs—wrecks—attacks flashed through their minds in the darkness. The silence increased the tension. Then a shot was fired, and immediately hundreds of rifles protruded from windows and were discharged. Bullets, hitting the stone walls of the tunnel, richocheted in all directions. The excitement was intense. That no one was wounded seemed a miracle. The incident served to show, however, that the German military machine was not entirely the nerveless thing of iron-clad discipline and precision that it was supposed to be.

Richthofen rode with his regiment across Luxemburg without incident other than his ill-advised capture of a Luxemburg policeman, whom he finally decided to release, inasmuch as Luxemburg had not opened hostilities or resisted the German invasion of its frontiers, and the policeman had not interfered with his march or his men.

Approaching the fortified towns on the Belgian frontier, the cavalry division rode as though on manœuvres. With this division, Richthofen crossed his second enemy frontier in the vicinity of Arlon, in which town he climbed the church steeple for observation purposes but learned nothing more than that the surrounding country appeared to be free of Belgian or French forces.

The townspeople were bitter, and the young Uhlan was forced to use all of his diplomacy and reserve to get out of the town alone and join his troop on the outskirts. Later, he wrote that it had become necessary subsequently to execute some of the citizens for sniping on troops passing through the main street.

His daring, which could also be called his lack of caution, did not mark him for any great success as a cavalry officer. The characteristics which later made him such a redoubtable foe in the air almost cost him his life, and did cost him the lives of most of his troop in his first armed encounter with the enemy. For all his years of military training, the young Uhlan officer fell victim to the simplest in mounted manœuvres. He allowed himself and his troop to be ambushed and almost annihilated.

It was on August 21st, in the little Belgian village of Etalle, twenty miles from the frontier, that Richthofen received orders to make a mounted reconnaissance toward the south in the direction of a little town called Meix-devant-Virton. His duty it was to discover the strength of French cavalry supposed to be occupying a large forest. With the war less than two weeks old, movement marked the efforts of the opposing forces to get into advantageous contact with one another.

From the height of a hilltop, Richthofen looked over the forest with his binoculars. The dew on the treetops sparkled in the brilliant morning sun. The scene was one of peace and quiet, and the Uhlan patrol of fourteen men felt itself off again on an objectless ride which would bring it back to camp late at night with nothing but fatigue and aching bones to pay for a long day's march. It was soon to have a rude awakening from such blissfulness.

After his two advance men had trotted into the forest without encountering resistance, Richthofen advanced with his patrol to the edge of the trees and easily discovered from the ground that a large number of horsemen had passed that way shortly before. The hoof marks were fresh in the damp soil. Here was the chance for action at last. Young blood tingled.

"In my mind's eye, I saw myself at last at the head of my little troop, sabring a hostile squadron," Richthofen wrote afterward. "I was quite intoxicated with excitement, and I saw the eyes of my young Uhlans sparkle."

They took up the trail immediately and advanced through the darkness of the forest at a sharp trot. At first they rode with the regulation caution of advance and rearguards, but, after twenty minutes, in which nothing was encountered, the entire patrol became bunched together, and eagerness increased the pace.

In thirty minutes, the first riders, making a turn in a leafy glade, were brought to a sudden stop by the presence of a barrier of felled trees lying across the road. On the left, there was a small rivulet, and beyond that a small meadow fifty yards wide. To the right rose a steep, stony slope. In all other directions, the darkness of the forest pressed in with menacing shadows on the sunlight of the small clearing. There was no other sound than the snorts and breathing of the sweating horses and the rattle of equipment.

Richthofen galloped up to the barrier and raised his binoculars. On that instant a volley of rifle fire blazed out on the little patrol from three sides. Trapped! A mounted force of French cuirassiers (light cavalry), estimated at one hundred men, had them at their mercy.

The carbines banged away. Horses reared and men fell to the ground, some to lie quite still, and some to struggle with the reins of their terror-stricken animals.

The path ahead was blocked by the felled trees. The river stopped a charge to the left. The rocky hill on the right barred progress in that direction.

Lifting his hand in signal for hasty retreat, Richthofen put spurs into his horse and dashed backward, but the Uhlans behind had mistaken his signal and had galloped up to his assistance. Bunched together in the sunlit clearing, they offered an excellent target for the cracking carbines.

Richthofen later described the exploit which reflected so sadly on his long years of cavalry schooling:

> As we were on a narrow forest path running across the clearing, one may easily imagine the muddle that followed. The horses of two men ran away in a panic because the noise of every shot was increased tenfold by the echoes of the forest. The last I saw of them they were leaping the barricade. I never heard again from the men, and presume they were taken prisoners. My orderly rode at my side. Suddenly his horse was hit and fell. As he was slightly in advance, I had to jump both of them. Other horses were rolling on the ground. In short, it was wild disorder.

In his first clash with the enemy, Second Lieutenant Richthofen had lost ten out of his small force of fourteen men. He himself escaped unscathed. In a letter to his mother, written that night upon his return, he described his escape as a miracle. He credited his French foemen with having surprised him "beautifully."

His defeat at the hands of the French hurt his pride. He had expected greater of himself. His injured pride, however, did not permit him to excuse himself. He acknowledged his fault. His code, as he applied it to himself, was as stern as when he applied it to others. His pride would not permit him to be dishonest with himself even to save his pride. Admitting his error as an officer still permitted him to retain his pride in himself as a man who valued courage above all. With his set of principles, an alibi would have cost him the pride he held in his courage. To Richthofen, a liar and a coward were the same.

Pride, truthfulness, and the little glimmer of jealousy are the characteristics revealed in his letters at that time to his mother. He wanted the trophies of the brave—decorations for valour. These baubles appealed to him tremendously, and he did not attempt to hide his ambition to win badges of credit for himself. To his mother he wrote of his frequent assignments on reconnoitring duty, with the addition, "I am trying hard to win the Iron Cross."

He knew the intrepid qualities of his younger brother, and he lived in the fear that Lothar would see more action than he did, or would have the first opportunity to distinguish himself.

> Unfortunately, we Uhlans have been attached to the Infantry [he wrote to "Liebe Mamma"]. I write "unfortunately" because I feel certain that Lothar has already been in big cavalry charges such as we will probably never ride in here.

This feeling extended even to a fear that the war would end before he was given the chance to win the coveted decorations. It made him restless and ill at ease during the intervals of inactivity that became longer as the fighting front solidified itself in the west and the war of attrition began. Transferred from Belgium to Verdun, he grew to despise himself as a "base hog" because the duties assigned to him seldom allowed him to go within a mile of the front-line trenches.

He saw the day of the cavalryman disappear. Trenches and barbed wire spelled their finish. He saw the infantry lay down their rifles and take up the lowly spade and pick. His cherished picture of war—waving standards, flashing sabres, the charge, the *mêlée*—slowly erased itself, and in its stead came a loathsome reality of muddy shell holes, water-filled ditches, damp, unclean dugouts, and bombproofs. Where was the glory of war?

> I hear that a cavalry division stands on the approaches to Paris [Richthofen wrote in September, 1914], and I nearly believe that Lothar [his young brother] is lucky enough to be there. But apart from that, he must certainly have seen more than I have here before Verdun.
>
> The army of the Crown Prince is investing Verdun from the north, and we must wait till the fortress surrenders. Its huge fortifications being what they are, any attempt to storm them would cost more in men and munitions than the strategic value

of the position would justify. Only, it's unfortunate that we Uhlans are tied up here by these considerations, and that presumably we will have to end the war here.

The battle of Verdun is very severe, and day after day a vast number of lives are sacrificed. Only yesterday, eight officers of the Seventh Grenadiers were killed in one attack.

One of the most decisive battles in the war is going on; thousands of men are being killed, but Richthofen is on the side lines and not in it. The war is quite unsatisfactory to him. His duties are almost clerical, to his mind. Early in the morning, as a communications officer, he approaches the front lines through filthy trenches. He returns at noon to his deep dugout behind the lines and directs the telephone lines for a sector. A fine job for "us Uhlans," and all the time his younger brother, for all he knows, may be taking Paris single-handed and winning the first Iron Cross in the Richthofen family.

He demanded action. On his hurried front-line visits, he would borrow a rifle and take a pot shot now and then at the opposing trenches. In places where the lines approached within ten yards of each other, he would "stir things up a bit" by tossing a hand grenade over among the French holding the opposing position.

Two or three similar presents usually came back, and one must presume that these little diversions of the visiting "base hog" did not increase his popularity with the men he visited.

His hunter instincts could not be denied. War was "killing time," and he was not in on the killing. After twelve hours' trudging duty through the trenches and in the foul air of the telephone dugout, he would spend the night tramping the woods back of the front in search of prey for his rifle. If they would not let him shoot at men, he must find other game.

Full moonlight nights, with the light snow of late fall, came to his assistance, and he followed the tracks of wild pigs through the dark forest of La Chaussée. With much effort he and an orderly built a shelter seat in a tree, and there he waited, night after night, for his quarry. Morning frequently found him cramped and stiff and almost frozen, but these hardships were like food to the craving within him.

One night there came a sow which swam the little woodland lake in the bright moonlight and broke into a potato field on the other side. Several miles away, the guns of Verdun boomed, and their flashes sometimes sent flickers of light across the night sky. From his tree nest, Richthofen awaited the return of the sow and sent a bullet into her body as she swam back across the lake from her midnight foraging. She was only wounded, and the hunter, descending from the seat, plunged into the cold water, bringing his victim out by the hind leg and finishing her life with a trench knife.

At another time, it was a boar that he faced, rifle in hand, at twenty yards, and sent a bullet crashing through its mighty head—a head which was carefully salvaged, skinned, cleaned, cured, stuffed, and mounted and forwarded, even in wartime, to the little bedroom in Schweidnitz, where one sees it on the trophy wall. If not the Iron Cross, then some over trophy, but symbol there must always be for the craving of the primitive.

At last the Iron Cross came—his first decoration, awarded in recognition of his repeated trips along the front line under heavy fire. It was his first trophy of the war, and he hastened to register it with his mother. In his dugout the following night, he wrote:

Dear Mamma:

I come with glad tidings. Yesterday I was decorated with the Iron Cross.

How are matters around Lemberg? Let me give you some sound advice. If the Russians should come, bury everything you want to see again deep down in the garden, or elsewhere. Whatever you leave behind you will never see again.

You wonder why I save so much money, but don't forget that, after the war, I must reëquip myself from head to foot. Everything I took with me is gone, lost, burned, torn—not even excluding my saddle. If I should come out of this war alive, I will have more luck than brains.

The Iron Cross helped: it brought some gratification to the pride after the tediousness of his unaccustomed duties as an infantryman, but there were long months ahead in which the accumulated boresomeness of the unchanging and never-ending battle of Verdun was to drive the restless young Uhlan to an act which approached insubordination. He stuck it out, but with little spirit.

There was excitement, but not of the kind he craved. He was helping to kill, but he was unable to see the foe he slew. His competitive spirit had no opportunity for expression. His individualism was lost in the great machine of which he had become a cog. Although he never put the thought in words, his desire was to come to close contact with the enemy, to cross swords face to face with an adversary, to kill him or be killed.

In October, he was almost killed. Death passed him by a hair's breadth. He was riding back of the front. A French shell came crashing through the trees and landed ten yards in front of him. With the explosion, the air was filled with earth, stones, pieces of wood, and shell splinters. One sliver of steel struck the saddle on which he was seated. His horse dropped beneath him with another splinter through the brain. Three other horses were killed, but the only harm to Richthofen was a hole in his overcoat and the destruction of his equipment and the contents of his saddlebags.

But where was the glory in such a death? An unseen, unknown Frenchman pulled the lanyard on an unseen fieldpiece thousands of yards away and sent forth an engine of destruction to deal death. An unseen, unknown, impersonal target received the charge and died. What a death! It was not Richthofen's idea of war. He wanted the personal element. He wanted to attack a man and kill him.

Three months of this stagnation without change and Christmas approached—the first Christmas of the war and the first one Richthofen had ever spent away from his mother's home. He wrote her continually that he was sick of the work assigned to him, and that he envied his younger brother, who, at least, was still a cavalryman and had the chance at any time to come into actual contact with the enemies of the Fatherland.

With the new year came a slight change when he was appointed Ordnance Officer of an infantry brigade, but the endless inspections and unending paper work brought to him the deeper realization that war was by no means what he thought it was going to be, and with this growing disappointment came disgust. Only when there were prospects of movement was he lifted from the gloom of depression into which the stalemate of 1915 had thrown him.

In February of that year, before Avillers, Allied pressure increased, and there was the possibility of a break through. There were frequent night alarms in which the brigade staffs were called upon to put all reserves in readiness to fill a breach in the line, but always it was the same. The break never came, and after each attempt life settled down to what it had been before.

At times he would give serious consideration to his own chances of being "bagged" in the game of war. He believed in his luck and liked the axiom that "He who hesitates is lost." He frequently made a mistake, but he never shunned a decision.

His schoolboy friend, Hugo Frei of the Fourth Dragoons, was killed, but his death made only a passing impression on Richthofen. He admired Hugo. Hugo was dead. Well, the best ones are always the first to go. "Weeds don't perish" was his comment on his own salvation when his comrades had been killed on both sides of him and he was as yet untouched by an enemy bullet.

But how long could he go on unscathed? That depended upon how long the war went on. Here it was April, and the conflict had raged for nine months, and there was no prospect of its abatement. Richthofen was not the only German, or for that matter the only Allied combatant, who was surprised at the duration.

"Struggling on" was not Richthofen's strong point. He could sit up in a tree throughout a winter night and keep his eyes open watching through the hours for the approach of game. He could track a quarry hour after hour through a forest and never give up the hunt. But he could not play at the war of waiting. It broke his spirit.

So it was that toward the 1st of May, he received instructions to prepare himself for another duty in the service of supply, still farther back from the front lines. Strong as army discipline was in him, he exploded, and the day after that the Commanding General of his Division received one of the shocks of his life when he read the following unmilitary communication from the restless Uhlan:

MY DEAR EXCELLENCY:

I have not gone to war in order to collect cheese and eggs, but for another purpose.

The rest of the letter was an official application for his transfer to the Flying Service. Richthofen's constructive work in either the infantry, the signal service, or the supply department seems to have been on a par with his failure as a cavalryman, and it is not recorded that his departure from the old services was accompanied by any great regret on the part of his superiors. His uncivil letter gained his end and his wish. At the end of May, 1915, he was transferred to the flying service and sent to Cologne for training.

With the old cavalryman's contempt for the gas engine, he knew nothing of what was under the hood of an automobile. He was a horseman, and he had held, with other horsemen, that the cavalry would never have to resort to rubber tires and smelly exhaust pipes. This pardonable ignorance, inherited from the proud spirit of his branch of the service, stood him in bad stead when he began his training for the air. It almost barred him from the pilot's seat.

His conscious inclination was not toward flying as a sport. To him, it offered an opportunity to get in touch with his enemies—to see the man he wanted to kill. At the front he had seen the few military planes then flying, but he had considered them only fads. He was not aware that the legend of his corps as "the eye of the army" had passed forever to another service.

He had watched the airmen aloft with not sufficient interest to learn the different markings that distinguished Allied flyers from German. In the fall of '14, his men had fired their carbines on all planes that passed over them, being unable to distinguish foe from friend, and also being unable to resist the temptation offered by so excellent a human target.

It never occurred to me to be a pilot [he wrote]. I was anxious to get into the air at the front as quickly as possible. I began to fear that I might get there too late; that the World War would be over before I could really get into it. To become a pilot would have required three months' training, and by that time peace might have been concluded.

It was upon his cavalry training, if not experience, that he depended to fit himself for an aërial observer, and at the airdrome in Cologne there was competition to stimulate him. He was in a class of thirty young officers, from which the most successful ones were to be selected and assigned to squadron duty. The others would be given the opportunity of taking the course a second time, and then, in case of a second failure, would be returned to the trenches. Richthofen had had enough of the trenches.

But even his cavalry training for reconnaissance duty failed him that morning in June, 1915, when he went up into the air for the first time. His sense of direction left him, and in his new world of three dimensions he was completely lost. The sensation is not new to anyone who recalls his first flight, but it pained Richthofen and deprived him of the fullest enjoyment of the sensation of flying, which he began to love from that moment.

He had gone to bed early the night before to be in the best possible condition for the early morning flight. He took his seat in a plane for the first time, and encountered the customary discomfort from the propeller's blast, which whipped the muffler from his neck and blew his helmet off before he had time to fasten it. His gloves blew from his hands, and the noise from the engine drowned his voice so that he could not communicate with the pilot in front of him.

In the dash across the flying field, he gripped the sides of his seat and tightened his muscles at every jolt. The machine finally left the ground, slid into the air like a knife blade, wheeled first to the right and then to the left, and then straightened out on a level course 800 feet above the ground. The future ace of all German flying men clutched the sides of the fuselage and peered over and downward. He wrote later that he was much surprised to find that he was lost over his own airdrome.

But there was glory in the motion. The wind tore at the buttons on his jacket and gave him the sensation of speed. Here was movement, here was the stimulation, the intoxication that he had felt taking the jumps on the hunting field.

No sign of sickness or dizziness—just speed and exhilaration. He wanted to sing. His eyes sparkled and his nerves tingled. Here was a steed worthy of a man hunt—with a machine like this beneath him, a man could fight and see what he was fighting.

Richthofen was drunk with enthusiasm when he landed. In the long glide to the landing field, he had been impressed by the heavy silence that followed the heavy noise when the motor slowed down and the plane skimmed over the ground at express-train speed. But he felt that he could know no fear in the air. It was all so simple, all so clean, and God! how he hated the mud of the trenches.

He won his brevet, and after two weeks' daily flights was sent to the Russian front, where Mackensen was hammering his way through the Russian lines at Gorlice. His pleasure was complete. Action at last—burning towns and fields and the forward and backward sway of battle, all unrolled below him every day like some great unnatural spectacle staged to tingle the craving in his heart.

To Richthofen, those months of June, July, and August, 1915, when he flew against the Russians, constituted a new freedom after the muddy drudgery of the trenches. His experience of and distaste for the filth and discomforts of land fighting gave him a new respect and admiration for the million weary ones who plodded on through the mud and grime throughout the war.

The air was clean and free and belonged to the brave, and he was glad to count himself among that care-free company that carried the war closer to God's heaven. To him it was like the war life he had expected to experience in the cavalry.

Morning and afternoon, he sallied forth on reconnaissance flights over the enemy lines and far into the rear, bombing railway stations and bridges, machine-gunning columns of troops on the roads, but most important of all, bringing back the information upon which Mackensen made his plans for new blows against his poorly equipped and none too well organized foes.

His first pilot was Zeumer—little Zeumer, the "lunger." Zeumer was a first lieutenant and one of Germany's earliest pilots. He was considered one of the aces of the Sixty-ninth Squadron, and his daring was a thing that officers and men alike talked about when out of the little fellow's hearing. Zeumer did not like them to talk about it in his presence.

He thought they suspected the reason for his daring. His eyes had a feverish light in them and his sallow skin was drawn tight over his cheek bones and temples. His voice was dry and weak, seeming to come from a mouth that lacked moisture. He frequently wet his lips with his tongue, and sometimes in the upper air he struggled vainly to suppress fits of violent coughing which shook his skinny shoulders and made it difficult for him to keep his fine, thin-skinned, birdlike hands on the flying controls.

Zeumer was dying. Beneath his shrunken chest, slow death gnawed. But his eyes were young and clear, his heart was stout and good, his mind was keen and quick. In the air he was as good as any pair of spotless lungs—yes, better, because he could dare with less to lose and more to gain. He would disprove the charge that war took the best and left the weak.

He would match his few remaining months against the full life span of any healthy human machine that wore the colours of the enemy. If he lost, he lost less in life than his adversary would. And if he lost, he gained that which was dear to him in his doomed silence. To meet quick death in the air as a fighting man would be a victory over the slow death that was gradually killing him from within.

Richthofen gained new lessons in fearlessness in those days when he flew with a dying man. Zeumer's flying was a race with the "bugs," and his goal was the hope of cheating them. His natural instincts of self-preservation had gone out in rasping exhalations. He courted any end other than the one that death had marked for him. Old flying officers shook their heads when they saw the chances he took in the air.

But the race was long. Death in the air evaded him, and the "bugs" gained daily. A year later, he was shot down near Verdun by a French flyer. He arose from the crash with only a few flesh wounds from glancing bullets. Three days later, with his growing weakness, he fell from the pilot's seat of a new machine while it was in the hangar and went into the hospital with a broken thigh. But the dying man's determination knit the bone with the heat of desperation. A month later, he limped out a cripple, but went aloft again trying to catch up his lost laps on the "bugs."

Another year, and it was June again, and France. The story was simple—several lines in a letter from Richthofen to his mother. They read:

> Yesterday, Zeumer was killed in air combat. It was the best that could have happened to him. He knew he had not much longer to live. Such an excellent and noble fellow. How he would have hated to have to drag himself on toward the inevitable end. For him it would have been tragic. As it is, he died a heroic death before the enemy. Within the next few days, his body will be brought home.

Little Zeumer had won his race. Richthofen's was still to be decided.

Chapter III

"To die a hero's death unnecessarily is stupid."

Two young fools once had this thought at the same moment. They believed the moment was their last. The thought flashed to them as they were falling three thousand feet into the fiery furnace of a burning town.

Below them was a sea of flames. Above and around them were dark billows of smoke which stung their eyes and choked them. The heated air through which they fell burned their cheeks and hands. They hurtled through showery clouds of sparks which dug at their leather flying jackets.

"What a fine pair of damned fools we are!"

The pair was in its early twenties. One was a baron and the other was a count. Both were German flying officers. The pilot count's name was Holck. The baron observer was Manfred von Richthofen. Both are dead now.

But they didn't die that day. The god of war and the fortune that favours fools were with them in their fall. One was saved to kill a hundred other men with his own hand before he went to the death that he had dealt to his victims.

The incident which was Richthofen's first brush with death in the air occurred in Russia in the autumn of 1915, when the man who was to become the ace of Germany's air fighters was still a humble observer with hardly a hundred hours in the air to his credit.

From Gorlice to Brest-Litovsk and beyond, the Russians were retiring before the hammering blows of Mackensen's advance. Behind them, they left ruin in the wake of their retreat. Villages, fields, farmhouses, and bridges were ablaze. From the air, it seemed as though the whole countryside were burning. It was the terrible panorama of war.

Richthofen, from the forward observer's seat of his Albatross plane, looked down on the picture and called it "beautiful." His side was winning, advancing. The enemy was withdrawing. The signs of victory were good to see. He shot an exultant smile over his shoulder to Holck, who was working the controls in the pilot's nacelle behind him. That was the way the machines were constructed in those days.

The two were flying back to their lines after a successful reconnaissance flight over enemy territory. They had seen the columns of Russian infantry and artillery moving eastward along the roads, and they had ascertained the direction of the retreat.

Flying at an altitude of 4,500 feet they approached the burning town of Wicznice, over which an enormous column of smoke towered to a height of 6,000 feet. The column looked to be several miles in diameter. It writhed across their path like a great black phantom. To have flown over or around it would have meant five minutes out of their way.

Richthofen smiled to Holck, who returned the smile with a nod. Both were flushed with victory. Around the smoke cloud was safety; through it was danger, and nothing to be gained. The decision had been made in the silent exchange of smiles while the engine roared away merrily and they came closer and closer to the smoke pillar. The plane sped forward with open throttle. It penetrated the smoke volume like a needle disappearing into a black velvet cushion. From sunlight and cool fresh air the two fools found themselves suddenly in hot, suffocating darkness.

The horizon was blotted out: directions became jumbled up, down—right—left—forward—backward—— How? Where? The three dimensions danced drunkenly. A sudden upward blast of almost withering heat, and the machine reeled, tipped, slipped. They coughed and choked. So did the motor.

Richthofen was almost thrown out of his seat, just saving himself by grasping a strut and hanging on. He could not see Holck behind him through the darkness. Out of control and seemingly helpless, they plunged downward. It was like falling down the working smokestack of a giant blast furnace. Then the darkness below them suddenly glowed red and the heat increased. They were looking into the flaming town.

There came a sudden jolt which drove both of them down into their seats with irresistible power. In a flash, their downward descent was changed by the plane catching itself and changing course from the perpendicular to the horizontal. In the next instant, it shot out through the wall of the smoke cylinder and was again the cool air and light of day.

In the few seconds that had passed they had fallen 3,000 feet and were now 1,500 feet above the ground with a smoke-choked motor which began to miss and bring the prospect of a new danger before their smoke-reddened eyes.

As the engine slowed down, they began to lose height, and at the same time bursts of machine-gun fire began to greet them from below. Russian infantry at that time was not noted for any fine feeling toward German aviators. The Russian regiments, many of them containing wild, bearded units from the Siberian steppes, had suffered greatly from the German flyers. Without a flying service of their own, and but very little and quite ineffectual anti-aircraft, the Russians had suffered the customary lot of the defenceless. German aviators falling into the hands of these desperate, hard-pressed mujiks could expect nothing but quick death—and a violent one.

"The motor is giving out!" shouted Holck. Motors with carburetor trouble have been fixed or adjusted in the air by flyers, but this was out of the question for Holck and Richthofen, both of whom, being from the cavalry school, were still ignorant of the simplest facts concerning the source of power upon which they had to depend while in the air. The situation reflects the pioneer stage of martial aviation at the time, and also detracts somewhat from the generally accepted idea of Germany's complete preparedness and the technical efficiency of her flyers.

With the weakened motor, the Albatross lost altitude steadily. Now, at less than a thousand feet above the ground, the Russian machine-gun fire from below increased, and bullets began popping through the fabric of the wings and hitting the taut wire braces. One struck a vital part in the motor and the propeller, after a few slow revolutions, came to a stop. They were gliding down without power.

Holck managed to keep the plane's nose up as they skimmed over the treetops of a small forest and reach a clearing on the other side. Richthofen recognized it as a position that the Russians had occupied with artillery the day before, but was the place still in the hands of the enemy infantry? The plane came to the ground, stripped off its under-carriage, tipped to one side, broke a wing, and came to a halt.

Richthofen and Holck jumped out of the wreck and ran to the shelter of the woods. Holck's little dog, which always flew with him, scampered after them, unmindful of the fears then running through its master's mind. The two flyers threw themselves flat on the ground at the edge of the trees and peered out across the clearing. Richthofen had a pistol and six cartridges. Holck was unarmed.

A man came running across the clearing from the other side. The hidden pair saw that he was in uniform, but they still could not distinguish which uniform, and the German spiked helmet, then worn, was ominously absent. The man was wearing a cloth cap. Was he Russian or German? Were they in the enemy lines or their own?

Holck answered the question with a shout of joy as he recognized the uniform as that of a grenadier of the Prussian Guard. These troops had stormed this part of the line that morning and had penetrated as far as the Russian artillery positions. The fugitives came out from their hiding place and learned from the soldier that a general advance all along the line was in progress.

By the narrowest margin of chance, the two young Uhlans

who had dared to dive through the smoke column over the burning town had escaped death both in the flames and at the hands of the retreating Russians. For their luck, they received the congratulations of the German Prince Eitel Friedrich, who soon rode across the old Russian position with his staff officers. He supplied the stranded airmen with horses upon which they returned to their airdrome.

Before the end of August, 1915, aërial activity on the Russian front came to a temporary halt, and Richthofen's itch of restlessness was gratified with orders which took him back across Germany and into Belgium again, this time to the renowned seaside resort of Ostend, where pilots and aviators were being trained on the latest German model, the *Grossflleugzeug,* or "Big Fighting Machine," from which great results were expected.

These machines, owing to their bulk and weight, lacked speed and manœuvring ability, which detracted greatly from their fighting capacity, with the result that their eventual utility was that of night bombers. In the slang of the air, Richthofen called it his "big apple barge."

Little Zeumer, the "lunger" who had been his first pilot in Russia, was again at the controls of his machine here, and Richthofen flew with him many times on bombing expeditions over Belgian towns occupied by the British forces.

Richthofen liked bombing, but he did not like the arrangements on his machine which prevented the observer from witnessing the burst of the bomb after it had landed.

> This always made me wild [wrote the future ace], because one does not like to be deprived of one's amusement. If one hears a bang down below and sees the delightful grayish, whitish cloud of the explosion in the neighbourhood of the object aimed at, one is always pleased.

To the right and left of the observer's forward seat in which the bomb-aiming device and the release levers were located were the two whirring propellers. On one expedition—a daylight raid over a village in the vicinity of Dunkirk—Richthofen had just released his first bomb and was peering over the side to see how close it burst to its target. As usual, one of the plane's wings came between him and the object, wiping out his view. He quickly extended his left hand in a signal to Zeumer to turn to the left so that he could see.

In his eagerness he forgot the whirring propeller blades and lost the tip of his little finger. He confessed that the pain, while slight, deprived him of further amusement in bombing for that day, and that, after hurriedly dropping the remainder of his missiles, he returned to the airdrome and a seven-day spell in the hospital. It was his first tiny drop of blood for the Fatherland for which he was later to give his life.

The war was not too bad, those happy, sunny days in Ostend. It was fun to bathe in the surf and loll in bathrobes on the beach, with orderlies to serve coffee and drinks from the big Palace Hotel that the army had seized. One drawback, however, was that the Belgian girls shunned the beach during 1915, both from choice and from the fact that the naval gun batteries which the Germans had installed in emplacements along the sand dunes were forbidden areas to the civil population.

There came one day an interruption to the peaceful scene, when bugles suddenly sounded, and the officers lounging on the beach hurriedly left their deck chairs and directed their field glasses seaward, where distant smudges of black smoke revealed the presence of a British naval squadron.

A tiny flash of light is seen against the black smoke, and in less than a minute a big shell arrives on the beach, sending up a geyser of sand, beach chairs, and striped parasols. Richthofen and a number of his fellow officers spent the remaining minutes of the fight in the deep dugouts which they laughingly called the "heroes' cellar."

Back in the air, on the next day, he and Zeumer tested out the auto-locking arrangements on the rudder of their twin motor machine, by which the plane could be made to hold a normal course if only one motor was working. The experiment took them far out over the English Channel, and, in the midst of it, Richthofen's keen eyes detected a submarine in the water beneath them.

The huge black hulk was travelling slowly under water when the two airmen caught sight of it. They went down to several hundred feet above the sea and flew back and forth across the spot.

Richthofen's face became tense and his hands reached for the levers on the bomb releases. Here was a battle to his liking—a new thrill: bird against fish—and this time with the bird having all the advantage of its blind adversary below.

The undersea boat was submerged too far to use its periscope, and yet it could be easily seen from the eyes in the air. But one thing could not be detected. That was the nationality of the submarine, and Richthofen had to suppress his destructive instinct through an inability to determine whether the craft was Allied or German.

His debate and regret over having to relinquish such easy prey was interrupted by warning heat from one of the motors, and a sudden realization that the water had disappeared from one of the radiators. They started for the coast at once with the auto-locking arrangement working on the rudder and thereby enabling them to reach land on the one working motor. It was just another close shave with trouble.

Stalking a submarine from the air offered greater possibilities for results than aërial combat in the fall of 1915, when the tactics of air fighting were still undeveloped. Hostile airmen were almost immune from danger from one another, because air armament and methods of attack were inadequate, if not totally lacking.

This was one of the reasons why the chivalry of the air at the commencement of war permitted the airmen of opposing sides to fly about their duties without molestation from one another. Airplanes were considered primarily for the purposes of observation, secondly for bombing. Actual fighting in midair was almost unheard of, and the airman's chief dread was from machine gun or shell fire from the ground.

This state of affairs did not last long. Pilots began to take up with them rifles, carbines, revolvers, and rifle grenades to attack one another. Air fighting commenced in that way, but with very little success. Machines moving past one another at several hundred miles an hour had little chance of winging one another with single shots. The machine-gun mounting had not been perfected.

Richthofen failed in his first air fight. It occurred in the month of September, 1915. Both he and Zeumer were impressed with the battling name of their machine, and both were eager to test its fighting capacity. Although they flew from five to six hours every day on bombing and reconnaissance flights, they had never encountered an enemy plane in the air. Their hopes materialized one day when they sighted a lone Farman plane with the British cockade, taking casual observations over the German lines.

Zeumer headed for the plane. Richthofen's heart beat faster and he gripped his repeating rifle. Neither had been in a fight before; neither had ever seen a combat between planes, and neither of them had ever heard the first-hand account of an air battle. Both knew that they wanted to knock the other plane down out of the sky, but neither knew how it was to be done.

The planes approached from opposite directions, but before Richthofen knew what was happening, they had passed one another and were out of range. He had had time in the passing to fire four shots at the whizzing comet, but the only apparent result was to inform the English flyer of his intentions. The latter swung his plane around and attacked the German machine from the rear. The Englishman in the forward observer's seat fired a repeating rifle into the tail of the German plane.

Zeumer, trying to avoid the fire, flew around in a circle

with the Englishman flying after him. After several minutes of this futility, both planes flew away. Zeumer and Richthofen landed at their airdrome and each blamed the other.

Zeumer held that Richthofen had shot badly. Richthofen charged Zeumer with not having manœuvred the plane right so as to give him the chance for a good shot. The air relations between the pilot and observer became decidedly strained.

They tried it again the same day, but still with no result. Zeumer, who was considered one of the best pilots, regretted that he could discover no means of flying that would enable his observer to fire a fatal shot. Richthofen, who prided himself on his marksmanship, began to feel that he would never be able to bring down a hostile plane, no matter how many shots he had at it. Both were puzzled and discouraged. War in the air was young.

A month later, when activity commenced on the Champagne front, Richthofen and Zeumer and the "Apple barge" tried their luck again against the French, but still without result. It was not until afterward, when Richthofen flew with Osteroth, another pilot who had a small machine, that his nature was able to exult with the feeling that he had shot down a human victim from the air.

Osteroth's machine was equipped with a machine gun that could be moved from one mounting to another on the two sides of the observer's cockpit, which in this plane was behind the pilot. The French plane was a Farman two-seater, and, strange as it may seem, it does not appear that its two occupants had any hostile intentions toward the German plane, which they permitted to approach them from the rear and to fly along with them side by side.

Richthofen, with his machine gun mounted on the side facing the French plane, opened hostilities with a rapid burst of ten or twenty shots, which was stopped by the jamming of the weapon. None of the shots had struck the French plane, but the fire had been noticed, and the Frenchman began to fire back, also with a machine gun.

Richthofen worked at the jammed gun, and got it going again while Osteroth held the plane to its course. The two machines sailed along at equal altitudes like two rival cruisers, exchanging broadsides after the fashion of sea warfare. Both of the flyers ignored the manœuvring possibilities of the third dimension.

With the gun working and Osteroth reducing the range by flying gradually closer to the Frenchman, Richthofen poured out the last of his hundred rounds of cartridges, firing all the time with the picture of the French observer across from him firing at him. Then it happened with a suddenness that surprised Richthofen. He said later that he could not believe his eyes when he saw the French plane begin to go down in a spiral.

Osteroth was busy with the controls, so Richthofen reached forward and tapped him on the head to call his attention to the adversary's descent. Richthofen's eyes never left his prey. Osteroth circled slowly downward, keeping the falling machine in view all the time. They saw it land head first in a shell crater with its tail pointing to the sky.

Hurriedly, they located the spot on the flying map and marked it with a circle, noting that it was located three miles behind the French lines. Neither ever knew whether the two Frenchmen survived the descent. From the fact that the tail of the plane was still pointing skyward, the landing was not as bad as it might have been, and there is the possibility that the first two men that Richthofen shot down in the air may have survived.

But of particular regret to the future German ace at that time was the rule then prevailing in the German Air Corps, to the effect that planes brought down behind the enemy lines were not placed to the credit of the flyer or flyers who downed them. Richthofen was proud of his success, but never forgot that his record of officially credited victories, which amounted to eighty before his death, should have been one more.

His experience with Osteroth, and it was a happy one, convinced him that his chances of killing many adversaries in the air would not be great as long as his flying was confined to large two-seater planes. He realized early that these planes were too clumsy for manœuvring, and that the small, speedy single-seater had every advantage in a combat with the bigger plane. It is to be noted from his record of victories after he became the pilot of a single-seater that almost three quarters of them were big double-seater planes.

Little Zeumer graduated to a Fokker single-seated monoplane as soon as this type reached the front, and Richthofen, still an observer, found himself shifted to another two-seater plane with another pilot. This hurt his pride. His restless spirit demanded action and progress. He wanted to become a pilot, and his desires gained their greatest impetus when, on October 1, 1915, he met for the first time the great Boelcke.

To Richthofen, Boelcke was the German air god. That day, in the fall of 1915, when he met the young and insignificant-looking little lieutenant in the dining car of a train, marked the birth of a new ambition in Richthofen. Boelcke had shot down four hostile airplanes, and he was the only man in the armies of the Central Powers who had accomplished such a feat. At that time, he was the greatest individual killer in the German Air Corps. His name had been mentioned in dispatches. His appearance was not impressive, but his successes in the air, then widely known, gripped the imagination of the young Uhlan.

"Tell me how you manage to shoot them down," Richthofen asked the idol as the two sat over a bottle of Rhine wine in the dining car.

"Well, it's quite simple," he said. "I fly close to my man, aim well, and then, of course, he falls down."

Richthofen, who had asked the question in all seriousness, reflected that he had followed somewhat the same method, but his opponents did not seem to come down so easily. He became more convinced than ever that the difference lay not so much with the flyer as with the plane he flew. He could not shoot them down in a "big fighting plane," but Boelcke could in a Fokker. He resolves to do two things: to cultivate Boelcke and to fly a Fokker.

Little Zeumer, his first pilot, came to his aid and flew with him in an old training machine, a two-seater which had dual controls, so that the student pilot in the observer's cockpit could operate the machine from that point, and any mistakes of his could be corrected immediately by the instructor in the pilot's cockpit. Richthofen hurled himself into the work with desperation and studied harder than he ever had in his life. Upon their landing after the twenty-fifth instruction in the air, Zeumer announced that the lessons were over and that the pupil was fit to take the plane into the air by himself, fly it, and return it safely to the ground.

It was in the stillness of a late October afternoon that the man who was to become the ace of all German airmen took a plane into the air alone for the first time. In spite of his long experience now as an observer and a student pilot, Richthofen had fears. He did not think he could fly and land safely. His fears were well grounded. He couldn't.

His head was buzzing with Zeumer's parting instructions when he climbed into the pilot's familiar cockpit, tested the controls as he had been taught, made his ignition contact, and felt the vibration of the plane as the motor started in response to a swing on the propeller by a mechanic.

The chocks were removed from the wheels—the plane moved off across the field into the wind and, with the motor full on, left the ground. Richthofen was in the air and with the knowledge now that his safe return to earth depended solely upon himself. His fears left him as the exhilarating tingle of motion stole over him. Acting under Zeumer's last instructions, he circled to the left, and flying over a ground mark, previously arranged, shut off his motor and headed the plane back for the landing field, as he had been told.

Now came the test—the landing. His actions were entirely mechanical. He followed instructions to the letter. He did exactly as he had been told to do, but he lacked the "feel" of the air and of his machine. His flying was by the book and not by instinct. He noticed that the plane's responses to his controls were different from what he had expected. Something was wrong. He was not on an even keel. The plane was approaching the ground at a high rate of speed.

CRASH!

Men came rushing across the field from the hangars as Richthofen, shaken but uninjured, extricated himself from the pile of splintered struts, twisted wire braces, and torn fabric. On his first solo flight he had failed.

Smarting under the gibes and jokes of his comrades, he returned to his quarters, and made a vow that nothing would stop his mastering the art of flying. He plunged passionately into studies and instructions, working days and nights on the machines, both in the air and on the ground. After two weeks' intensive cramming, he believed he had overcome his faults, and presented himself for his first examination.

This time he got off the ground well, circled left and right, described figure eights in the air several times, and landed evenly and easily. He repeated the demonstration several times, and glowed with pride when he brought the plane down safely on the final landing. He received the greatest disappointment of his life when the examining officer, who had witnessed his performance in the air, told him that his flying and landings were faulty, that he did not appear to be in full control of the machine, and that he had failed in his examination again.

Richthofen developed perseverance and grim determination in the weeks of hard study and training that followed. In spite of his failures, he persisted in his ambition to become a pilot. On the 15th of November, he flew as an observer in a big Gotha from the front to Doberitz, near Berlin, to make another effort toward mastering the pilot's controls.

For five weeks he and another young lieutenant, of the name of Lyncker, applied themselves entirely to the task. Both of them had the ambition to become pilots and fly single-seater Fokkers in a fighting squadron on the western front. Boelcke was their ideal, and no work was too hard that brought them any closer to walking in the footsteps of the great air fighter.

Christmas Day that year—1915—brought him the reward he craved. He was notified that he had passed his third examination and was now a pilot. Although he had been successful in the tests, it does not appear that his instructors had sufficient confidence in his ability to send him to the front.

During spells of fair weather in January and the following

months, he made practice flights about Germany, landing at Breslau and Luben, and once at his home in Schweidnitz. Another flight took him back to Schwerin, where he reduced somewhat his ignorance of gas motors by a study of the engines in the Fokker plant.

He arrived at the front as a pilot in March, 1916, being assigned to the so-called "Second Fighting Squadron" then stationed in the line behind Verdun. Richthofen was eager for combat. He wanted a fight in the air, with himself operating both the flying controls and the machine gun. Although he was a pilot, he had not yet achieved his ambition to fly a single-seater machine. He was still assigned to the heavier two-place planes and had to carry an observer with him.

As the planes were then constructed, this would have left all of the fighting to the observer and all of the flying to the pilot. This arrangement did not appeal to Richthofen. He had another machine gun built into his plane, so that he could operate it from the pilot's seat. The plane was an Albatross, with the observer sitting behind the pilot and operating a rear machine gun.

The forward machine-gun mounting was copied from that in use at the time on the French Nieuports. It was fixed above the upper plane in such a manner that it could be pointed upward or straight ahead in the direction of the machine. Other pilots rather ridiculed the idea, but Richthofen was proud of it and hoped for any early opportunity to test its practical value.

The chance came on the morning of April 26th, when Richthofen and his observer sighted a Nieuport machine wearing the French cockade. The two observed the enemy plane for some time and then flew toward it, although Richthofen had not made up his mind how he would attack the plane. It is apparent from the tactics that followed that the Frenchman was almost as much of a beginner as Richthofen, because, as the two planes approached, the Nieuport swerved and started to fly away.

This manœuvre would have been safe had the German plane been equipped only with a rear machine gun. A gun so placed could not shoot forward at a pursued plane, but the pursued plane would be able to fire on the pursuer from its own rear gun. It is possible that the Frenchman did not observe the unusual mounting of the forward gun on the German two-seater.

Richthofen approached within sixty yards of the French plane. His disappointments in flying had been so great that he had small hopes of winging his prey, but he did want to reap the full benefits of practice. Sighting the machine gun on the tail of the plane directly in front of him, he fired a short burst of shots.

The Nieuport answered by zooming upward and side-slipping on one wing. The German plane shot by to one side, and Richthofen was surprised to see the French plane fall over and over in the air. He became wary immediately, suspecting that the Frenchman was manœuvring his machine in this manner in an endeavour to trick the German plane into an unadvantageous position.

From a safe distance they watched the descent of the Frenchman. It became apparent that the machine was completely out of control. It never righted itself once. The observer tapped Richthofen on the head.

"Congratulations!" he shouted, trying to make his voice heard above the idling motor. "He's falling! He's done for! You hit him."

The fluttering white machine crashed among the treetops of the thick forest behind Fort Douaumont. The Frenchman fell behind his own lines, and Richthofen never knew his fate.

The German plane flew back to its airdrome, where Richthofen proudly reported that he had had an aërial combat and had shot down a Nieuport. For that day the German war communiqué read:

> Two hostile flying machines have been shot down in aërial fighting above Fleury, south and west of Douaumont.

Early next morning, Richthofen wrote his exultation to his mother in the following letter:

Before Verdun, April 27, 1916.

LIEBE MAMMA:

In haste—some gladsome news. Look at the communiqué of yesterday, April 26th. One of these planes was shot down by my machine gun and is to my credit.

MANFRED.

He had brought down his prey—he had tasted nameless acknowledgment in the communiqué, but his craving for the credit for the kill was again thwarted by the army rule which ignored, in so far as the flyer's record was concerned, any planes brought down behind the enemy lines. His pride in his achievement was great, but he had a certain feeling of pique in being denied what he considered his just due, namely, a public acknowledgment of his victory over the unknown French flyer.

Chapter IV

With a bullet through his head, he fell from an altitude of 9,000 feet—a beautiful death."

Baron Manfred von Richthofen employed this sentence in a letter to his mother to describe the end of his closest friend and oldest flying comrade, the young Count von Holck with whom he had had his first air adventures in Russia.

Flying almost two miles above the battle lines in front of Verdun, Richthofen, from a distance, saw his old friend battling for his life with a number of French fighting planes. A contrary wind, a slow engine, and the intervening distance between him and the scene of the fatal combat prevented him from going to Holck's assistance, and he was forced to stand off helplessly when the latter started on his fatal plunge.

The spectacle occurred May 1, 1916, just four days after Richthofen himself had shot down a French flyer in the same sector. The German war machine was still pounding away at Verdun, and a violent drum fire was playing on the battered, shell-pocked ruins of Fort Douaumont, still valiantly held by the French. A strong wind was blowing from the west.

The Flying Uhlan, from the pilot's cockpit of his biplane, saw three French Caudrons savagely attacking a Fokker single-seater machine which he suspected was Holck's, although he hoped that it was not. The Caudrons dived repeatedly, but always managed to maintain a position between the Fokker and the German lines.

Gradually, the fight circled over the French position in the town of Verdun. Richthofen and his observer, still too far away to get into the *mêlée,* watched the unequal combat with frequent exclamations of admiration for the hard-pressed German pilot who, although outnumbered three to one, was giving an excellent account of himself.

It soon became apparent, however, that Holck was on the defensive. Other French machines were between him and the German lines, and his numerous adversaries dived on him relentlessly, spraying lead from all angles. Holck lost altitude with every manœuvre, and Richthofen and his observer both knew that this was fatal. It's the man on top who wins in the air.

They could not fly to Holck's assistance. Their two-seater machine was too heavy and its motor too weak to make headway against the wind and arrive on the scene of the fight in time to be of use.

Holck plunged downward through some small clouds, and Richthofen's heart beat faster in the belief that his old friend had evaded his adversaries by this move. But it was not a ruse. It was Holck's last dive. One of the French bullets had gone through his head. The German pilot's lifeless body was strapped in the seat when the Fokker nosed downward and plunged almost two miles to the earth.

It was no time for regrets. Air activity in the Verdun sector increased steadily during that summer of 1916, and the French Nieuports were exacting regular toll from the German flyers who dared to meet them. Death was a frequent visitor to Richthofen's squadron. Under date of June 22d, he wrote to his mother:

What did you say about Immelmann's death? In time, death comes to us all—also to Boelcke. The leader of Lothar's fighting squadron also did not return from the bombing flight. The day before, the leader of my old fighting squadron No. 1 was also shot down. He was the Baron von Gerstoff, one of the most efficient squadron leaders. I liked him very much.

The death that Richthofen predicted almost came to him two weeks after writing that letter. To the satisfaction of his great ambition, he had obtained permission to make some test flights in a single-seater Fokker, in which he believed he could duplicate the easy and multiple air victories of Immelmann and Boelcke.

But air equipment was not plentiful, and he had to share the new machine with a fellow pilot, who was equally ambitious to get away from the heavy two-seater planes and cruise the air lanes as an individual fighting unit. An element of security was not entirely foreign to this mutual ambition.

Richthofen and his comrade both knew that by far the largest number of victims in the air were amongst those who flew the heavy two-seater planes. They were the prey of the speedy little one-seaters. The fighting capacities of the two types measured up like a comparison between a butterfly and a wasp. Richthofen was sick of butterflies. The wasps got too many of them. He wanted to be a wasp and hunt butterflies.

The joint ownership of the new Fokker was unsatisfactory to both Richthofen and his comrade. Each feared that the other one would smash the plane. One flew it in the morning and the other flew it in the afternoon.

Richthofen made his first trip without encountering a single enemy plane, and, returning to the airdrome, made a difficult but safe landing. His comrade flew off with the prize Fokker that afternoon, and that was the last Richthofen ever saw of it. It crashed in No Man's Land, but the pilot escaped uninjured and managed to return to the German lines after lying in a shell crater until darkness.

The young Uhlan became the sole owner of the next single-seater that was issued to the squadron. Just as he left the ground on his third flight, the motor stopped and he had to make a forced landing in a near-by field. All that remained of the machine was a scrap pile, but the flying Baron again escaped death without a scratch.

Advancement he craved, but it came hard for him. The failures that marked his efforts to progress from observer to pilot still plagued his attempts to advance from the two-seater to the single-seater types. Although only responsible for one, he was really charged with crashing two Fokker single-seaters, and this record was taken into consideration when he was once more definitely assigned to the heavy two-seaters and suddenly transferred from the Verdun front back to the eastern theatre of war, the scene of his martial début in the air.

The fighting squadron functioned as bombers and travelled as a "circus." It had special trains for the flyers, the mechanics, and the planes. They were equipped with dining and sleeping cars and repair shops. Everyone's baggage and personal effects remained on board, so there were none of the delays and troubles of breaking camp whenever the squadron changed its base of operations.

Bombing ground troops from above gave him a "tremendous pleasure." His enthusiasm was tireless. There were times when, after dropping one load of bombs on a camp or a troop train, he would fly back to his airdrome, load up with explosives and fuel, and return to the last scene of carnage with another delivery of death.

It was more fruitful from the standpoint of results than seeking victims in the air. So often the fighting pilot had to return with an empty bag from a hunt in the sky. Maybe he didn't find the quarry, or it was too wary for him, but not so with the bombing expeditions. There was always something that could be done with bombs, and one need never return with a feeling of unrewarded efforts.

The Russian army in the field, almost defenceless from the air, constituted an excellent target. Anyone who could throw a missile out of a boat and hit the surrounding water, was almost equally capable of registering a hit if he dropped a bomb from the air anywhere immediately behind the Russian front lines.

Sweating under the heat of the August midday sun, Russian troops were being massed for an attack in front of a rail centre in the town of Manjewicze, twenty miles back of the lines. Under orders to disrupt the Russian communications, demoralize their reserves, and thereby weaken the force of their attack, the bombing squadron left its airdrome at noon.

Their "C" type planes of the two-seat reconnaissance variety were heavily loaded with bombs to the limit of their capacity, which was about three hundred pounds of explosive each, in addition to the extra fuel, ammunition for two machine guns, and the weight of the pilot and the observer.

They rose heavily in the light, hot air of midday, and reeled perilously as they left the ground. Once in the upper air, beyond the danger of sudden sinkings from low air pockets, pilot and observer breathed freer. The anticipation of a ground crash with three hundred pounds of explosive suspended under one is not without a tingle to the dullest imagination.

Richthofen had a fat observer, whose extra weight he begrudged because it meant that he must carry less bombs. With his 150-horsepower motor turning over under a full throttle, he managed to get the plane off the ground. The engine hummed regularly during the several preliminary circles that he made up above his own airdrome. This was a precaution taken by all flyers, especially those on the east front, because all of them knew that a descent behind the Russian lines on account of a motor failure meant death. Owing to the almost complete absence of Russian aircraft and the scarcity and inaccuracy of Russian anti-aircraft artillery, "dead motors" represented the principal risk.

They flew over Manjewicze, easily recognizable from its web of hurriedly constructed side tracks, and the hundreds of tents and wooden barracks which had been erected around it. Houses and barracks were smoking, and one end of the railroad station was wrecked, all indicating that some of Richthofen's comrades had already reached the target and "laid their eggs."

They dropped bomb after bomb on the railroad station, and damaged the one remaining line, so that a locomotive which happened to be moving out slowly at the time was forced to stop at the place where the bombs had torn up the rails and made a large hole in the right of way. They flew so low that they could see the engineer and fireman hurriedly abandon the engine and dive into a ditch beside the track.

It was all quite easy. No enemy airplanes to watch out for; no intensive fire from the ground to fear. Richthofen thought that flying on the east front was joy-riding as compared to the difficulties encountered on the west front. He was right, because at that time, which was immediately after the beginning of the 1916 battle of the Somme, the British Flying

Corps had swept the German air force from the air and made their flyers the butt of stinging jokes on the part of the undefended German infantry.

Many German flyers paid with their lives for the British air offensive on the Somme, and Richthofen's happy assignment during that period to the eastern front may be looked upon as one of the reasons for his survival throughout that year.

That season on the Russian front was a carnival of unimpeded daily slaughter for the young sky Uhlan. Computation of the lives he took on the ground is obviously not possible, but it is quite possible that he killed many more men in this manner than he did in his entire career of combat in the air. It was wholesale. He liked that. It fed the killing hunger, but his spirit of combat starved. It was all killing and no fighting. Richthofen preferred a mixture of the two.

Once the squadron was sent to break up a concentration of Russian troops which were crossing the Stokhod River in preparation for an attack. A long column of Cossacks were riding four abreast over the single bridge when Richthofen arrived above the spot with a plane heavily laden with bombs and machine-gun munitions. He circled low over the target, and the Cossack column went into a gallop.

Depressing the nose of the plane, he dived and swooped low over the crowded bridge. He and his observer could see the bearded Cossacks bending low over their horses' necks and urging them to greater speed upon the appearance of this new enemy from a quarter in which they could not defend themselves. Richthofen's observer, with his eye glued to the bomb sights, pulled the lever that released the first missile.

It missed the bridge, but landed beside the crowded approach on one bank. A cloud of dust and smoke, a terrific detonation, and the galloping column was cut in half by the appearance of a large white half circle of roadway dotted with the prone figures of men and horses.

Some horses on the bridge leaped the stone side parapets and landed with their riders in the stream below. Others on the shore edge of the circle bolted. But the column closed up again, and the charge across the bridge continued.

Three times the air guerilla swooped low, and each time another bomb landed among the massed horsemen, creating terrific havoc. Men and animals were rushing and dragging themselves away in all directions from the centre of the bomb burst. The disorder was complete, with officers urging their men to re-form and proceed, but with every mind intent above anything else on the danger from the air.

With all bombs expended, the two flyers repeated their

swoop manœuvre, spraying the column with machine-gun lead. Men toppled off their horses and were trampled underneath their comrades who were galloping behind them. Horses rolled on the ground, and others fell over them. "We enjoyed it tremendously," Richthofen wrote, "and I imagined that I alone had caused the Russian attack to fail."

It was an orgy of blood for the Flying Uhlan, and he was in high mood to receive a reward for his efforts. In the space of twenty minutes, he probably killed more men than his air combats would total in his busiest month, but the slaughter did not show on his record, and he loved the trophies of victory—the symbols of his prowess. The prize he received was even greater than he had expected.

On that day, the great Boelcke arrived at the airdrome at Kovel.

Everyone in the squadron knew the purpose of his visit. The great German flyer was selecting flyers for a crack squadron which he would take to the west front to fight under his command against the British. The German air force, driven down on the Somme, left German artillery blind and German infantry defenceless from air attack and subject to terrific punishment from British and French artillery, which was well directed from the air.

The day after his arrival at Kovel, Boelcke, wearing the star of the order Pour le Mérite, called in person at Richthofen's quarters.

"Would you like to go with me to the Somme and see some real fighting?" Boelcke inquired. Richthofen almost fell on his neck. Three days later, he was speeding across Germany on a train with his greatest wish fulfilled. Boelcke, his god, had chosen him to be one of the great new fighting squadron. "From now on began the finest time of my life," he wrote as he thrilled to the new joy and distinction.

Jagdstaffel No. 2 was the military designation of Boelcke's new combat organization, whose mission was to put the German air force back into the air on the western front. These selected pilots were assigned specially fast and new one-seater planes whose sole use was fighting. Bombing and reconnaissance and artillery direction from now on became the duty of the slower, heavier machines.

The Jagdstaffel reached the Somme basin during the second week of September, and Boelcke began at once to inculcate a new fighting spirit into his cubs, most of whom were young and, although at home in the air, had but little or no experience in the rapidly developing tactics of air fighting. The cubs trained on the ground and in the air hours every day, improving their marksmanship by firing thousands of rounds of machine-gun ammunition into the target butts and practising fighting evolutions.

Boelcke flew early every morning, returning to the airdrome to take the first meal of the day with his cubs. Three days in succession he reported to them that he had been able to shoot an Englishman for breakfast that morning.

He told them how he killed them, and they leaned anxiously over their plates with their eyes glued on those of the master. With each new tale of death, their fighting spirit and eagerness increased.

Richthofen became impatient for the arrival of the new planes on which they were to make their grand début.

They came, and the cubs took off with their master on the first test flight. Behind the German lines, they played "follow the leader," Boelcke going through his fighting manœuvres and then ordering the cubs to perform the same feats. He put them through the stunts one after another, and then flew them in squadron formation and signalled orders to them by movements of the wings of his planes. When they returned to the ground, he congratulated all of them and told them that the squadron would receive its baptism of fire on the following day.

It was the 17th of September and a glorious fine day when the Jagdstaffel, the first of the famous German flying circuses, went into battle for the first time. It was the date on which young Richthofen was to taste blood officially in the air for the first time.

The morning sun shone brightly as the air fighters went aloft. They did not have to go far before sighting the enemy. The British were out early, and as usual were seeking combat with the enemy over the enemy's ground. Boelcke was the was the first to recognize a hostile squadron of British planes flying far behind the German lines in the direction of Cambrai.

He signalled the intelligence and his intentions to the V formation of his young disciples, and they followed him as he manœuvred into position between the English planes and the front line. The Germans were between them and their base. The Britishers would have to fight to get back.

Ritchthofen counted seven planes in the enemy formation which contained units of the Eleventh Squadron of the Royal Flying Corps, composed of heavy bombing planes and an escort of two-seater fighting planes of the F. E. type. The English flew steadily on their course, which was a mission of destruction behind the German lines. The German manœuvre seemed neither to startle them nor to deflect them from the object of their regular flight. They kept on toward their goal.

Boelcke and Richthofen and three more of the Jagdstaffel approached the squadron. The altitude was about ten thousand feet. Richthofen and the other cubs kept their eyes on their leader and hoped for the chance to show their ability under his eyes. They all thirsted for a "kill."

They watched Boelcke in the lead as the master approached the first English machine quite closely, but refrained from firing. Richthofen followed immediately behind the squadron leader. The enemy plane closest to him was a large two-seater F. E. painted in dark colours.

At its controls was Second Lieutenant L. B. F. Morris, and in the observer's seat behind him was Lieutenant T. Rees. Both were youngsters. Rees manned a Lewis machine gun, mounted on a turntable pivot over the observer's seat, and Morris had another Lewis fixed to the fuselage and shooting forward through the propeller arc.

Richthofen's plane was a single-seater and speedier. His two machine guns were fixed to the fuselage and fired only forward through the propeller. He approached within fifty yards of the English plane and opened fire.

At the same instant a stream of lead poured from the rear machine gun on the English plane. Rees was on the job, and his aim was good because Richthofen was forced to change his position immediately. He dived out of range, but zoomed upward again and regained his position above and in the rear of Morris and Rees.

Whenever he approached within range, Rees opened fire, and Richthofen would see the English tracer bullets zipping through the air quite close to him. The English plane with its forward and after machine guns could shoot in almost all directions, while Richthofen's weapon shot only forward, so that, in order to land a telling shot, he had to get behind the Englishman.

Morris was young but experienced. Every time Richthofen attempted to get behind him, he would swerve into a circle, during which time the German flyer, coming under the muzzle of Rees's movable machine gun, would find himself in danger of being riddled. Morris twisted and turned and flew in zigzag spurts, increasing Richthofen's difficulty in bringing his guns to bear on the plane. Rees met every attack and succeeded in keeping the overeager Uhlan at a healthy distance.

Appearing to accept failure for the time being, Richthofen changed his tactics and dived into a cloud. He made a large circle and returned at a lower altitude. With his speedy machine, he soon had the English plane in view again and noticed that Morris was now flying straight on instead of twisting and turning. From this he presumed that the two English flyers had lost sight of him.

He recalled the instructions of Boelcke. He had studied the model of the F. E., and he knew that directly to the rear and slightly below the English plane was a "blind spot"—a small angle of vision which could be covered neither by the pilot nor the observer nor their guns. He had manœuvred himself into this safe angle, and Morris and Rees above him were unaware that he was "under their tail."

He pulled up on the stick sharply and, with his motor roaring under a wide-open throttle, zoomed upward under the dark red belly of the English plane. In the flash of a few seconds, he was within thirty yards of his quarry, and his twin machine guns were trained on the bottom of the plane.

His finger pressed the trigger button, and the speeded-up Spandaus poured forth a stream of lead which raked the under belly of the Britisher machine from nose to tail. The first part of the stream shattered the crank case of the engine, releasing the compression and destroying the motor. The spray next ripped through the fabric and wooden bracing above which Morris was seated. The last of the stream sewed a long seam of lead under the cockpit in which Rees was sitting.

In describing the fight, Richthofen said:

> At that time, I did not have the conviction, as I later had in similar cases—the conviction best described by the sentence "He must fall." In this, my first encounter, I was curious to see if he would fall. There is a great difference between the two feelings. When one has shot down one's first, second, or third opponent, then one begins to find out how the trick is done.

After delivering the burst of lead into the bottom of the English plane, Richthofen found himself so close under the F.E. that he had to swerve suddenly to one side to avoid colliding with it. As he came out from under and swept by, he saw that the propeller of the English plane had stopped. "I nearly yelled with joy," he said afterward.

The English plane reared and side-slipped. Morris at the stick had received some of the bullets from below and was, temporarily at least, out of control of the plane. As the machine fell, Richthofen dived on it and, looking down into the after cockpit, saw Rees crumpled up on his seat. He was either dead or unconscious. The disabled F. E. plunged downward in a mad spiral toward the earth—almost two miles below.

Morris revived sufficiently to bring his shattered plane to a safe landing in a field. Richthofen, his heart pounding and his eyes burning with the excitement and exultation of the moment, had never let the English plane out of his sight. So great was his eagerness that he landed in the same field and almost smashed his own plane, so intent was he upon keeping his eyes on his victim. He wanted to be sure of his prey.

He jumped out of his plane immediately and rushed over to the English machine. The field was behind the German third line, and reserve infantry men were running out from all directions. Morris and Rees were unconscious, their bodies both riddled with bullets. Richthofen's shots had gone home with telling effect. The burst of lead from underneath had shattered the motor and severely wounded both the pilot and the observer.

With the assistance of the soldiers, Richthofen lifted his two victims from the bloodstained cockpits. He laid them as tenderly as possible on the ground, and loosened the leather flying coats and the collars of their tunics.

Rees opened his eyes once with a boyish smile and died.

A medical officer and two stretcher bearers arriving, Morris was placed on the stretcher and carried to a dressing station. He was dead when he arrived there.

Returning to his airdrome, Richthofen found Boelcke and the rest of the Jadgstaffel in the midst of a joyous victory breakfast. He proudly reported his "kill" and learned that Boelcke had "had another Englishman for breakfast," and that the other flyers of the unit had each brought down their first plane.

He walked into Cambrai and went to the hospital in the centre of the town and out into the backyard, where there were two fresh graves in a lot set apart from the graves of German dead. The crosses over the two fresh mounds of earth bore the names of Morris and Rees.

He placed a stone on each grave. They were his first official victims in the war. He honoured them and their graves.

Standing silently at the foot of the two graves, Richthofen did not know that, by his own hand, he was to fill many dozen more like these until he himself came to rest in a similar one. It was only the beginning.

Chapter V

Boelcke, the master, had watched his fledglings with happy pride that September morning when young Richthofen shot down and killed his "first two Englishmen."

High in the sky above them, his eagle-trained eyes observed every feature of their performance. It pleased him to note that his pupils, by following his instructions to the letter, reflected great credit on the commander who had personally selected and trained them.

His pleasure and pride found immediate expression in a sudden descent into the *mêlée,* where he engaged one of the enemy squadron and brought it down. It added another victory to his "bag," which then amounted to twenty-six.

One other thing he saw that day, and it was something that was entirely new to his experience and, at that time, unprecedented in the records of martial aviation.

It happened as the Jagdstaffel was flying back to its airdrome after the fight with the enemy squadron. The German formation was approaching a small bank of clouds floating on its exact level. Just before reaching the clouds, an English two-seater plane, with motor full on, suddenly emerged from the bank of fleecy white vapour and flew straight for the centre of the German V, but did not fire a single shot.

Several of Richthofen's flying mates swerved to attack, and one was forced to dive suddenly to avoid a head-on collision with the onrushing English plane. Boelcke's fledglings dived on it from above and from the right and left, pouring round after round of machine-gun lead into the machine.

Apparently undamaged by the repeated attacks, the English plane continued onward without firing a single shot in reply. It flew apparently under good control, and its course was that of a large circle to the left.

Boelcke himself dived to a position over the tail and, with his eyes along the sights of his twin Spandaus, pressed the machine-gun trigger. From above and behind he saw his bullets go into the bodies of both the pilot and the observer, who were sitting bolt upright in their cockpits. Still there was no return fire from the English plane, and still no deviation in its course—apparently no attempt to manœuvre out of range and shake off its pursuers.

These were weird tactics. The German ace was puzzled. He was well acquainted with English daring and audacity, but the conduct of this plane was beyond his understanding. He flew closer and closer, holding his fire, and ready at any minute to meet any sudden surprise attack from the strangely acting plane. Gradually, he flew directly over it, fixing the speed of his plane so that he kept a position fifteen yards above the enemy machine.

Banking his wings slightly to depress one side of the fuselage, he peered down into the two cockpits of the English plane and into the bloodstained faces of two dead men, sitting rigidly strapped to their seats.

The plane was a derelict of the air.

Death had placed its controls in neutral, holding it to an even keel as it sped onward across the sky, its motor roaring with life from a wide-open throttle.

Boelcke wiggled his wings as a signal to his pupils to cease the attack. Hovering above and around, the fledglings watched the master fly some minutes above the derelict, escorting it like a funeral plane as it flew westward with the bodies of its air Vikings on their last flight. Before changing course to return, Boelcke dipped his wings in a parting salute to the dead.

The German squadron reported the death plane but did not claim it as one of its victims. Boelcke was certain that the English pilot and observer were dead when the plane first appeared out of the cloud bank. Where the fight had occurred, with whom, and when, remained enigmas of the air. The death flight would continue until another trick of circumstance changed the controls or the motor stopped for want of fuel—then, down to the last landing.

Derelicts of the air—planes that fled on through space with the lifeless bodies of their occupants seated at the fixed controls—provided many of the weird tales that went around the mess tables of the cavaliers of the air on both sides during the war. Boelcke's derelict—named after him as a comet bears the name of its discoverer—formed a brief topic of conversation that night in the mess of Jagdstaffel 2 when Boelcke's fledglings compared their experiences of the day.

"A glorious death," was the comment of young Baron von Richthofen. "Fight on and fly to the last drop of blood and the last drop of benzine—to the last beat of the heart and the last kick of the motor: a death for a knight—a toast for his fellows, friend and foe."

They drank it standing, and with feeling, drank it in red French wine from the large silver victory cups which had been the reward of each of the five young fledglings that had brought down their first victims in the air that day.

Boelcke had presented the cups in the name of the air commander, who had inaugurated this method of spurring his young eagles to greater endeavours aloft. They were large, heavy, beaten-silver mugs of mediæval German design, capable of carrying a full quart inside and an ample inscription on the outside.

Richthofen's cup pleased him and gave him an idea. It was a proper trophy commemorating a great achievement. On a trophy table in his quarters in the field, or in the home of his mother in Schweidnitz, it would look good and well reflect his prowess as a hunter of the war. But one trophy was not enough. There must be more. The young Uhlan decided to inaugurate a system of cup presentation all his own.

Instead of the one official cup for his first victory, he would present himself with a silver victory cup, not only for that victory, but for each successive one.

He ordered the first one of his special set that night by mail from a jeweller in Berlin. He described the kind he wanted in detail: small, plain, two inches tall, and a little more than an inch across the top, with slightly sloping sides to a base smaller than the top, the whole to be done in finely polished sterling, and the inside of the cup to be plated with a dull gold finish. He instructed the jeweller to engrave on one side of the first cup the following inscription:

1. Vickers 2. 17. 9. 16.

The numbers and the word indicated that the cup commemorated his first victory, that the type of the enemy plane he had shot down was a Vickers, a two-seater, and that the combat took place on the 17th of September, 1916. That inscription and the many subsequent ones were at fault in the use of the name "Vickers" as the type of the plane, but among the Germans the British F. E. plane was generally known by the other name.

In his letter to the jeweller, Richthofen advised that he would forward successive orders for more cups, and warned the artisan to preserve the same design and the same type of engraving, as he desired to build up a uniform collection, one for each plane he shot down, after each victory had been officially acknowledged and placed to his credit.

In the bedroom of the Flying Uhlan in his mother's home in Schweidnitz, one may see how that collection of dead men's cups grew as the war in the air progressed. On a table under a large photograph of the dead ace one may count sixty of the small silver drinking cups, and read from the inscriptions on them the type of each machine, the number of its occupants, and the date on which Richthofen shot each one down from the sky.

The Berlin jeweller made a good thing out of Richthofen. The Flying Uhlan's trophy lust spurred him on, and the orders were repeated so frequently that it might in fact be said that, by his wholesale killings in the air, Richthofen greatly depleted Germany's fast-diminishing supply of silver.

Almost a year later, after engraving the inscription of the sixtieth victory on the last silver cup, the Berlin jeweller had to decline further orders. He had run out of silver and could get no more. The result is that Richthofen's last twenty victories in the air, from his sixtieth to his eightieth, are commemorated only by reports and the graves of his victims, and not by dead men's cups.

But in the flush of his first "kill," and still tingling with pride to be flying under the eyes of Boelcke, his admired master, Richthofen renewed his determination to pursue his game without stint.

On the sixth day after the killing of Morris and Rees, he posted another letter to the jeweller in Berlin. And a week later, on the 30th of September, 1916, he shot down another two-seater, and the happy little German jeweller in Berlin screwed his funny eyepiece into one eye again and scratched the record of victory on another silver tombstone.

His fourth and fifth victorious combats were with two more English machines, one a D. D. 2, a cumbersome pusher type with openwork tail spars instead of fuselage, and hardly a match for the speedy Albatross tractors that Richthofen and the other members of Boelcke's squadron flew. Richthofen downed his fifth on October 16th and his sixth on October 25th, just nine days later.

Although winter was approaching and the changing elements added to the difficulties of the conflicting forces, the long series of bloody encounters known as the "Battles of the Somme, 1916," comprising a part of the Allied offensive of that year, continued with unrelenting fury.

The British had opened the offensive on July 1st with the battle of Albert, which was marked by the capture of Montauban, Fricourt, Contalmaison, and the bitter attack on the Commercourt salient. It had continued with increasing frenzy and terrific losses on both sides through July, August, and September, with the battles of Bazentin Ridge, Delville Wood, and Pozières Ridge, and the battle of Flers-Courcellette, marked by the British capture of Martynpuich, during which Richthofen had shot down his first British plane.

By October, when the fighting had swung through Thiepval and the Transloy ridges to the heights of the Ancre, Richthofen had flown so many times up and down and across the Bapaume-Albert road, which stretched out below like a straight and tight but somewhat frayed ribbon of white, that he felt perfectly at home in the area. It was indeed his happy hunting ground. The woods, rivers, hills, mine craters, trench systems, and ruined villages below were as familiar to him as the street signs and lamp posts in his native Schweidnitz.

The German flying service, though slowly regaining morale and strength under new leadership, new model machines, and the adoption of formation-flying tactics, was still hard pressed by the British air forces, which continued their offensive policy of carrying the fighting to the German side of the line, bombing the German airmen in their own airdromes, and offering battle whenever a squadron of Maltese cross planes appeared in the sky.

And then, on October 28th, came a disaster which went deep to Richthofen's heart. His master, his hero, his air god, Boelcke the Great, was killed.

It happened toward the end of the battle of the Ancre Heights, after the British ground forces had captured the Schwaben and Stuff redoubts and parts of the Regina trench system.

The conflict was raging over a territory from Le Sars to Contalmaison and from La Boiselle to Hamel, and was incessant day and night from the 1st of October until the 11th of November.

There were many clouds in the sky that October day, and the wind blew fitfully. It was cold aloft, but the unfavourable weather had not prevented British patrols from daring the choppy air lanes above the German back areas.

Boelcke was leading his Jagdstaffel of six fighting planes on his last flight. His spirit always animated his pupils, Richthofen often said. "We always had a wonderful feeling of security when he was with us. After all, he was the one and only" are the words that his most famous pupil used to sum up his opinion.

Although outnumbered three to one and far away from their own lines, two British planes immediately accepted battle with the six Germans. Boelcke gave the signal for a united formation attack, and the struggle began.

The Jagdstaffel swooped downward on the two Englishmen. Boelke dived on one of the enemy planes, and Richthofen, right behind his master, fastened himself above the tail of the other machine and poured in a murderous stream of lead. But the Flying Uhlan had to pull out of the fight because of the return fire he encountered, and, further, because of the fact that one of his comrades, flying in close formation, dived in between him and his intended quarry.

From a distance of several hundred yards, Richthofen watched Boelcke and the English plane flying round and round in circles, each endeavouring to shoot into the tail of the other.

Then down from above came another German Albatross with another of Boelcke's pupils, a favourite, at the controls. He was diving at a terrific speed to the assistance of his master. His eyes were on the enemy plane as he manœvred to train his machine guns on the Englishman, who was busily engaged watching Boelcke.

But the newcomer watched too closely his enemy and not his leader. As he swooped past to the attack, the tip of one of his wings touched the tip of Boelcke's right wing.

"Collision" was the thought that sped through Richthofen's mind as he observed the entire incident from a flying position close to one side. The lightness with which the two wing tips had appeared to touch surprised the Flying Uhlan, who had thought that a collision in midair had an entirely different aspect. He did not realize then that the slightest contact between two bodies moving at such terrific speed through space is sufficient to produce the most disastrous effects.

Boelcke's Albatross responded immediately to the wing contact. It swerved leftward and nosed slightly downward in a large curve. Its descent did not appear to be out of control, but Richthofen was able to notice from above that a part of his plane tips had broken off, leaving splintered edges and flapping fabric at which the wind tore. Soon the plane was lost from view as it sank through the level of the clouds just below.

The pupil who had collided with Boelcke followed him down, and as the master's plane came out on the under side of the cloud curtain, the horror-stricken pupil saw that the falling Albatross was minus one complete plane.

Weakened by the jolt of the collision, it had been torn off by the rush of air in the increasingly rapid descent. It plunged downward, entirely out of control. Thus perished the man whom Richthofen held to be the greatest air fighter in the world.

Richthofen's admiration was unconsciously based on the fact that Boelcke possessed something which Richthofen did not have. It was personal magnetism.

Oswald Boelcke was a Saxon and the son of a schoolmaster. Richthofen was a Prussian and the son of a Junker family. Killing was a duty with Boelcke and his training in engineering was responsible for his presence in the air force. Killing was an instinct as well as a duty with Richthofen, and he took to the air simply because there he was able to kill more and could see those he killed.

Boelcke began his army life in a battalion of telegraphers and took his early training in Coblentz, where he first came in touch with the German Air Force in 1913. An asthmatic affliction barred him from strenuous physical exercise, and this, together with his interest in motors and aëronautics, was responsible for his entering the Halberstadt flying school just before the war.

He became a pilot in seven weeks' training and on September 1, 1914, the anniversary of the battle of Sedan, he flew to the western front, where, with his brother as his observing officer, he did aërial reconnaissance and, later, some fighting in the 1915 battles of the Champagne and the Argonne. In June of that year, he had transferred to the single-seater fighting division, where he flew in company with Immelmann.

After their eighth victory in the air, the two were cited for the Pour le Mérite, the Empire's highest military decoration for bravery. When, on May 21, 1916, he had downed his sixteenth plane, the high command issued strict orders forbidding him to fly, for the reason that his experience in the air was considered so valuable that he was worth too much as an authority and instructor to be risked further in individual combat.

Boelcke was sent to the eastern theatre of war and instructed Austrians, Bulgarians, and Turks in airmanship, but always under specific orders which prevented him from flying. He met Enver Pasha, Mackensen, Ludendorff, Hindenburg, and many celebrities, but wearied of the hero worship to which he was subjected and insisted upon being sent back to the front.

During the battle of the Somme, when the German air service was driven from the sky over or near the British lines, he was assigned to organize a special squadron to regain superiority of the air. Reaching the front early in September with Richthofen as one of his pupils, he was able by daily flying and fighting to increase his victories to the then unprecedented number of forty, when death overtook him.

Among both his mates and his foes, Boelcke had a great reputation for bravery and chivalry. He seemed more human than Richthofen. He devoted many of his rest hours to visiting wounded prisoners of war he had brought down. He motored to their hospitals or sent cigarettes to the men that survived a fight with him, and he made them believe he liked them. He actually did. Once, back of the German lines, he risked his life to save a French boy from drowning.

> It is a strange thing [Richthofen later wrote] that everybody who met Boelcke imagined that he alone was his true friend. I have met about forty men, each of whom imagined that he alone had Boelcke's affection. Men whose names were unknown to Boelcke believed that he was particularly fond of them.
>
> This is a curious phenomenon which I have never noticed in anyone else. Boelcke had not a personal enemy. He was equally pleasant to everybody, making no differences. His death shocked us.
>
> Nothing happens without God's will. This is the only consolation which we can put into our soul during this war.

Boelcke's body lay in state in the military hospital at Cambrai, from which place it was taken on a special funeral train to Germany. His military funeral behind the front was one of the most impressive ceremonies of the war. British planes flew high over Cambrai and sent down parachutes to which were attached wreaths with the following inscriptions:

To the memory of Captain Boelcke, our brave and chivalrous foe. From the British Royal Flying Corps

and

To the Officers of the German Flying Corps in service on this front: We hope you will find this wreath, but are sorry it is so late in coming. The weather has prevented us from sending it earlier. We mourn with his relatives and friends. We all recognize his bravery.

Please give our kind regards to Captain Evans and Lieutenant Long of the Morane Squadron.

(Signed) J. SEAMAN GREEN, Lt.

Richthofen, as one of the three survivors of the original twelve pilots of Jagdstaffel 2, was placed in command of the formation, which from that time on, by special citation of the high command, was designated as the "Jagdstaffel Boelcke," and the plan was that the group should carry the name of its great leader forever as one of the greatest traditions of the German air service.

With his sparse but hard-won seven victories, the Flying Uhlan found himself stepping into the command vacated by the man who had shot forty enemy planes from the sky. It sobered him, and made him look older than his twenty-three years. His Prussian seriousness increased. He suddenly became aware that the discipline that had always been so irksome to him, and which had been one of the factors responsible for his transfer to the air service, was now the very thing that he needed if he was to remould Boelcke's old unit from its several nerve-shattered veterans and the enthusiastic new replacements, freshly arrived from training schools to fill the gaps left by death, wounds, and collapse.

He gathered the pilots of the Jagdstaffel in the mess-room and talked to them in the uninspired, quiet seriousness of a man who suddenly feels great responsibilities on his shoulders. In ponderous, hesitating fashion, he reviewed the fighting of the previous six weeks, referring individually to each of the units' fallen comrades, and with profound respect, approaching adoration, to the departed leader, in whose name he asked them all to take a solemn vow to carry on his great work, if need be at the cost of their lives.

He told them that changes were slowly taking place in air tactics, and success, now more than ever before, depended upon organized flying and fighting. Individual combats, he said, there would be, of necessity, but the flying force that maintained the best formation and discipline in the air was the only one that could meet, and even overcome, the English superiority in the air. In Boelcke's name, he dedicated the Jagdstaffel to the solemn duty of restoring the confidence of the German land forces in their auxiliaries in the air.

He flew daily with them in close formation, and for those pilots who failed for any reason to keep their prescribed position in the uptilted, flying V he had only frowns of displeasure, which were accepted as prophecies of the early transfer of the offender to some less distinguished unit. Twelve days after Boelcke's death, the Flying Uhlan had opportunity to test the fighting capacity of the Jagdstaffel in an air battle, which, for the number of machines engaged, was the greatest that had ever occurred in the war up to that time.

Eighty airplanes, and more than a hundred knights of the blue, took part in that aërial tourney of death—at least, that is the aggregate of the estimates of both sides as to the strength of the enemy they encountered, although both the English and the Germans recorded that they were outnumbered by the others. The English reported the German planes as numbering forty, and Richthofen estimated the English planes at between forty and fifty. Each side admitted having about thirty of their own planes in the battle. As the majority of the machines were two-seaters, it is safe to estimate that about one hundred winged men-of-war took part in the hostilities.

It was on the morning of the 9th of November, 1916. The current battle of the Somme was drawing to its conclusion, leaving behind it a gory trail of death and destruction spread over four months of night-and-day fighting on a scale and a ferocity seldom approached before in the history of the world. It was during the last phase of the Allied offensive of 1916, which was to end ten days later with the capture of Beaumont Hamel.

His Royal Highness, the Grand Duke of Saxe-Coburg Gotha, a noble relation of Emperor William and King George, stood with folded arms on the stone portico of the French country house from which he commanded the German troops of that sector.

His headquarters was located close to the occupied French village of Vraucourt, in the centre of which was a large beet-sugar factory that had been taken over by the Germans for the storing of vast quantities of material, mostly explosive. It was the principal munition dump for the sector: It was near Laigncourt, not far from Richthofen's airdrome.

Some forty or fifty eyes of the air looked at the spot marked Vraucourt on their flying maps shortly after eight o'clock, when sixteen heavy English bombing machines, with their escort of fourteen fighting planes, climbed into the morning sun and nosed their propellers eastward.

It was not many minutes afterward that Richthofen and his flight of six planes, flying at an altitude of 12,000 feet, sighted the English air flotilla as it came across the lines.

At similar altitudes, far to the right and left of him, but still within sight, were five or six more V-shaped groups of planes on whose brilliantly painted sides the black Maltese cross of the Fatherland could be seen. The spread-out German formations wheeled and changed their several courses toward a common centre in the path of the oncoming British group, which took the form of a deep, moving wedge, with bombers below and fighting machines above.

The opposing forces moved toward each other.

The objective of the English operation was to bomb Vraucourt and its environs, and particularly the sugar factory, with a couple of carefully selected and martially correct visiting cards, to be dropped on His Royal Highness the Grand Duke of Saxe-Coburg Gotha.

It was the duty of Richthofen and his comrades to thwart the English plan and shoot down the bombing planes before they could reach their objective.

The Boelcke Jagdstaffel of fighting Albatrosses, with the Flying Uhlan in the lead, dived downward on a long steep swoop toward the slow-going bomb carriers, plodding along at their best speed several thousand feet below their escort.

The fourteen British fighting planes of the Eleventh and Sixtieth squadrons, R. F. C., saw the move and dived from a similar altitude almost at the same time to intercept them.

With motors full on, and the air shrieking through struts and bracing wires, the belligerent planes sped downward toward one another like swarms of winged furies sliding down the opposite and converging sides of a mile-high letter "V," the apex of which was the covey of sixteen English bombing planes flying in close formation.

The pilots of the bombing planes saw the avalanche coming down from heights before them. Also they saw with some measure of comfort the similiar descent of their own protectors from positions above and behind them.

The observers crouched in the forward cockpits of the bombing planes, elevated the barrels of their movable machine guns, and prepared to meet the onslaught with lead.

With a roaring and the staccato gibbering of machine guns, the speeding, human-driven missiles of steel, wood, and fabric whizzed by and around one another, missing collision by scant margins of yards.

Zooming, swerving, swooping, diving, the tourney of the air was on. The winged knights of the Black Cross directed their attention always to the big bombing planes. The air cavaliers of the tricolour cockade tried to fasten themselves to the tails of the black-crossed falcons and drive them from their prey. The falcons in turn tried to shake them off.

The heavy-laden bombers met each attack to the extent of their defensive ability, and endeavoured to maintain their covey formation, which had been disrupted in the *mêlee.* They were the quarry, and they knew it.

The dizzy whirl of gyrations caused the fighting planes to lose height, so that now they engaged one another hundreds of feet below the plodding bombers, who continued on their course. Their only part in the fight was defensive. They carried bombs. They had objectives. They must deliver the goods—their "eggs."

Then down from the upper lanes came more diving black-crossed falcons, spitting new streams of lead on the bombers. They attacked from left and right, and the formation was shattered again.

The machine gunners on the bombing planes tried to hold them off by spraying them with bullets. English fighters, disengaged from their outranged enemies below, climbed to meet the newcomers.

Again the combat went into the *kurvenkampf,* the circular whirlwind of seemingly endless tail chasing, with death the penalty for the tail that's caught.

Richthofen returned aloft and dove again. Little Immelmann, a cousin of the great Immelmann, was also diving some yards on his right. Their targets were two bombers who, as a result of the last *mêlée,* found themselves detached from their covey.

Immelmann's victim went down in flames from a well-directed stream of lead, but the bomber that Richthofen picked out put up a stubborn resistance.

At the machine gun was Second Lieutenant J. G. Cameron. He met the Flying Uhlan's first dive with a burst of hot lead from his Lewis gun. Richthofen, seeing the English tracer bullets flashing by him, swerved quickly and made a turn which enabled him to deliver a burst of bullets full into his selected victim.

Cameron crumpled in the cockpit, and his machine gun swung aimlessly toward the zenith. The same burst stopped the motor and severed the control wires.

Lieutenant G. F. Knight, at the useless controls, was helpless as the powerless bomber nosed earthward, saving itself from a stall in midair. It descended in a wide spiral followed by Richthofen's still pursuing gun. Knight faced the prospect of landing out of control, while suspended beneath the fuselage of his machine was his unexpended load of bombs. The bomb release levers were in the cockpit of the helpless Cameron.

The plane came to earth near Laigncourt, not far from the airdrome of the Boelcke squadron, which reveals how far the English were carrying the fight into the enemy's country. The bombs did not explode. Knight escaped uninjured, and from his prison camp at Osnabrück wrote to his aunt a story of the fight and the further fact that Cameron died of his wounds.

With the fight over, Richthofen and Immelmann, eager to see their latest victims, flew directly to their airdrome and landed. Considerable havoc had been wrought in their vicinity and around the sugar factory in Vraucourt by the English bombs, but without stopping to inspect it, the German airmen jumped into a motor car and sped away in the direction of their fallen prey.

After the cool air aloft, it was hot on the ground, and Richthofen left his flying coat and cap in the car when he started out across the fields in the direction of Knight's plane. Before reaching the spot, he encountered a group of German officers returning from the scene and asked them how the fight had looked from the ground. The officer described the combat vividly, not omitting to tell about the bombs which the British had dropped and their effect. He then inquired the flyer's name and presented him to the group of officers, whose uniforms were in scrupulous order and whose boots were all well polished.

One of them appeared to be someone of particular consequence. He wore peculiar epaulettes and the distinctive trousers of a general. His face was young, and the star of a high order dangled from the throat of his tightly hooked, stiff military collar. Richthofen, covered with grease, oil, sweat, and mud, felt ill at ease in the presence whose identity he did not learn until that evening, when an aide telephoned him that His Royal Highness the Grand Duke of Saxe-Coburg Gotha had enjoyed meeting him and ordered his presence at the Vraucourt headquarters. For accounting for at least one load of bombs which were not aimed at his Royal Highness, Richthofen that night received the bravery medal of the Grand Duke's duchy.

The medal looked well on his Uhlan tunic together with the black-and-white ribbon for the Iron Cross of the second class that he had won in the trenches at Verdun. He was the only one in the squadron who had the Gotha decoration, and the distinction was by no means unpleasant, but . . .

Richthofen thought a long time about it that night as he wrote another letter to the Berlin jeweller instructing him to get busy on one more "Victory Cup."

Eight victorious combats in the air was by no means a bad record, he felt. He reflected that when the great Immelmann and the great Boelcke had shot their eighth victim down from the sky, they had been decorated with the order Pour le Mérite, the highest award for bravery in the gift of the Kaiser. It corresponded to the British Victoria Cross, the French Médaille Militaire, or the Congressional Medal of Honour in the U. S. A. But he had received only a provincial decoration.

It had not become any easier to shoot down enemy planes than in the days of Boelcke and Immelmann.

On the contrary, it had become much more difficult. The Flying Uhlan, in the privacy of his quarters, recalled that the first opponent Immelmann shot down did not even carry a machine gun. No chance to find any easy meat like that in these days.

Aërial equipment and armament had undergone tremendous improvement in the space of a year; the motors had doubled in horsepower and efficiency, the ceiling had been pushed up from 10,000 to 18,000 feet, and organized fighting tactics had evolved from the old individual fighting.

True, the knight of the air had more engagements aloft now than he had before, and consequently more opportunities to shoot down enemy planes, but, at the same time, the chances of being shot down himself had increased in proportion.

Whether Richthofen made his thoughts on this subject known, or whether some of his immediate superiors, sharing the thoughts with him, bestirred themselves on his behalf, is unknown, but the records show that on November 11, 1916, just two days after he had accounted for his eighth victim and received the Gotha medal, he was cited for the Hohenzollernschen Haus Order mit Schwertern (The Order of the House of Hohenzollern with Swords), and that helped somewhat. At least, the ruling family of the Empire was aware of his existence and his efforts for "Gott und Kaiser." This knowledge further whetted his desire for the Pour le Mérite.

After a week of almost daily combats in which he failed to bring down a single enemy, the Flying Uhlan redoubled his efforts on November 20th and "shot a double," which, in the parlance of the corps, meant that he brought down two enemy planes in one day. The first was a two-seater bombing plane, and the second was a single-seater fighting plane. Both were British.

This success, which to Richthofen was unprecedented, set his mind running back to his trophies, in quest of some means by which the dual victory could be symbolized in a manner to distinguish it from single affairs.

His first thought was to mark the double event with a cup twice the size of the eight little cups that now formed his collection. But, by doing so, he would reduce the number of trophies by one, and this would conflict with the original purpose of the collection. He pondered this and then abandoned the idea for a compromise.

Writing to the jeweller, he ordered two more cups, the first one after the usual fashion, the second to be of the same design but just twice as big.

The similarity of the dates registered the fact that both were brought down in one day, and the double size for No. 10 would mark the passing of his first decade. He instructed the jeweller that, hereafter, every tenth cup was to be just twice the size of the little ones that commemorated the intermediate victories.

The little bespectacled jeweller in Berlin chuckled when he received the new orders and exhibited them and the cups to his customers. His pride in the collection was almost as great as Richthofen's. How droll, how care-free, how happy these knights of the air who faced death aloft every day and then joked about their risks! The Fatherland would be forever safer with sons like these to protect it. The jeweller, with the wartime spirit of the land, gloried in his task as a maker of silver tombstones for the enemies of his country.

If any one of Richthofen's conquests in the air deserved distinction above the others, it was the next one, his eleventh, which occurred a few days later—on November 23rd. On that day, he killed the first and foremost ace of the Royal Flying Corps, an accomplished air fighter of long experience and fame, and one who carried on his breast the purple ribbon and the bronze emblem of the Victoria Cross. His victim was Major Lanoe George Hawker, V. C., D. S. O., R. E., R. F. C.

With the example of Boelcke before them, Richthofen's flying mates arranged a military funeral for their fallen foe, but the man who brought him down did not attend the ceremonies, which was according to the custom then in vogue.

He personally dropped a note from the air behind the English lines, addressed to Hawker's comrades of the Royal Flying Corps, stating briefly the death of the English ace and expressing the widespread admiration of German airmen for him as an exceptionally brave airman and a chivalrous foe.

But in the hearts of the R. F. C. and the English people he left a tradition that will live as long as that of any hero of the Great War. Hawker was twenty-five years old when Richthofen shot him down. He was one of the few pre-war airmen in the greatly extended Flying Corps of the British forces.

Like the Flying Uhlan, he was from the regular army, in which he had received his commission as a second lieutenant on July 20, 1912, at the age of twenty-one. His interest drew him immediately to military flying. On March 4, 1913, he received his pilot's license after successfully flying one of the old Deperdussin monoplanes three times around the airdrome at Hendon.

Two months after the outbreak of the war, he graduated from the Central Flying School at Hendon and flew to France with the Sixth Squadron of the Royal Flying Corps. Within seven months, his daring exploits in pioneer war flying had pushed him to a most prominent position in his branch of the service. He gained public distinction and a citation for the D. S. O. on April 18, 1915, when he destroyed a Zeppelin hangar on the ground.

To protect himself from the fire of machine guns and artillery from the ground, Hawker had spiralled down around a German balloon, throwing hand grenades at the machine gunner in the basket. The German gunners on the ground were prevented from firing on him for fear of hitting their own balloon. Even then, Hawker's machine was found to have 23 bullet holes in it when he returned after laying his eggs on the Zeppelin nest.

Three months later, while flying alone over the lines, he encountered three German two-seater planes armed with machine guns, which were a novelty in the air at that time. Hawker attacked the three successively.

The first one managed to escape. The second one he damaged and drove to the ground, and the third, which he attacked at an altitude of 10,000 feet, he drove to earth behind the English lines, with the result that the pilot and observer were killed. For this exploit he won the Victoria Cross.

Richthofen felt that, in killing Hawker, whose bravery and fighting capacity he highly admired, he had in a degree wiped out the loss of Boelcke. His mechanics brought him the fabric numbers from the English ace's F. E. fighting plane and several other souvenirs, among them Hawker's machine gun, which may be seen over the doorway of Richthofen's old bedroom in his mother's home at Schweidnitz.

In the following month of December, bad flying weather reduced the activity of the air forces in the Somme sector, but, in spite of this, Richthofen led the Boelcke Jadgstaffel on line patrols, and often there were combats, with occasional successes. His twelfth victim, an English one-seater fighting plane, went down under his guns on the 11th of that month, and nine days later he sent two more of the same type to destruction.

Richthofen's father was a major of reserve infantry stationed back of the Somme line not far from the son's airdrome. Lothar, his younger brother, had transferred from the cavalry and was taking his final training for the air in a front flying school near by.

Young Lothar's initial flight alone was an event that Richthofen watched with confidence, but with some degree of anxiety, because he still remembered the difficulties and the dangers he had encountered and survived in order to get the coveted licence to be a fighting pilot.

The younger brother came through with flying colours, passing the examination by a wide margin of safety and receiving the assurance of both his instructors and his brother that he was now well trained for the front.

They celebrated the event together on New Year's Day, and three days later Lothar was watching from the ground when his elder brother brought down his sixteenth British plane in a hot air fight almost immediately above the airdrome.

The silver cups of death, ranged in a row on Richthofen's desk, now numbered sixteen. They told the story of his victories over a period of as many weeks.

Looking at the cups on his desk, Richthofen could reflect with some degree of pride upon his achievement. He had shot down sixteen planes in four months: three in the last half of September; three in October; five in November; four in December; and one in the first four days of January.

As eight of the planes had carried two occupants and eight of them had carried one occupant, he individually had accounted for twenty-four of his enemies.

The Flying Uhlan, as the result of his work on the Somme, could report a personally inflicted casualty list that would read as follows:

Killed: 16 (12 unidentified).
Wounded or Made Prisoners of War: 8 (7 unidentified).
Total Casualties Inflicted: 24.
Enemy Planes Destroyed: 16.

But the most important aspect of his record to Richthofen at that period of his career was the fact that his sixteen victories placed him in the lead of all the living air fighters in the service of his country.

He had reached the zenith. He was the ace of German aces.

Chapter VI

With the new young year of 1917, fame came to Richthofen.

Jade or goddess, she came to feed with her own delicious sweets the hunger of a spirit proud and brave and young.

The twenty-four-year-old Uhlan had with his own hand killed more enemies of his country than any other living man in the ranks of the millions of the Central Powers.

He answered the old Teuton demand of a nation of fighting people for a personal champion, a blond youth with shining armour and flaming sword to be its war god.

Boelcke and Immelmann, the old heroes, though not forgotten, were dead. The war was on, and it was the day for the live, the quick, the strong. Richthofen succeeded to the favours the old heroes had once received from the hands of Fame.

From his throat she suspended the coveted gold-and-white enamelled cross of the order Pour le Mérite with a special citation from the Emperor. And on his breast she pinned the Austrian war cross from Francis Joseph.

She brought him telegrams and illuminated messages of congratulations and felicitations from notables of state, army, and navy.

Before his eyes she unfolded the newspapers that welcomed the new d'Artagnan of the air with front-page pictures of himself and large black headlines that blazoned the name, "RICHTHOFEN"—his name, to the world.

She decked his quarters at the front with floral wreaths and conqueror's palms, sent from admiring organizations and individuals from all over Germany, Austria-Hungary, and Turkey.

She filled his mail with hundreds of letters from sighing maidens, who expressed the pangs of their hero worship and adoration in passionate phrases.

Richthofen smiled as he read these letters from unknown admirers, many of whom looked up to him with soulful eyes from scented photographs. Some of them he showed to Voss and Schaefer, who clapped him on the back and told him that he was a gay young blade. Sometimes they read some of the burning epistles aloud, and discussed the writers with gales of laughter.

One series of letters, he never showed. The handwriting was distinctive. One of them turned up every time the mail arrived at the front. There was almost one for every day in the week.

It was from the same girl—the same fraulein—the one who has since remained the mystery in the haze of legend that now surrounds the life of Germany's greatest air fighter.

Her penmanship was well known to the mail orderly and to Richthofen's personal orderly. The letters were thick. They could not be mistaken. The mail orderly always removed them from the flutter of general mail, and they were turned over to Richthofen separately.

At times, returning from a raid in the blue, in which he had added another victim to his string, he would be met at the hangar doors by his personal servant, who would hand him the one missive that he wanted. The Flying Uhlan, still tingling with the thrill of his latest kill, would go to his quarters alone and devour the contents of the note.

She was the one who shared his joy. She was the one he believed, among all the crowd of blind worshippers. Her words seemed to mean more to him than all the rest. Everyone in the Jagdstaffel knew about her, although none knew who the mystery girl was, and Richthofen never permitted any discussion of her.

His mother knew but she would not remove the veil of secrecy that still surrounds the identity of this girl her son loved above all other women.

Friends of both said that the romance was one of suppressed desire on both sides. They both wanted to be married, but Richthofen feared, and rightly, he would not survive the war. He knew Death stalked him.

"I cannot indulge myself in the right of marriage," he once said, "as long as I am liable to die any day."

But the exchange of letters between him and the girl continued until he met his expected end in the air. Richthofen kept her letters, and she kept those from him. The present whereabouts of those love notes is one of the mysteries of the affair. Those who have studied Richthofen hope that some day those letters will come to light to reveal the human side of a man whose reputation rests now upon his power and spirit to kill.

Unknown as the mystery girl remains, she is credited with having been his inspiration and confidante in those days when his name stood forth with those of Ludendorff and Hindenburg. She was with him at the peak of his distinction.

That distinction was uncontested in Germany and was recognized amongst the fighting forces of all the Allied countries. It was spoken of along the fronts in the first days of January, when the Flying Uhlan took the lead of his countrymen in the air.

It was a general recognition that Richthofen liked, but he desired more.

He wanted each of his adversaries in the air to know who it was they fought. As the knights of old distinguished themselves by the colour of the plumes waving atop their steel casques, so he identified himself personally in the tilt yard of the sky.

It happened during the days when the flyers on both sides were experimenting with camouflage in the air. Richthofen, with the rest, had tried out many different colours to make his plane less conspicuous, but the search for "invisibility" remained fruitless. Seen from below with a sky background above, all airplanes, by their very opaqueness, showed distinctive silhouettes.

Once the ace daubed his wings with blotches of yellow, green, and brown on the theory that, if seen by an enemy from above against the background of the earth, the outline of his machine would appear less perceptible, but as most of the flying done by the fighting scouts carried them into the higher altitudes, the earth camouflage appeared of little advantage and was discarded.

Convinced of the futility of these efforts, Richthofen went to the other extreme with a gesture of daring that gave new impetus to his reputation for fearlessness among friend and foe. He had his plane completely painted a bright and glaring red. He mixed advertising with his chivalry.

The assumption was that in so doing he made himself more conspicuous and thereby invited more attacks. It was a gauntlet thrown down to the enemy, proclaiming that his prowess as a knight of the air was such that he could handicap himself with the brightest hue and did not have to seek ambush in schemes of neutral colouring. Actually it was no handicap.

The Allied flyers accepted the challenge, and the air soon became kaleidoscopic with colour. Richthofen was allowed by common consent to maintain a copyright on the use of "all red." When all the distinctive solid colours of the rainbow had been adopted and exploited, the use of combinations came into vogue. Thus in the spring of that year the cavaliers of the air sallied forth in pink planes with green noses and black planes with yellow wings, blue bodies, and orange tails.

Out of these efforts the German evolved one system of differing the colours of the surfaces and wings on one airplane so that it increased the difficulty of an English flyer in determining at a glance whether the other craft was flying right side up or not, or was approaching or going away. This colour confusion might have carried a shade of advantage during the excitement of a "dog-fight."

Richthofen, however, having made the gesture, stuck to his all red plane and had the satisfaction of learning from prisoners of war that his machine was known above all the rest. Later, when rumours reached the squadron that special rewards and inducements had been offered for Richthofen's head, his flying comrades prevailed upon him to let them share his special colour. He consented, but always made them carry an additional colour on some part of the machine, so that he still retained the distinction of being "all red."

Thus it was that Lothar Richthofen's plane was red with a splash of yellow, Schaefer's was red with the elevators and tail black, Allmenröder's was red with a white tail. Although each had a distinctive colour, from the ground or at a distance, they appeared as though all of them were red.

Richthofen maintained his colour monopoly, so that when, during the first two weeks of the new year, he was suddenly transferred and placed in command of a new flying formation, he took the colour with him, and the old Boelcke squadron had to adopt different adornment.

The new formation was Jagdstaffel 11, and although just as old as the Boelcke unit, it started out under its new commander without a single killing to its record. Richthofen did not like to make the change. He was accustomed to his old flying mates, and he cherished the traditions connected with Boelcke's name, but orders were orders, and he had to go. The methods and discipline of the new unit and its personnel of a dozen officers did not appeal to him.

Just to show them how it was done, he led them over the English lines for the first time on January 23d and "knocked down" the first victim to be registered on the unit's victory book. For Richthofen it was his seventeenth "kill."

At dinner time, when his twelve officers gathered around the mess table, he explained the technique of his first demonstration, called attention to some flying blunders his pupils had made, and answered their questions. At the close of the meal and the lecture the Flying Uhlan and his disciples retired to their quarters with the knowledge that they were "going over" again in the morning.

At high noon the next day, the Richthofen swarm found its prey in the air just west of Vimy Ridge, then held by the Germans. It was an English photography plane from the Twenty-fifth Squadron, Royal Flying Corps, engaged calmly in taking mosaic photographs of the ridge.

Richthofen's machine was the latest word in German production, a single-seater B. U. Albatross with two synchronized guns firing through the propeller, and fitted with a 200-horsepower Mercedes motor. At that time, it was considered the fastest plane in the war. So swift was the German plane, and so capable its master in availing himself of the advantage of clouds and sun spots that the Englishman was taken completely by surprise. Richthofen had his eighteenth victory.

During the following week, the Jagdstaffel assigned itself seriously to the business of building up its score of killings so that it would make a showing against the old intrenched record of the Boelcke squadron.

There were daily patrols in the bitter winter air high above the lines, and brushes occurred with the English during every flight. Richthofen opened the month of February with another successful combat in which two more English flyers paid with their lives.

Just two weeks later the Flying Uhlan was given credit for a double victory. The second English plane he shot down that day landed on the English side of the lines, but the English records reveal no air casualty at the time stated, so it is presumed that the occupants of the machine escaped without sufficient injuries to place them on the casualty lists, although Richthofen's report would make such an outcome seem almost a miracle.

The report reads:

Requesting Acknowledgment of My 21st Victory

Date: Feb. 14, 1917.
Time: 4:45 P.M.
Place: Station 1,500 yards southwest of Mazingarbe.
Type of Plane: B. E. two-seater. No details as plane landed on enemy side.

About 4:45 P.M. in company with my Staffel, I attacked an enemy squadron of five artillery flyers in a low altitude near Lens. Whilst my gentlemen attacked another B. E. I attacked the one flying nearest me.

After the first 100 shots, the enemy observer stopped shooting. The plane began to smoke and twist in uncontrolled curves to the right.

As this result was not satisfactory to me, especially over the enemy's lines, I shot at the falling plane, until the left part of the wings came off.

As the wind was blowing at a velocity of twenty yards a second, I had been drifting far over to the enemy side, and consequently I could observe that the enemy plane touched the ground southwest of Mazingarbe. I could see a heavy cloud of smoke arising from the place where the plane was lying in the snow.

As it was foggy and already rather dark, I have no witnesses either from the air or from the earth.

(Signed) BARON VON RICHTHOFEN.

This is the only one of Richthofen's early claims that was

acknowledged and credited to him as a victory when there were no witnesses to the event. After his sixtieth victory in the air, witnesses were no longer required to the reports he made of his combats, because, after that time, he seldom appeared with less than twenty planes with him.

Although he flew almost every day and fighting was always his principal duty, there was other work required of the German ace, and this principally concerned his ingenuity in creating or perfecting new methods of both individual and organized attacks and also in analysing the air tactics of the enemy.

One of the reports he made at this period was found under date of February 16, 1917, with regard to air fighting in general and the training of pursuit flyers. In this report, which was addressed to the commander of the Sixth Army air forces, Richthofen wrote:

The adversary often slips downward over one wing or lets himself fall like a dead leaf in order to shake off an attack. In order to stick to one adversary, one must on no account follow his tactics, as one has no control over the machine when falling like a dead leaf.

Should the adversary, however, attempt to evade attack by such tricks, one must dash down [*sturzflug*] without losing sight of the enemy plane.

When falling like a dead leaf, or intentionally falling wing over wing, the best pilot loses control of his machine for a second or two, therefore, it is a manœuvre to be avoided.

Looping the loop is worse than worthless in air fighting. Each loop is a great mistake. If one has approached an adversary too close, a loop only offers a big advantage to the adversary. Change of speed should be relied on to maintain the position desired, and this is best effected by giving more or less gas.

The best method of flying against the enemy is as follows: The officer commanding the group, no matter how large, should fly lowest, and should keep all machines under observation by turning and curving.

No machine should be allowed either to advance or to keep back. More or less, the whole squadron should advance curving. Flying straight on above the front is dangerous, as even machines of the same type of plane develop different speeds. Surprises can be avoided only when flying in close order. The commanding officer is responsible that neither he nor any of his pilots are surprised by the enemy. If he cannot see to that, he is no good as a leader.

In analysing and giving his opinion of English air tactics prevailing in the spring of 1917, he wrote:

The English single-seater pilots always fly in squad formation

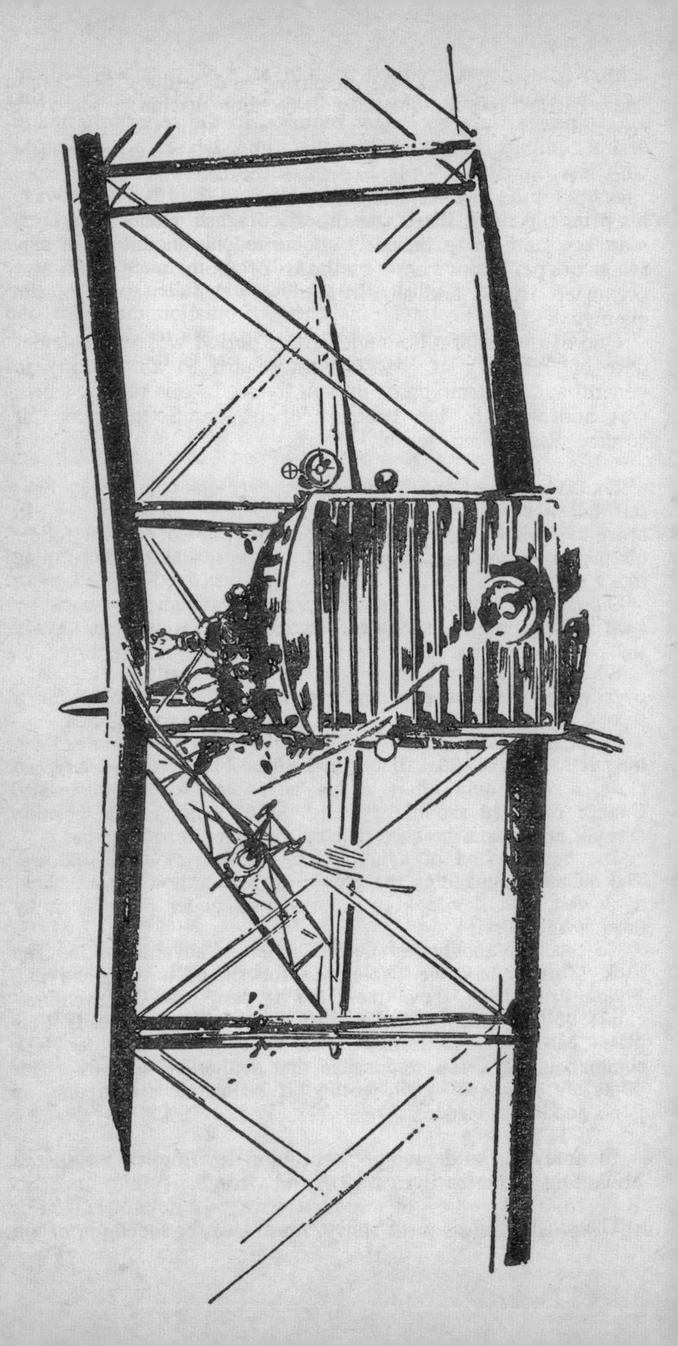

when on pursuit work. Reconnoitring and artillery fire is also now carried on by squads of two-seater machines, sometimes containing as many as twenty machines. Many English airmen try to win advantages by flying tricks while engaged in fighting, but, as a rule, it is just these reckless and useless stunts that lead them to their deaths.

When flying in large squads, the English planes keep close together in order to be able to come to one another's assistance at any given moment. When attacked, they maintain even closer formation. If an English plane which has fallen behind is attacked, the first planes of the enemy formation make left and right turns and hurry to its assistance. After the rest of the formation has passed them, they close up the rear as the last planes.

As squadron and close formation flying developed on both sides, it became the tactics of the successful air scouts to lie in wait for the plane that dropped out of formation and fell behind for any reason. The lone plane was almost "cold meat" to an experienced scout pilot.

On March 4th, Richthofen "singled out" and shot down his twenty-second plane, adding two more dead men to his list of casulties inflicted. The affair occurred as the result of a clash between a German and an English formation.

Richthofen's victims were two more English lieutenants of the Forty-third Squadron. The Flying Uhlan reported the affair as follows:

Requesting Acknowledgment of My 22d Victory

Date: March 4, 1917.
Time: 4:20 P.M.
Place: Acheville.
Type of Plane: Sopwith two-seater.
Occupants: Lieutenant W. Reid and Lieutenant H. Green, both killed, buried by local command, Bois Bernard.

Accompanied by five of my planes, I attacked an enemy squadron above Acheville. The Sopwith I had singled out flew for quite a while in my fire. After my 400th shot, the plane lost a wing while trying to do a sudden turn. It plunged downward.

It is not worth while to have the plane taken back, as parts of it are scattered all over Acheville and the surrounding country. Two machine guns were seized by my Staffel. (One Lewis gun, No. 20,024 and one Maxim gun, No. 17,500.)

(Signed) BARON VON RICHTHOFEN.

Earlier on the same day that he killed Green and Reid, Richthofen had encountered another English plane and shot it down, but "credit" for the victory was not acknowledged by the high command until some time later, on account of the dearth of witnesses and the fact that the plane fell in the English lines. In consequence, the combat, while really his first one of that day, is registered to him as his twenty-third, and not his twenty-second.

Concerning this fight, which took place just before noon, one kilometre north of Loos, Richthofen reported:

> I had started out all by myself and was just looking for my squadron when I spotted a B. E. two-seater, all alone. My first attack was apparently a failure, as my adversary attempted to escape by curves and dives.
>
> After I had forced him downward from 7,500 to 3,500 feet, he imagined himself safe and started to fly once more in a straight line. I took advantage of this and, putting myself behind him, I fired some 500 shots into him. My adversary dived, but in such a steep way that I could not follow him.
>
> According to our infantry observers, the plane crashed to the ground in front of our trenches.

The English casualty list reveals that this plane was from the Eighth Squadron and was being flown on an artillery patrol by Pilot Sergeant R. J. Moody, with Second Lieutenant E. E. Horn in the observer's seat. English infantry witnessed the air fight and watched Moody's plucky attempts to regain his own lines. The plane crashed between the lines and could not be reached during daylight. That night, when patrols reached the wreckage, they found Moody and Horn both dead.

In the German records there are sufficient inconsistencies to reveal that great pains were taken to verify the claims made by flyers for combats that took place over the enemy lines, and as a result of this, earlier victories sometimes bear a record number not in keeping with the date on which they occurred.

On March 3d, Richthofen claimed to have shot down an English plane behind the English lines, but acknowledgment of his report was withheld until some days later, and subsequent victories having been acknowledged in the meantime, the March 3d claim was entered on the records as Victory No. 24.

He said that the plane was a B. E. two-seater, and that the fight occurred at 5 P.M. over Souchez, but it is apparent that a mistake or a misrepresentation exists in one of the two records, because the English records report no air casualty on that day.

On his silver victory cups, Richthofen inscribed his twenty-fourth victory under date of March 6th. In that Valhalla where the heroes of the air must meet some day, there will be ample material for argument.

For example, the shade of Richthofen will undoubtedly want to know who it was that shot him down on March 9, 1917, just after the official acknowledgment of the twenty-fourth "victory." The Flying Uhlan has written at length on that experience, which gave him a chance to feel some of the things that his victims felt when they fell under his guns.

It occurred early in the morning over the German artillery positions around Lens, where the English flyers, in accord with their customary offensive policy, were out in force, making observations, photographing trench lines, bombing ammunition dumps, and directing artillery fire. Richthofen's squadron was attacked by a formation of English pursuit planes, and the fight was on.

> I watched whether one of the Englishmen would take leave of his colleagues [Richthofen wrote afterward], and soon I saw that one of them was stupid enough to do this. I could reach him, and I said to myself, "That man is lost!"
>
> I started after him, and when I got near, he started shooting prematurely, which showed he was nervous, so I said, "Go on shooting, you won't hit me." He shot with a kind of ammunition that ignites. [Tracer bullets containing a phosphorous mixture that leaves a trail of smoke behind, and shows the gunner where his bullets are going. These fiery bullets are deadly to petrol tanks.]
>
> At that moment I think I laughed aloud, but soon I got my lesson. When within 300 feet of the Englishman, I got ready for firing, aimed, and gave a few trial shots. The machine guns were in order. In my mind's eye I saw my enemy dropping.
>
> My excitement was gone. In such a position one thinks quite calmly and collectedly and weighs the probabilities of hitting and being hit. Altogether, the fight itself is the least exciting part of the business, as a rule. He who gets excited in fighting is sure to make mistakes. He will never get his enemy down. Calmness is, after all, a matter of habit.
>
> At any rate, in this case, I did not make a mistake. I approached within fifty yards of my man. I fired some well-aimed shots and thought that I was bound to be successful. That was my idea. But suddenly I heard a tremendous bang when I had fired scarcely ten cartridges, and presently again something hit my machine.
>
> It became clear to me that I had been hit, or, rather, my machine had been hit. At the same time I noticed a fearful stench of gasoline, and I saw that the motor was running slow. The Englishman noticed it too, for he started shooting with redoubled energy, while I had to stop it.
>
> I went right down. Instinctively I switched off the engine. I left in the air a thin white cloud of gas. I knew its meaning from my previous experience with my enemies. Its appearance is the

first sign of a coming explosion. I was at an altitude of 9,000 feet and had to travel a long distance to get down. By the kindness of Providence, my engine stopped running.

I have no idea with what rapidity I went downward. At any rate, the speed was so great that I could not put my head out of the machine without being pressed back by the rush of air.

Soon I had lost sight of the enemy plane. . . . I had fallen to an altitude of perhaps 1,000 feet, and had to look out for a landing. These are serious occasions. I found a meadow. It was not very large, but it would just suffice if I used due caution. Besides, it was very favourably situated on the high road near Henin-Liétard. There I meant to land, and I did, without accident.

My machine had been hit a number of times. The shot that caused me to give up the fight had gone through both the petrol tanks. I had not a drop left. My engine had also been damaged by bullets.

A German officer who had watched the fight and the forced landing rushed into the field and found Richthofen sitting in the cockpit of his bus with his legs dangling over the side.

The officer took him to a near-by officers' mess, but failed to recognize the German ace either by face or name.

"Have you ever brought down an Englishman?" the officer asked.

"Oh, yes, I have done so now and then," replied Richthofen, proud but a little pained.

"Indeed," he replied. "Maybe you have shot down two?"

"No, not two," replied the Flying Uhlan, "but twenty-four."

Richthofen said later that the officer looked at him as though he were talking to a colossal liar. The explanation came when the German ace removed his flying togs and stepped forth in uniform wearing the order Pour le Mérite hanging from his neck. The mess feasted Richthofen with oysters and champagne.

Before noon that same day of his forced landing, Richthofen had entered the fight again and "bagged" his twenty-fifth victim. This was Lieutenant A. J. Pearson, a young mechanical and electrical engineer from civil life.

Pearson had joined up with the Royal Fusiliers in September, 1914. Although of officer material, he went into the ranks and earned his commission there in March, 1915, and won his Military Cross one year later when he carried one of his wounded men back from No Man's Land under heavy fire. He learned to fly at Upham in Wiltshire, where he won his wings and flew to France in December of 1916.

Pearson wrote his mother in March, 1917, that he had just brought down a German flyer alive and unwounded, and that the prisoner at that, the moment of writing, was having a good feed in the squadron mess. The German had presented Pearson with his helmet, which the English flyer had promptly forwarded to his mother as a trophy.

Two days later came the War Office telegram announcing that he had been shot down in flames over the German lines, and later, through the International Red Cross at Geneva, came the evidence upon which the name of this young M. C. went on the casualty lists as killed in action.

Identification had been difficult because, as Richthofen states in his report on the fight, Pearson's body was not recognizable as it had been almost completely cremated before his flaming coffin struck the earth. Richthofen's report was as follows:

Requesting Acknowledgment of My 25th Victory

Date: March 9, 1917.
Time: 11:55 A.M.
Place: Between Roclincourt and Bailleul, this side of the line, 500 yards behind the trenches.
Type of Plane: Vickers one-seater. Tail number A. M. C. 3425 a.
Occupant: Not recognizable, as completely burned.

With three of my planes, I attacked several enemy machines. The plane I had singled out soon caught fire. After I had fired one hundred shots into it, it burst into flames and plunged downward.

The plane is lying on our side of the lines but cannot be salvaged because it is nearly completely burned and is too far in front.

(Signed) BARON VON RICHTHOFEN.

Richthofen, who had followed his flaming victim almost to the ground, saw at close hand the fearful death that fate had spared him just three hours earlier that day. The sight did not unnerve him.

Two days later, he killed two more.

One of these was Eddie Byrne, whose death deserves particular attention because he was one of those ardent spirits who refused to recognize the generally accepted dictum, that air fighting is a young man's game. Byrne was thirty-seven years old and an old soldier of the regular army, with twelve years' service in China, India, and Africa to his record.

When war broke out, Byrne, having retired from the army with an honourable discharge, was managing the establishment of a wealthy Scotsman in Edinburgh.

He went to France at once with the Australian volunteer hospital corps, and finding this too dull and different from his old army life, switched over to the armoured motor-car corps for more excitement. When the armoured cars went into the limbo of bows and arrows after the end of the war of movement, the commanding officer of the Corps, the Duke of Westminster, recommended the old Tommy for a commission. He received one in the Fourth Gordon Highlanders, with whom he served in the trenches until severely wounded.

Two weeks after leaving the hospital, he was undergoing instruction for the air, and a month later saw him a qualified observer on flights over the German lines.

Byrne met death on March 11th. At ten-thirty that morning, Byrne, in the observer's cockpit and with Second Lieutenant J. Smith in the pilot's "office," went aloft in one of the old B. E. two-seaters and crossed the lines under orders to photograph certain German artillery positions. The plane was armed with two Lewis machine guns.

Over Givenchy, another English flyer saw a lone German plane drop out of the upper blue and rip a merciless volley of lead into the photography plane. They saw Byrne and Smith go down on the German side of the line with smoke pouring from the plane. On the next day, German prisoners told the English infantry that both of the airmen had been killed.

As a rule, Richthofen did not like to see the bodies of his victims. He would send a young officer of the squadron to the scene of his latest kill, with instructions to obtain the particulars necessary for the Flying Uhlan's report, so that he could obtain credit for another victory.

Wherever possible, this officer would bring back some trophy of the fallen plane or its occupants. Most frequently this souvenir consisted of a strip of fabric bearing the printed number of the plane and this was affixed to the wall of Richthofen's office at the airdrome in Douai. As the number of these strips grew, they soon filled one whole wall of the Staffel commander's office, which then became known as the room of "dead men's numbers."

Several days after his next victory, Richthofen received in the military mail a postcard photograph of the body of the English flyer he had killed.

It was gruesome and pitiful, but yet the Flying Uhlan was so fascinated by the grisly trophy of his prowess that he kept it as carefully as hunters keep and frame the photo of prize victims of the chase or the finny captives of their rods and lines. On the back of the photograph was the following inscription:

BARON MANFRED VON RICHTHOFEN

SIR: I witnessed on March 17, 1917, your air fight and took this photograph which I send to you with hearty congratulations, because you seldom have the occasion to see your prey.

Vivat sequens! (Here's to the next!)

With Fraternal greetings,

BARON VON RIEZENSTEIN.

Colonel and Commander of the 87th Reserve Infantry Regiment.

The photograph is that of the body of Lieutenant A. E. Boultbee. It shows Boultbee where he fell, near the German reserve line trenches in the neighbourhood of Oppy, over which place he and his observer, Air Mechanic F. King, fought Richthofen to the death at about eleven-thirty in the morning of that day.

Boultbee and King "went west" before noon that St. Patrick's Day, but for Richthofen the day was only half over. He was in excellent form. He had killed two men in the morning. In the afternoon, he killed two more.

One of them was Second Lieutenant G. M. Watt, a twenty-seven-year-old pilot of the Sixteenth Squadron, and the other was his observer, Sergeant F. A. Howlett, who had come into the Flying Corps from an East Kent regiment in which he had distinguished himself in the ranks.

On the afternoon of March 17th, Watt, with Howlett in the observer's box, left the airdrome at three-thirty and flew for the lines. They had a job of artillery observation to do over the little village of Farbus, which was several miles behind the German lines.

For almost two hours they ranged the guns of the English battery with which they were in wireless communication. They indicated targets, reported the shorts and overs, and contributed considerably to the afternoon's discomfort of the German residents of Farbus.

Although the anti-aircraft guns were banging away at them, Watt and Howlett disregarded the safer altitudes above and carried out their "shoot" around the more perilous 2,500-foot level. English fighting planes hovered above them as an escort, and Watt depended upon them to protect him from aërial interference, while, with the Archies, he simply trusted to luck and the best speed and manœuvring that he could get out of the old B. E. two-seater, which, in addition to its wireless equipment and armament of two Lewis guns, carried a pair of twenty-pound bombs.

They were so close to the front lines that English Tommies witnessed the fight at five o'clock, when Richthofen swooped down upon them and raised his day's toll of lives from two to four. Watt tried to shake Richthofen off by throwing the old B. E. into sharp curves, which also gave Howlett opportunity to rip out streams of lead toward their faster adversary every time he approached within range.

Then the Tommies saw the tragedy. At a height of 1,000 feet, the hard-pressed B. E., suffering from the strains of the curves and dives into which Watt was throwing her, collapsed in midair.

In falling, the wreckage was carried by the wind back over the German lines and landed in No Man's Land, where it instantly became the target for the German infantry and artillery. That night, English patrols crawled out in the dark and extracted the crushed and bullet-riddled bodies of Watt and Howlett and buried the remains.

That night, in the messroom of the squadron at Douai, Richthofen received the congratulations of his cubs on his double victory for the day. The Flying Uhlan accepted their praise modestly but reminded them that, as an organization, the squadron had not yet equalled the record of the old Boelcke squadron, and he would not be completely satisfied until the number of victories credited to the unit he commanded was greater than that of any other unit in the German air force.

He gravely directed the attention of his flyers to the current situation on the front, and repeated what they well knew, that the High Command would be forced to depend now more than ever upon the courage and cleverness of its air-force fighters.

Without being marked by battles of major importance, the months of January, February, and March had been punctuated with numerous fierce actions and engagements which have been placed under the general heading of the operations on the Ancre and which, beginning January 11th, had continued until the 13th of March.

Richthofen's squadron had participated in the fighting around Miraumont on February 17th and 18th, which had extended from Thiepval to Hamel and Beaumont. The unit had bitterly fought the English airmen, who endeavoured to dominate the air during the last week of February while their wet and freezing land forces were pushing forward to the capture of Thilloys. They had exacted a heavy toll of planes when the English took Irles on March 10th.

Four days later, the Allied world had been sent into a delirium of delight by the commencement of the German retreat to the Hindenburg Line. The German press agencies broadcast the story of the retreat as one prearranged for the purpose of disrupting the carefully laid Allied plans for the spring push. The flyers of the Maltese cross were kept aloft every daylight hour to interfere, if not to prevent, Allied observation of the new positions to which the Germans were retiring.

On that 17th of March when Richthofen snuffed out the lives of Byrne and Smith and Watt and Howlett, English ground forces pushed their way into Bapaume in the face of considerable resistance and on the following day occupied Péronne.

The German retreat and the Allied advance to the Hindenburg Line continued from March 14th until the 5th of April, and in the confusion of rearrangement and readjustments of forces due to the changed positions of the opposing armies, the respective commanders were forced to depend more and more upon aërial reconnaissance.

The activity in the air increased daily, the Allies concentrating every effort on finding out the details of the new German positions, while the Germans put every available plane in the air to frustrate these efforts.

Although he spent from three to six hours every day in the air and engaged in numerous hot combats, it was not until three days after the English occupation of Péronne that Richthofen succeeded in registering his next victory, which he did at the cost of two more English lives.

This was the last air fight that Richthofen had as "second louie." On the following day, March 22d, he received his first promotion of the war. The Uhlan of the sky became a first lieutenant, which, in consideration of his age—he was still only twenty-four years old—was an exceptional advancement under the strict regulations of the German army.

Two days later, he celebrated the promotion with another successful combat which he described in his report as follows:

Requesting Acknowledgment of My 30th Victory

Date: March 24, 1917.
Time: 11:15 A.M.
Place: Givenchy.
Plane: Spad with Hispano motor. The first I have encountered. Plane No. 6706. Hispano Suiza Motor, 140 H. P.; Machine Gun Maxim No. 4810.
Occupant: Lieutenant Baker, wounded, taken prisoner.

I was flying with several of my gentlemen when I observed an enemy squad passing our front.

Aside from this squad there were two new one-seaters which I had never seen in the air before, and they were extremely fast and handy.

I attacked one of them and ascertained that my machine was better than his.

After a long fight, I managed to hit the adversary's gasoline tank. His propeller stopped running. The plane had to go down.

As the fight had taken place above the trenches, the adversary tried to escape me, but I managed to force him to land behind our line near Givenchy.

The plane turned completely over in a small shell hole, and remained upside down. It was taken by our troops.

(Signed) Baron von Richthofen.

The day after his capture of Baker, Richthofen took another prisoner of war, this one being Second Lieutenant C. G. Gilbert, a pilot of the Twenty-ninth Squadron, who was flying a speedy French Nieuport machine on escort duty.

The Flying Uhlan was proud of the ease and dispatch with which he handled this English adversary, because it was the first time he had had an opportunity to perform in the air on the same mission as his younger brother, Lothar.

Lothar was with him that day, and Lothar himself attacked one of the English planes. It was his first combat as a fighting pilot, and he succeeded in disabling his adversary, but was not fortunate enough to shoot him down out of control. He still had his first victory to register. He was eager to duplicate the big brother's success in the air.

His first brush with the enemy was a great event for the boy. It was a red-letter day for his elder brother also, because it recalled to him the thrill and the tingles he had felt that day hardly seven months earlier when he, under the watchful eyes of Boelcke, the great master, had shot down his first victim from the sky.

Back in the flying baron's quarters in Douai, Lothar watched with a mixture of pride and envy over his brother's shoulder as the latter filled out the inevitable report with its reiterated petition for credit.

It was all so easy if one made one's self letter perfect and exercised care, was the gist of the lesson Richthofen repeated to the men of his Staffel, and especially to his kid brother. He repeated that the successful flyer had to know the possibilities of his plane, he had to be able to recognize different types of enemy planes and be thoroughly aware of the capabilities of each type. Then he had to learn how to take advantage of wind and sun and put them to his own use against the enemy. Combine an offensive spirit based on knowledge instead of blind sporting courage with the proper degree of carefulness, and one would go far and fare well in the air. Lothar learned well under his idolized brother, and some say he did even better. He followed his brother's rules and survived the war. The Flying Uhlan did not.

At this period of his career Richthofen's spirits were high. He reflected them in his current letters to his mother. On March 26, 1917, he wrote.

LIEBE MAMMA:

Yesterday I brought down my thirty-first, and the day before my thirtieth. Three days ago I received my appointment as First Lieutenant, and have thus gained a full half year. My squadron is shaping well. It really gives me great pleasure.

Lothar had his first air encounter yesterday. He was satisfied with it because he touched his adversary who, in our parlance, "stank," leaving a black, smelly trail behind him. He did not come down, of course—that would have been too much luck. Lothar is very conscientious and will do well.

How is Papa, and how did you like yesterday's official army report?

MANFRED.

The little silver cups of death now ranged on Richthofen's desk numbered thirty-one. It was not quite three months since he had been placed in command of his own squadron, and he had jumped his individual bag of victories from sixteen to thirty-one, almost doubling the score.

In four months' flying in the old Boelcke squadron, from September, 1916, to January 4, 1917, he had shot down his first sixteen planes.

In less than three months' flying with a squadron under his own command, from January 4 through March 25, 1917, he had shot down fifteen more, almost equalling his former bag.

He had downed two in January, two in February, and in the month of March had established a new record for himself by downing eleven. Four of the planes had been single-seater fighters, and eleven of them had been two-seater machines, whose principal functions did not include air fighting.

SUMMARY THROUGH MARCH 25, 1917

Number of planes shot down in 1917	15
Previously reported (1916)	16
Total planes shot down	31
Killed in 1917	16
Previously reported (1916)	16
Total killed	32
Wounded and prisoners of war in 1917	5
Previously reported (1916)	8
Total wounded and prisoners of war	13

Richthofen's books with death stood well in his favour. There was still more than a year of carnage ahead of him before he himself was to go the way of his many victims, but before that day arrived, he was to double and almost treble the terrible score that now stood beside his name.

Of all this following period, his record for the next month, April, 1917, was to be the reddest.

Chapter VII

To kill, to wound, or to capture a man a day, for a month is the unprecedented war record which young Von Richthofen wrote in blood during the thirty days of April, 1917.

It was the month America entered the war.

The appearance of this new and formidable ally in the ranks of Germany's foes had the effect of adding fresh fuel to the killer spirit that dominated the Uhlan of the skies.

With renewed energy and determination, with increased ferocity and aggressiveness, he applied himself and his fighting pilots to the ambitious task of forcing a conclusion at arms before the weight of American force could be brought to the fighting lines.

At the head of his pursuit group, he coursed the skies daily in search of fresh victims, and found them. Plane after plane he shot down in flames, finding new and keener exultation in following his disabled prey to the ground.

He produced results and demanded increased "production" from the members of his unit. He kept careful records of their flights and combats and became intolerant of those who lagged on the record. His own "bag" increased almost daily.

It was partly Richthofen's red score for April that Ludendorff had in mind when he said the flying Baron was worth as much as three divisions of German infantry.

Killing in individual personal combat on such a scale was beyond the experience, knowledge, and even the imagination of Prussia's ruthless war lords. It became the boast at German headquarters that Richthofen's appearance on any new sector was sufficient to cause extensive troop movements on the part of the enemy.

The Uhlan gloried in his success. On his closely cropped blond hair rested a grisly crown which distinguished him above all others as the foremost killer in the ranks of his militant people, and the ablest single executioner in the service of the grim reaper.

He made "Bloody April" a month of death and carnage in the air. In the number of casualties inflicted, the German air service achieved the zenith of its power.

Reorganized under a general air commander and greatly

reinforced, it was able to take from the Allies the aërial superiority which the latter had so decisively achieved in 1916.

During the period from March 31st to May 11th, the Germans claimed to have shot down 4 British planes for each German plane that was lost, and they put down the British losses at 120 planes as against 30 German planes. It would seem that the Germans even understated the losses of their enemies, because the records of the Royal Flying Corps show that, during the month of April, 151 British planes were ominously "missing."

Germany's technical genius and industrial efficiency were responsible in no small degree for the April successes of her flying forces. They had stolen a march on the British by bringing out their new spring model planes at least six weeks before the British could deliver theirs at the front.

For this failure on the part of home production in England, scores of young British flyers paid with their lives. Their old last-year machines—slow, cumbersome "B.E.'s" and "F. E.'s" and De Haviland pusher scouts—were hopelessly outclassed by the new Halberstadt and Albatross scouts.

The German flyers had all the advantage. Their machines were the latest word in aviation. In speed, they could literally fly circles around their adversaries. The Halberstadt and Albatross could outclimb and outmanœuvre any British plane in the air.

But in spite of this mechanical superiority, the British, with characteristic tenacity, refused to change their offensive policy and continued to carry the war in the air to the enemy's side of the line. Whereas, during the British superiority in the air in 1916, the German air force had been completely swept from the skies, the turning of the tables did not bring the same results in 1917.

The severity of the British losses broke all existing records, but they were not allowed to interfere with the orders to "carry on" as usual. There were still plenty of last year's machines, and there was never a dearth of young Englishmen from the army and navy eager to escape the monotony of trench and sea and to fight it out in the clouds.

There are few examples of more sterling courage than that shown by these cavaliers of the air with their hopelessly inferior equipment. Even the most expert and courageous flyer in one of the old British machines was almost a certain victim to any novice who flew one of the new German models. But, in spite of the inequality of the contests, the English knights of the blue went up day after day to almost certain death. It was like sending butterflies out to sting wasps.

Although the butterflies might conduct offensive observation and bombing patrols in the air over the enemy lines, they were

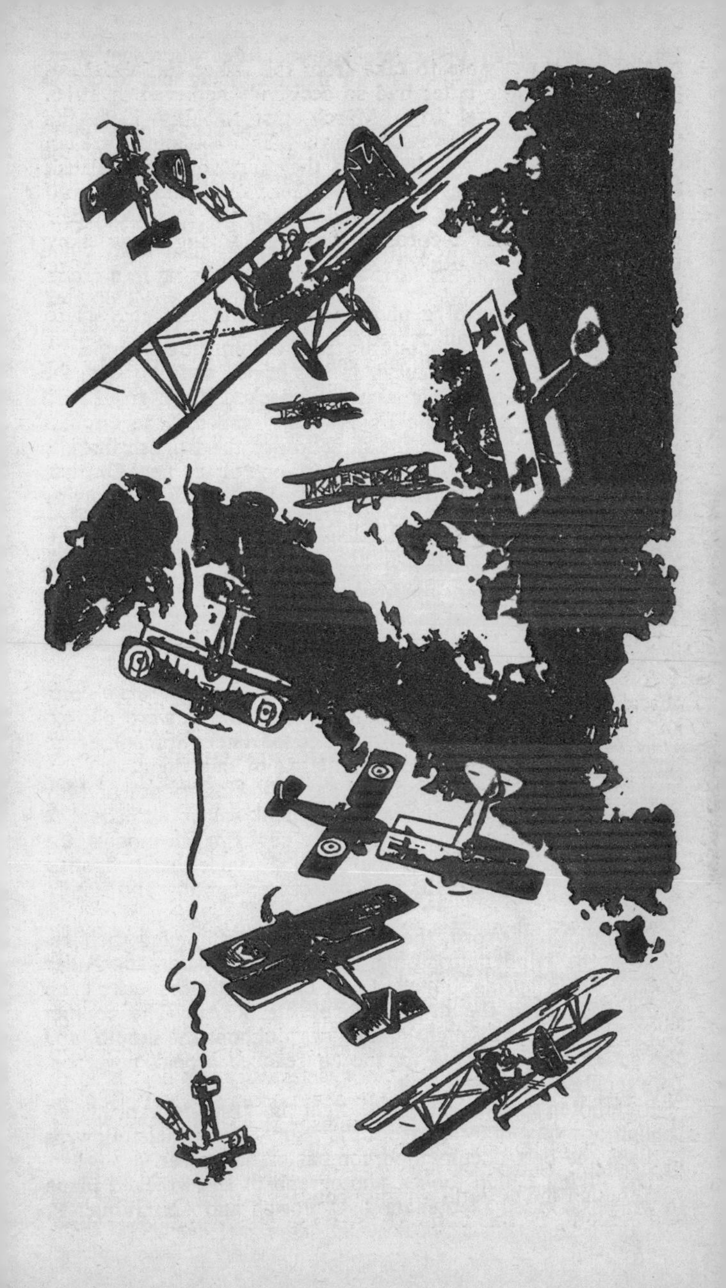

forced to rely solely upon defensive measures when they were attacked by the new German air fighters. They had to create new tactics to protect themselves.

It was a game of trying to ward off the other fellow's blows and never being able to deliver one at him. The price of the game was death. Two defensive measures were created by the hard-pressed Englishmen.

First, they learned to play "ring-around-a-rosie," or "tail-chasing," as it became known later. An English unit, when attacked, would close its formation and start flying in a circle, with each plane chasing the tail of the plane in front of him. To a degree this made it possible for each plane to protect the tail of the plane immediately in front of him in the circle.

If the formation were lucky in this device and closed in the circle just as quick as planes were knocked down from it, it was possible to get home by gradually shifting the circular course more and more in the direction of the English lines.

When flying alone, and attacked by one of the new German models, the trapped butterfly could only depend upon diving to within four or five hundred feet of the ground and then streaking for home by zigzagging and hedgehopping. This method was adopted when it was found that the new German planes were sometimes unable to pull out of a dive as low as five hundred feet from the ground, and, in consequence, their pilots were loath to follow their quarry to such a low height.

But even with the best of luck, it was a game in which the odds were greatly against the English. Few flights were completed without losses, and amongst these losses were old experienced men who were sorely needed later. Sometimes an entire formation would be annihilated in one flight.

It was not until the middle of the following month of May that the lagging British supply department was able to equalize matters by delivering numbers of the new English models, the two-seater Bristol fighters, the S. E. 5 single-seater fighting planes, and the De Haviland 4 two-seater fighting and bombing planes.

By the 5th of April, the Germans had completed their retreat to the Hindenburg Line, and four days later, the Allies opened their spring offensive of 1917, with the attack on Vimy Ridge and the first battle of the Scarpe. The conflict waged unremittently night and day throughout the month, and the activity of both sides in the air reached a peak never before touched in the war.

Richthofen's first successful fight in "Bloody April," although not very different from the many others that follow, is perhaps the best documented combat of his career.

The Flying Uhlan took a photograph of the wrecked plane in which he killed Lieutenant J. C. Powell and Air Gunner P.

Bonner. It remains, with his notations on the back of it, in one of his several scrapbooks in his mother's home at Schweidnitz.

Further documentation comes in a detailed account of the fight which Richthofen wrote for publication and another account of it written by his younger brother Lothar, who was now a full-fledged member of the Jasta. In addition to the above, Richthofen's official report on the combat has been found in the German Reichsarchiv in Berlin.

Jasta 11, composed of eight pilots, was divided into two groups or "chains" of four planes each. Richthofen flew alternately with each group. Lubbert the "bullet catcher" had been shot down and killed three days before, and the second chain now consisted of Richthofen's brother Lothar, and Lieutenants Wolff and Allmenröder, all of whom were decorated with the Pour le Mérite before they were killed.

On this day (April 2d) [Lothar wrote], our group had been assigned to an early morning start, that is to say, it had to be prepared to take the air first at any moment. Our duty began between 4 and 5 A.M. We had just got up and were sitting in the starting house, when the telephone rang.

"Six Bristols coming across from Arras in the direction of Douai" was the message.

We jumped into our planes and started. High up above us at about 9,000 feet there was a broken cover of clouds. We could see the English planes below the clouds not far from our airdrome. My brother's red bird was standing ready at the doors of its hangar, but my brother was not to be seen.

We came into contact with the enemy, but the Englishmen were too clever with their machines, and we could not bring any of them down. Whenever we thought we had one of them, he disappeared in the clouds. After flying around for an hour without having brought down a single plane, we flew back and landed.

My brother's red plane was in the open hangar door, apparently in the same spot where we had last seen it, but anyone could see, judging from the activity of the mechanics working on it, that it had been up in the air. We asked the mechanics.

They told us the Lieutenant had left the ground five minutes after we had started, and that he had returned twenty minutes later, after having brought down an English plane. We walked back to our quarters and found that my brother had gone back to bed and was sleeping as though nothing had happened.

Only a few bullet splashes and holes in his machine and the report of his having shot down another Englishman indicated that he had been flying. We were just a little bit ashamed of ourselves. We had been three, and we had started earlier and landed later than my brother, and we could show no results.

While we were getting ready for our next start, my brother turned up, and it seemed to me that he was cross with the

English who had interrupted his sleep and who forced peace-loving men to leave their beds at unseemly hours.

Richthofen himself described the fight as follows:

The second of April, 1917, was a very warm day for my Jagdstaffel. From my quarters I could clearly hear the drum fire, which was again particularly violent. I was still in bed when my orderly rushed into the room and exclaimed: "Sir, the English are here!"

Sleepy as I was, I looked out of the window, and, really, there were my dear friends circling over the flying ground. I jumped out of bed and into my clothes in a jiffy. My red bird had been pulled out of the hangars and was ready for starting. My mechanics knew that I would probably not allow such a favourable moment to go by unused. Everything was ready. I snatched up my furs and went up.

I was the last to start. My comrades had started earlier and were much nearer to the enemy. I feared that my prey would escape me and that I should have to look on from a distance while the others were fighting.

Suddenly, one of the impertinent Englishmen tried to drop down upon me. I allowed him to approach me quite near, and then we started a merry quadrille. Sometimes my opponent flew on his back and sometimes he did other tricks. He was flying a two-seater fighter. I realized very soon that I was his master and that he could not escape me.

During an interval in the fighting, I assured myself that we were alone. It followed that the victory would belong to him who was calmest, who shot best, and who had the clearest brain in a moment of danger.

Soon I had got him beneath me without having seriously hurt him with my gun. We were at least two kilometres from the front. I thought he intended to land, but there I had made a mistake. Suddenly, when he was only a few yards above the ground, I noticed how he once more went off on a straight course. He tried to escape me. That was too bad.

I attacked him again, and to do so I had to go so low that I was afraid of touching the roofs of the houses in the village beneath me. The Englishman defended himself up to the last moment. At the very end, I felt that my engine had been hit. Still I did not let go. He had to fall. He flew at full speed right into a block of houses.

There is little left to be said. This was once more a case of splendid daring. The man had defended himself to the last. However, in my opinion, he showed, after all, more stupid foolhardiness than courage. It was again one of the cases where one must differentiate between energy and idiocy. He had to come down in any case, but he paid for his stupidity with his life.

I was delighted with the performance of my red machine,

and returned to the airdrome. My comrades were still in the air, and they were surprised when we met later at breakfast and I told them that I had scored my thirty-second machine.

In his official report on the fight, Richthofen wrote:

Requesting Acknowledgment of My 32d Victory

Date: April 2, 1917.
Time: 8:35 A.M.
Place: Farbus (village).
Type of Plane: B. E. two-seater. No. 5841, Motor P. D. 1345/80.
Occupants: Both killed. Name of one Lieutenant Powell. Other occupant had no documents of identification.

I attacked an enemy artillery flyer.

After a long fight, I managed to force the adversary nearly on to the ground, but without being able to put him out of control.

The strong and lusty wind had driven the enemy plane over our lines. My adversary tried by jumping over trees and other objects to escape. Then I forced him to land in the village of Farbus, where the machine was smashed against a block of houses.

The observer kept on shooting until the machine touched the ground.

(Signed) BARON VON RICHTHOFEN.

Powell and Bonner were from the Thirteenth Squadron, R. F. C. They had left their airdrome a few minutes before 8 o'clock to photograph German artillery positions, and their comrades heard nothing more of them until the Germans dropped a message announcing they had been killed.

Richthofen learned the identity of his victims in the late afternoon of the same day he killed them. With Lothar, he motored over to Farbus village and examined the wreck of the English machine crumpled up against the wall of a house. A slight snow had fallen, effacing the dark red stains left by the life blood of the two English war birds. The Uhlan of the sky did not see the bodies of his victims. He did not want to, but he took a photograph of the plane.

Concerning the visit of the two brothers to the scene of Powell and Bonner's fatal crash, Lothar wrote:

It was a sad sight which we saw. Half of the machine was hanging from a roof, and the other half was on the ground. After inspecting the remnants, we went home. The soldiers around the place had in the meantime recognized my brother and cheered us madly.

Before noon of that same day, Richthofen had gone aloft

again and brought down another. There are three accounts of this fight, which took place more than two miles above the earth. Two of them are by Richthofen himself, and they contradict each other vitally. The third account is by the only living survivor of the combat, and it differs from the other two.

In the wartime account, which Richthofen wrote for publication and which has every appearance of careful editing under the hands of the military censor, the Flying Uhlan takes credit for having spared the lives of his victims because, in the persistence with which they defended themselves, they displayed most sterling courage. On his military report of the affair, he wrote that he deliberately killed one of the English flyers after the plane had landed behind the German lines.

The Prussian was in gay spirits after his early morning triumph. Visiting him at the airdrome was Lieutenant Werner Voss, a crack flyer and an old comrade from the Boelcke squadron. Of all the German aces, Voss was closest to Richthofen in the score of planes downed. On the day previous to this meeting, he had been accredited with his twenty-third victory and was only nine behind the flying Baron. They joked with each other about their competition.

The weather had turned out bad, with a strong wind and frequent flurries of snow and hail. Richthofen went aloft with Voss to accompany the latter back to his airdrome. They flew above the clouds in the direction of Arras, over which place they were joined by Lothar, who had recognized his brother's red machine from afar.

Suddenly, we saw an English air patrol approaching from the other side [Richthofen later wrote]. Immediately the thought occurred to me "Now comes number thirty-three." Although there were nine Englishmen, and although they were on their own territory, they preferred to avoid battle. I began to think that it might be better for me to repaint my machine. Nevertheless, we caught up with them. The important thing in airplanes is that they shall be speedy.

I was nearest to the enemy and attacked the man at the rear of the formation. To my great delight, I noticed that he accepted battle, and my pleasure increased when I discovered that his comrades deserted him, so I had once more a single fight.

It was a fight similar to the one I had had several hours earlier. My opponent did not make matters easy for me. He knew the fight business, and it was particularly awkward for me that he was a good shot. To my great regret, that was quite clear to me.

A favourable wind came to my aid, and it drove both of us over the German lines. My opponent discovered that the matter was not as simple as he had imagined. So he plunged, and disappeared in a cloud. He had nearly saved himself.

I plunged after him and dropped out of the cloud, and as luck would have it, found myself quite close behind him. I fired and he fired, without any tangible result. At last I hit him. I noticed a ribbon of white gasoline vapour. He must land, for his engine had stopped.

But he was a stubborn fellow. He would not recognize that he was bound to lose the game. If he continued shooting, I could kill him, for meanwhile we had dropped to an altitude of about nine hundred feet.

However, the Englishman continued to defend himself by shooting at me exactly as his countryman had done in the morning. He fought on until he landed.

When he had come to the ground, I flew over him at an altitude of about thirty feet in order to ascertain whether I had killed him or not, and what did the rascal do? He levelled his machine gun and shot holes into my machine.

Afterward Voss told me that, if that had happened to him, he would have shot the aviator on the ground. As a matter of fact, I ought to have done so, for he had not surrendered. He was one of the few fortunate fellows who escaped with their lives. I felt very merry as I flew home to celebrate the downing of my thirty-third airplane.

That was the account of the fight that admiring millions read in Germany during the war. It threw an even brighter mantle of chivalry around the Uhlan of the skies. He gave quarter to his foes after he had downed them. He could be merciful.

But read Richthofen's official report of the same combat, and it will appear that somebody is lying somewhere. Here it is:

Requesting Acknowledgment of My 33d Victory

Date: April 2d, 1917.
Time: 11:15 A.M.
Place: Givenchy.
Plane: English Sopwith two-seater. Clerget Blin motor, type 2, without number.
Occupants: Sergeant Dunn and Lieutenant Warren.

Together with Lieutenants Voss and Lothar von Richthofen I attacked an enemy squadron of eight Sopwiths above a closed cover of clouds on the enemy's side of the lines.

The plane I had singled out was driven away from its formation and tried to escape me by hiding in the clouds after I had put holes in its gasoline tanks.

Below the clouds, I immediately attacked him again, thereby forcing him to land 300 yards east of Givenchy. But as yet my adversary would not surrender, and even as his machine was on the ground, he kept shooting at me, thereby hitting my

machine very severely when I was only five yards off the ground.
Consequently, I once more attacked him already on the ground and killed one of the occupants.

(Signed) BARON VON RICHTHOFEN.

From my study of Richthofen's character, I don't believe he would have shrunk from publishing the statement that he killed one of his victims on the ground. It would have been the sporting thing to ignore the final shots of the downed flyer, who was a prisoner anyhow, but military ethics would have given the captor a perfect right to kill a prisoner that resisted.

If Richthofen's official report to his superiors is the true account according to his best belief, then it is my opinion that the change in the published account was made by the German censor for the purpose of destroying any possible material for "Hun atrocity" stories that might find its way to the hands of Germany's foes.

But now comes the third account of the affair, and this one is from Lieutenant Peter Warren, who was the pilot of the plane Richthofen shot down. His observer was Sergeant R. Dunn, and Dunn died shortly after the plane landed. Death came as the result of a bullet through his abdomen, but it was a bullet which he received at 12,000 feet in the air and not after he was on the ground.

"Really, I am afraid Richthofen in his report on his fight with Dunn and me must have mixed us up with somebody else," says Peter Warren. "I certainly wish Dunn and I had been able to put up as much resistance as the Baron credits us with, but actually it was rather a one-sided affair almost entirely in Richthofen's favour. Poor Dunn was hit early in the fight and was unconscious through most of it.

"It was the first time I had ever taken Dunn up, although he was a veteran observer with, I believe, three Hun machines to his credit. My regular observer, an infantry officer who had been in the air about three months, had fallen off a horse the day before and broken his knee. Dunn was assigned as a substitute. The fact that we had never flown together before would be a disadvantage if we were attacked.

"We left the airdrome at ten-thirty in the morning. The weather was bad—rain and hail, with almost a gale blowing in the direction of the German lines. Our faces were covered with whale oil to prevent frostbite. So many flyers had been laid up with frostbitten faces that the use of the grease was compulsory, and a case of frostbite became an offence calling for a court martial.

"Our flight consisted of six machines from the Forty-third Squadron, with Major Dore as patrol leader. Our planes were

Sopwith two-seaters armed with Lewis and Vickers machine guns, firing fore and aft. Our job was to photograph a section of the Second Hindenburg Line, east of Vimy Ridge, which, as you remember, was attacked just a week later. My plane and one other carried the cameras. The other four were escort.

"We were flying in a V at about twelve thousand feet, and our direction was northerly. I was flying at the end of the V, in the last position, which made me the highest.

"Richthofen dove down out of the sun and took Dunn by surprise. The first notice I had of the attack was when I heard Dunn from his seat behind me shout something at me, and at the same time a spray of bullets went over my shoulder from behind and splintered the dashboard almost in front of my face.

"I kicked over the rudder and dived instantly, and just got a glance at the red machine passing under me to the rear. I did not know it was Richthofen's. I looked back over my shoulder, and Dunn was not in sight. I did not know whether he had been thrown out of the plane in my quick dive or was lying dead at the bottom of his cockpit.

"I realized that he was out of action, however, and that I was quite defenceless from the rear. I endeavoured to get my forward machine gun on the red plane, but Richthofen was too wise a pilot, and his machine was too speedy for mine.

"He zoomed up again and was on my tail in less than half a minute. Another burst of lead came over my shoulder, and the glass faces of the instruments on the dashboard popped up in my face. I dived again, but he followed my every move.

"I had lost several thousand feet, but still below me at about nine thousand feet was a layer of clouds. I dove for it, hoping to pull up in it and shake him off in the vapour. Bad luck again.

"The clouds were only a thin layer, you know, and instead of remaining in them, I went completely through them, came out below, and found that the red Albatross with those two sputtering machine guns had come through with me.

"Another burst of lead from behind, and the bullets spattered on the breech of my own machine gun, cutting the cartridge belt. At the same time, my engine stopped, and I knew that the fuel tanks had been hit.

"There were more clouds below me at about six thousand feet. I dove for them and tried to pull up in them as soon as I reached them. No luck! My elevators didn't answer the stick. The control wires had been shot away.

"There was nothing to do but go down and hope to keep out of a spin as best I could. I side-slipped and then went into a dive which fast became a spiral. I don't know how I got out of it.

"I was busy with the useless controls all the time, and going down at a frightful speed, but the red machine seemed to be able to keep itself poised just above and behind me all the time, and its machine guns were working every minute. I found later that bullets had gone through both of my sleeves and both of my boot legs, but in all of the firing, not one of them touched me, although they came uncomfortably close.

"I managed to flatten out somehow in the landing and piled up with an awful crash. As I hit the ground, the red machine swooped over me, but I don't remember him firing on me when I was on the ground.

"I looked into what was left of the observer's cockpit and saw poor old Dunn crumpled up on the bottom. He was quite heavy, and I had some difficulty in lifting him out. He was unconscious. I laid him down on the ground and tore open his coat. He had been plugged through the stomach, apparently from the back.

"I lifted his head and spoke to him.

" 'I think I'm done,' he mumbled, and then became unconscious. German infantrymen rushed out from dugouts near by; some of them brought a stretcher. We carried Dunn to a dressing station in a stone hut. I was kept outside under guard. The doctor came out and told me that Dunn was alive but would not last much longer. I never saw him again. Later, they told me that he died six hours afterward. He was a stout fellow.

"My guards marched me back some distance to a headquarters, where I was put into a car and taken to Douai. There I was placed in a room in the old French military barracks. The dirty plaster walls were covered with many names, so I presume a lot of prisoners had preceded me there.

"In one corner there was a bed with a blanket on it. An electric light bulb hung down from the centre of the ceiling. There was a high barred window in one wall and a small wood stove stood by one of the side walls.

"The German sentry, who frequently looked at me through a wicket in the door, came in twice and relighted the fire in the wood stove, which I had allowed to go out. I sat on a wooden stool in front of the stove and felt pretty miserable. I presume it was my nerves. I couldn't get my mind off poor old Dunn. I felt completely dejected.

"About six o'clock in the evening, when it had become rather dark, I heard someone unlocking the door. I looked up as it was opened. An enormous great Dane dog—biggest one I ever saw—walked into the room and right across to me.

"He wagged his tail and, putting his nose up in my face, started licking the whale grease which I still had on my cheeks. We were friends at once. I needed a wash badly, anyhow.

"The electric light flashed on, and in its yellow light I saw the dog's master standing in the doorway smiling at me. He was a thin dark man of medium height, thin intelligent face, pince-nez glasses, well-trimmed moustache. He wore a very smart and dapper uniform with highly polished boots and looked to be about fifty years of age.

" 'Good-evening,' he said in flawless English. 'I am Captain Baron von Karg Bebenburg. It is needless to tell you that I am from the intelligence section. I have come to talk with you and ask you if there is anything I can do for you. I am sorry to tell you that your comrade, Sergeant Dunn, is dead.'

"There was nothing that I could say. I remained silent. He offered me a cigar, which I accepted, and repeated his offer to do anything for my comfort within his power. I told him that I could make good use of some soap and water and a towel. He sent these up late during the night, together with a packet of cigarettes and a French novel.

"Of course, I would answer none of his questions about the number of my squadron, its strength, location of its airdrome, and the reason for our renewed air activity during the last week.

" 'I appreciate your reticence,' he said, 'but, as a matter of fact, we have most of that information. Our intelligence system is working quite well on this front. I have just perfected a new organization of charts and telephone communications whereby our airdromes are notified whenever your squadrons start on a mission over the lines. I know, from my charts of your past performances, almost what your destination is and just about what time you will arrive there. Your flying corps operates so closely on schedule and with such regularity that we are now able to recognize your intentions before you have time to execute them.'

"I told him this was all very interesting, but I offered no opinion on it. He told me that he was a Bavarian and had been a professor of history in the University of Munich. He was a most interesting talker, and conversation with him became almost a temptation.

" 'What the world needs to-day,' he said, 'is two good strong nations to divide it and run it as it should be run. Germany and Great Britain are the only nations that could do this. France—Paris—they could be just a common playground for all of us. What do you think?'

"I told him I had never thought of it.

"'How do you think the war is doing?' he asked.

"'Very favourably for the Allies,' I replied. 'It seems almost certain that America is coming in with us.'

"It seems strange, as I recall that conversation to-day, to realize that America did enter the war just four days afterward. My opinion at the time, however, did not shock or seem to disturb my interrogator.

"'Yes,' he said, 'we recognize such an eventuality, and have made our dispositions accordingly. Our intensive submarine campaign will neutralize any effects the United States might have.'

"He smiled, but I just continued petting the dog.

"He left me, and I never saw him again. I was moved the next day to the prison camp at Karlsruhe, and later to Schwarmstadt, where I attempted an escape but was caught. I spent the rest of the war caged up."

British G. H. Q. still demanded more accurate information and photographs of Vimy Ridge, against which a massed attack was to be launched within a week. The lives of thousands of infantrymen depended upon this information, and it was up to the flyers to get it. Photographic patrols went over daily on this hazardous mission, and the next victims that went down under the guns of the German ace were engaged in that work at the time. The fight occurred on the afternoon of the next day. Richthofen reported it briefly as follows:

Requesting Acknowledgment of My 34th Victory

Date: April 3d, 1917.
Time: 4:15 P.M.
Place: Between Lens and Liévin.
Plane: Vickers two-seater, No. A6382. Motor unrecognizable.
Occupants: Lieutenant O'Beirne, killed. Observer MacDonald, prisoner.

Together with Lieutenant Schaeffer and Lieutenant Lothar von Richthofen I attacked three enemy planes. The plane I myself attacked was forced to land near Liévin.

After a short fight, the motor began to smoke and the observer ceased shooting. I followed the adversary to the ground.

(Signed) BARON VON RICHTHOFEN.

It must have been rainy or otherwise inclement weather on the Somme on April 4, 1917, the day after Jack O'Beirne's fatal fight, because Richthofen, whether he took the air or not, appears to have missed one day without having, as his friends liked to say, "his customary Englishman for dinner."

But, on the following day, he made up for it by knocking down two planes in less than fifteen minutes. In these two successful combats, he killed one man and captured three, two of whom he wounded.

These were not photography or artillery planes this time, but offensively armed fighting machines, quite worthy of his most careful attention. The fight occurred when a flight of the Fourth Squadron, Royal Flying Crops, while on a scouting patrol across the lines, bumped into Richthofen and four of his fighting pilots almost directly above the Flying Uhlan's airdrome at Douai. The English were out to attack the Baron in his lair.

Requesting Acknowledgment of My 35th Victory

Date: April 5, 1917.
Time: 11:15 A.M.
Place: Lewards, southwest of Douai.
Plane: Bristol two-seater, No. 3340, Motor 10,443.
Occupants: Lieutenant McLicker and Lieutenant George both seriously wounded.

It was foggy and altogether very bad weather when I attacked an enemy squad while it was flying between Douai and Valenciennes. Up to this point, it had managed to advance without being fired upon.

I attacked with four planes of my Staffel.

I personally singled out the last machine, which I forced to land near Lewards after a short fight. The occupants burnt their machine.

It was a new type of plane, which we had not known before, and it appears to be quick and rather handy, with a powerful motor, V-shaped and twelve cylindered. Its name could not be recognized.

The D 111 Albatross was, both in speed and ability to climb, undoubtedly superior.

Of the enemy squad, which consisted of six planes, four were forced by my Staffel to land on our side.

(Signed) BARON VON RICHTHOFEN.

And—

Requesting Acknowledgment of My 36th Victory

Date: April 5, 1917.
Time: 11:30 A.M.
Place: Quincy.
Plane: Bristol two-seater, details unobtained as machine burned.
Occupants: Pilot Lieutenant Adams. Observer Lieutenant Steward, unwounded.

After having put the first adversary near Lewards out of action, I pursued the remaining part of the enemy squadron and overtook the last plane above Douai.

After a rather long fight, the adversary surrendered. I forced him to land near Quincy. The occupants burned their machine to ashes.

(Signed) BARON VON RICHTHOFEN.

Richthofen revealed in the two reports the anxiety with which each air force watched the other for new types, devices, or mechanical improvements that could give one side an advantage over the other. The Uhlan felt convinced, however, that this new English type was still inferior in speed and climbing to the German plane then in use.

Whether there was anything new on the Sopwith two-seater that the Germans would care to copy and apply to their own machines is not apparent, but from the care with which the occupants of the vanquished planes immediately destroyed their machines upon landing, it would seem that the English flyers thought it embodied features not known to the Germans.

The arrival of the new English air steeds was the subject of many reports and much discussion that night—April 5th—at Richthofen's airdrome at Douai. After the dinner débris had been cleared away at the long mess table, the flyers gave heated accounts of their encounters during the day, pointing out the strength and the weakness of the "Sops" as they had found them. All of them shared their knowledge from experience to develop the best way in which to attack the new bus and also how to evade its attack.

During that dinner, events were shaping themselves not many miles away that would rudely disturb the evening's discussion before it was finished.

In an airdrome close by the village of Izel le Hameau, behind the English lines, there were indications of unusual activity.

Mechanics bustled back and forth in the dark carrying bulky metal objects in their arms. Others crawled over the machines in the hangars, making final adjustments under the furtive gleams of carefully hooded lights.

Occasionally a door of the O. C.'s office would open, and an orderly would stand framed in the light for a moment and then disappear into the murkiness of the moonlight.

In the elephant iron huts of the flyers and observers, cheery-faced youngsters tugged at hip-length flying boots lined with sheepskin and bundled themselves up in sweaters and mufflers, surmounting the resultant bulk with leather flying coats.

Soon the planes, with loaded bomb racks, fuel tanks, and landing flares fixed below the under wing tips, were pushed out of the hangars, like giant night birds surrounded by retinues of attending gnomes.

The orders for the night were simple. Every pilot and observer knew them. They read:

No. 100 Squadron will bomb Douai airdrome on the night of April 5th–6th if the weather is suitable.

There was no question about the weather. It was made to order. An early moon was rising to the full. The wind was light.

Eighteen planes of the squadron—F. E. 2b's they were—were lined up ready for the start. They had been painted from wing tip to wing tip a dull black, with the bodies of the plane in dull gray. On the under side of the lower wings, plain white circles took the place of the customary markings, but the upper surfaces of the top planes bore the regular red, white, and blue cockades. The tail planes and rudders were painted as black as the night itself. Their decorations were supposed to make the planes less visible in a searchlight's beam or against a moonlit sky.

The thirty-six youngsters of the squadron were off on a maiden venture. These were the squadron's first orders for a night raid, and they were received with enthusiasm. The job was to lay a few eggs in Richthofen's nest and "blow the stink off it." There were a lot of scores to settle with the "jolly old Baron," and the prospect of paying him a night visit was a happy one.

An officer read 10:30 on the illuminated dial of his wrist watch. The wave of his hand was answered by increased life in the idling motor of the first plane in the line. The volleys grew to a deafening roar. Flame and sparkling soot particles flashed down the wind from the red-hot exhaust pipes.

A sign from the pilot, and the wheel chocks were pulled away. The plane moved across the field, gathering speed. The watchers soon saw the glow of those red-hot exhaust pipes mounting from the ground, higher and higher, until a black-winged shadow, passing between the watchers and the moon, revealed that No. 1 is "on her way."

The rest of the planes pulled out at three-minute intervals, and with the departure of the last of the eighteen, the airdrome was painfully silent after the nerve-racking thunder of the motors.

Up aloft, the night riders of the sky were strung out in

eighteen sombre units, each framed in a halo of the young moon's pale murkiness. The tiny hooded lights of the instrument boards, reflected up into the goggled young faces of the pilots, whose eyes constantly watched the compass needle, the flying map, the altimeter, the "rev" meter, the water thermometer.

A large fire was burning in Lens—behind the German lines. It made an excellent landmark. The squadron could not mistake its direction. It climbed steadily in the hope of crossing the lines without the knowledge of the enemy. It was to be a surprise attack.

Back now in the long smoke-filled room of the officers' mess at the Douai airdrome the table was littered with coffee cups and wine glasses. Richthofen, sitting at the head of the table was, with the aid of two uplifted saucers, demonstrating in three dimensions a manœuvre by which an Albatross or a Halberstadter could reach the "blind spot" of the new Sops.

The telephone rang. An officer picked up the receiver.

"The English are coming," he shouted after a minute's conversation. The detectors at the lines had picked up the drone of the heavily burdened English motors, and the warning was being spread up and down the lines and to the rear, to be on guard and to extinguish all lights. Dozens of searchlight crews and anti-aircraft gunners rolled from their bunks and manned their posts in response to the summons.

The warning caused sufficient excitement in Richthofen's camp to indicate that the night visit was not expected. Officers and men dived down immediately into the bomb-proof shelters which Simon, the supply officer of the Jagdstaffel, had already constructed. Soon the hum of the motors was heard overhead, and beams of white light lashed the moonlit sky.

The enemy was still too far away to be attacked [Richthofen wrote later in describing the night]. Down in our bombproof shelters we were particularly merry. The only thing we feared was that the English would not succeed in finding our airdrome.

To find some fixed spot at night is by no means easy. It was particularly difficult to find us because our airdrome was not situated on an important highway or near water or a railway, which are guides most useful to night flyers.

But the night-time war birds of One Hundred Squadron found Richthofen's nest that night. They had studied the terrain carefully. They knew that the Douai airdrome lay exactly 270 feet below the level of their own flying ground at Izel le Hameau, and even this comparatively insignificant difference was taken into careful consideration in conjunction with the orders that not a single bomb was to be released at more than 500 feet above the target.

This is close work when the searchlights are full on the low, swooping plane, and machine guns and anti-aircraft cannon are popping away in a human "duck hunt."

The squadron hovered at its highest altitude above the airdrome but hung on to its bombs until the agreed signal. The target had to be illuminated first so that more of the pills would hit their mark. This was the work of the squadron leader, and now he is swooping to carry it out.

Off went the motor, and the plane pointed downward in a circling glide. Suspended from the racks under the wings were two forty-pound incendiary bombs of phosphorus and T. N. T. The rest of the squadron was waiting up above for "the great white way to be lit up."

Meanwhile, the suspense below was intense. Richthofen and his men made what jokes they could while sitting in the crowded darkness of the bombproof shelters. Sometimes there were periods of silence, easily understood by anyone who has ever had the experience of sitting under a load of dynamite and waiting for it to fall. The uplifting stimulation which comes from the excitement of action is entirely missing.

We had begun to think that our friends had given up their job and were looking for another objective [Richthofen wrote in describing his impressions and sensations during those weighty minutes before the first bomb fell].

But suddenly we noticed that one low-flying plane had shut off his motor. So he was coming lower. Lieutenant Wolff, who was standing beside me, said, "Now we are in for it."

We had two carabines, and we began shooting at the Englishman. We could not see him. Still, the noise of our shooting was a sedative to our nerves.

Suddenly the searchlights reveal him in their glare. A shout rises all over the flying ground, "There he is." Shots ring out from all sides.

Our friend was sitting in one of the prehistoric English packing cases, and we could clearly recognize the type. He was half a mile from us, but was flying straight toward us.

He came lower and lower. At last he had come down to an altitude of about 300 feet. Then he started his engine again and came straight toward the spot where we were standing.

Wolff thought he took an interest in the other side of our establishment. Before long, the first bomb fell, and it was followed by many others. We were amused by some very pretty fireworks.

The wartime censor would not permit Richthofen to reveal further results of that night, but they are to be found in the excellent accounts written by Captain W. E. Collinson, who compiled a record of the many exploits of One Hundred Squadron.

In the swoop of the first plane, the two incendiary bombs exploded right on the airdrome. Richthofen's nest was lit up like the last night of a carnival. From above, the rest of the squadron could easily see the three sides of the triangular flying field with the hangars ranged at regular intervals on two sides.

Two of the hangars were blazing bright when the seventeen remaining planes started downward. One after another they skimmed low over the flying field, dropping their loads of twenty-pound high-explosive bombs.

The engines roared as the pilots "gave the gun" to the old F. E.'s, which swept across the danger arc at top-most speed. The observers sitting braced in the "front porch" offices worked the release levers on the bombs and at the same time fired their machine guns straight down the beams of dazzling light which held the planes in glares as bright as midday. Some of the lights went out, either damaged by the sprays of lead or deserted by their crews. Others carried on in their place.

The downpour of fire and explosive lasted about twenty minutes and ended as suddenly as it had started. The night riders, after dropping their bombs, climbed faster and higher, being relieved of their loads, and soon gained safer altitudes, although searchlight beams still whipped the heavens, and the night sky was punctured with the bursts of anti-aircraft shells and flaming strings of "Spanish onions."

Richthofen and his flyers rushed from their shelters and directed their attention to preventing the flames from spreading to other hangars. The planes were pushed out of the threatened hangars, ancient French fire apparatus was rushed from the town, fire extinguishers were applied to the flaming ruins of the hangars, and men were put to work at once to fill in the holes made by the bombs in the flying field.

Back to the airdrome at Izel le Hameau, the exultant pilots of One Hundred Squadron returned one by one, flashed on their landing lights, received their signals from the ground, and landed down the broad beam of the station searchlight, flattened out across the flying field to make a pathway of light.

All returned. As each plane landed, it was surrounded by its crew of mechanics, who first asked if everything had been in order and then hurried themselves to the task of immediate inspection, refuelling, and lubrication. The crews vied with one another in counting the bullet holes through the planes.

In the messroom, pilots and observers clapped one another on the back and lifted glasses to the "jolly Baron."

Thirty minutes later, with bomb racks replenished, they took the air again and went back over the same route. They arrived over Douai airdrome just in time to interrupt the reconstruction work then going on.

Down went the squadron leader again, and two more phosphorous forty-pounders were released to provide the footlights for the second show. They landed close to two hangars, which immediately went up in flames. The illumination thus provided, plus the glow of the burning phosphorus which ignited everything inflammable that it touched, revealed the target in a glare almost as bright as day. The gentlemen "upstairs" swooped down as before to do their stuff.

Down in the bombproof shelters again, Richthofen and his flyers heard the roar of the low motors as the "flying pianos" sped across the airdrome at heights of from two to three hundred feet, dropping their twenty-pound presents of trinitrotoluol. They heard splitting crashes as these deadly missiles exploded and filled the air with steel splinters that populated the night darkness with humming birds and bumble bees.

Knife blades of flame spurted from the muzzles of rifles and machine guns as the ground defences released their venom on the deadly night birds. The English observers returned the fire as best they could, directing most of it toward the searchlights and their crews. Anti-aircraft guns barked up at them from all sides, their bursting shells blinking and twinkling in the night sky, which resounded continuously with the thump and wallop of the explosions.

With its mission performed, the squadron reached for the ceiling again and headed for home, always followed by the groping beams of the searchlight and the angry puffs of shell and shrapnel. One by one, the planes landed on their home grounds to celebrate the night's work, which in the daybook of war consisted in dropping 4 phosphorous and 128 high-explosive bombs, more than a ton of highly concentrated death and destruction, in a place where it could be expected to do a lot of good. Again the waiting crews tended the returning planes, repaired fabric rents, replaced stay wires that had been cut by bullets, or laid new piping that had been destroyed by shell particles. One crew waited in vain, looking long and eagerly into the night sky toward the north. The bird did not come back to roost.

The missing machine was that piloted by Second Lieutenant A. R. M. Richards with Second-Class Air Mechanic

E. W. Barnes presiding over the "lump sugar" and the "pepper box." What happened to them was not known for some time. Their old F. E. during its low swoop over Ritchthofen's home grounds had been mortally wounded by a burst of machine-gun lead which found its way to the motor's vitals. The propeller stopped spinning, and Richards and Barnes made an unconventional landing in the dark in a field close to Douai. They escaped the resulting crash and spent the rest of the war as guests of the Kaiser.

The Flying Uhlan's camp ground the next morning looked as though a cyclone had struck it. Four hangars had been burned completely to the ground, all the rest of them had been burned or ripped up in spots, and many of the Jagdstaffel's machines had been temporarily, if not permanently, put out of action. The grounds, which had been carefully smoothed off for landing and starting, were pockmarked with so many bomb craters that a plane could leave the ground only with the greatest difficulty and danger.

It is significant that the squadron leader's almost daily record for the month so far, shows no registration for a victory of April 6th, the day after One Hundred Squadron had left its cards, and it is quite probable the all-red Albatross was among the wounded birds that couldn't take the air.

The day was well spent in arranging for a hot reception should the visitors return again that night. Richthofen openly admired the nerve of the English flyers in clumsy "flying pianos" swooping as low as 200 feet above his airdrome on a moonlight night. He considered it also an impertinence amounting to an insult to his well-known ability as a marksman.

He reflected that he had shot wild pig at that distance at night; why not an Englishman? He had shot plenty down from above; how about winging one from the ground? He decided it would be a worth-while novelty. At least it would be better than the nerve-racking uncertainty of huddling supinely and inactively in the dugouts waiting for all hell to fall.

While extra gangs of workers repaired the hangars and filled in the holes in the flying grounds, the mechanics busied themselves with the damaged machines, and others were put to work ramming piles and posts into the ground, on which machine guns would be mounted for high-angle fire.

Extra machine guns mounted on old steel tripods after the fashion employed by the infantry were rushed to the airdrome from the nearest supply dépôt, and these were placed in position erect, as though standing on their hind legs, with just sufficient room under the breech to permit a gunner to aim.

As there were not enough German machine guns to go around, Richthofen dealt out machine guns that were the squadron's trophies—weapons that had been captured together with ammunition from the enemy. Together with his flyers, he practised at the butts with the captured guns, and then returned them to emplacements from which they could be used that night.

Richthofen placed great reliance upon the dependability of the English. If they had come last night at a certain hour, they would be certain to come at the same hour the following night. He had reason.

> Again we were sitting in our mess [he wrote concerning that night of April 6th]. Of course, we were discussing the problem of the night flyers. Suddenly an orderly rushed into the room shouting:
>
> "They are there. They are there," pointing above. He was only half dressed, and he finished his warning by diving into the closest bombproof.
>
> We all rushed to our machine guns. Some of the men who were known to be good shots had also been given machine guns. All the rest were provided with carabines. The whole squadron was armed to the teeth to give a warm reception to our kindly visitors.
>
> The first Englishman arrived, exactly as on the previous evening, at a very great altitude. Then he came right down to about 150 feet and, to our greatest joy, was making for the place where our barracks were. Just then he got into the glare of the searchlight.
>
> When he was only 300 yards away someone fired the first shot and all the rest of us joined in. A rush of cavalry or of storming troops could not have been met more efficiently than the attack of that single impertinent individual flying as low as 150 feet.
>
> Quick firing from many guns received him. Of course, he could not hear the noise of the machine guns. The roar of his own motor prevented that. However, he must have seen the flashes of our guns. Therefore I considered it tremendously plucky that our man did not swerve but continued going straight ahead in accordance with his plan. He flew exactly over our heads.
>
> At the moment when he was directly above us, we jumped quickly into our bombproof. It would have been too silly for flying men to die by a rotten bomb. As soon as he had passed over our heads, we rushed out again and fired after him with our machine guns and rifles.

That first swoop as on the night before was the one that turned on the light. Two more hangars blazed upward as a pair of phosphorous bonfires landed neatly between them.

The resultant conflagration made every detail of the airdrome stand out in bright relief. As before, the rest of the squadron swooped down and across, but this time there were only 13 "flying pianos" instead of 18 as on the night previous. In addition to the captured bus of Richards and Barnes, four other machines had been so badly hit by anti-aircraft fire that they were unable to take part in the second night's excursions.

If the intensity of the German reception was a surprise to the English visitors—and it was—then the German defences had a surprise in store for them also. The wise ones of One Hundred Squadron had put their heads together, and re-membering the experience of the previous night, had evolved some new tactics.

As soon as each machine had dropped its bombs, it re-mained at the low height and started looking for more trouble instead of climbing immediately for the upper levels. They directed their attention particularly to searchlights, diving straight down the beams and spraying the lamps and their crews with lead.

Many of them were thus put out of commission, with the result that the following bombers had things easier, as they could approach the target without being revealed in the air and targeted by the ground defences.

Machines that had released their bombs would circle the field and watch for a searchlight to open up on one of their comrades descending with bombs. The instant the light went on, it suddenly received a rain of lead from another quarter of the darkness and usually it went out while the crew scampered for safety.

This was the beginning of a new form of air fighting which later found complete exploitation at the battle of Messines. It became known as "ground strafing," and there are but few records of it having been employed before this date.

Richthofen's closest friend in his squadron was Lieu-tenant Schaefer, who prided himself on being as good a shot as his commander. Like a trap-shooter sitting at the butts, he emptied hundreds of rounds into the air as each English plane swooped across his zone of fire.

Schaefer insisted that he had hit one of the night birds, but Richthofen refused to believe him, stating with reason that, as so many were firing at each machine at the same time, it would be impossible to tell which one had hit the target.

The Germans believed, however, that the intensity of the ground fire had caused some of the bombs to be dropped rather aimlessly, although Richthofen admitted that one of the missiles did explode only a few yards from his own plane where it stood in the hangar.

During the night, the fun commenced again [he wrote, indicating that One Hundred Squadron was determined to duplicate its double raids of the previous night].

I was already in bed fast asleep when I heard, as though in a dream, anti-aircraft firing. I awoke to find the dream a reality. One of the Englishmen at that moment was flying so low over my quarters that, in my sudden fright, I pulled the blankets over my head.

The next moment, I heard an incredible bang just outside my window. The glass fell in, a victim to the bomb. I rushed out of my bedroom in pajamas in order to get a few shots in after him, but unfortunately I had overslept my opportunity. He was being fired on from everywhere.

That night, back at Izel le Hameau after the second raid, One Hundred Squadron counted noses and found that another plane was missing. This time it was one piloted by Second Lieutenant L. Butler, with Second-Class Air Mechanic Bobbie Robb in the observer's seat.

The survivors were silent a moment over their good-night pegs and drank silently to the hope that Butler and Robb had had a "happy landing."

The outfit hated losing Butler. He was one of the best bridge players in the squadron. Down in the men's quarters Robb's comrades rolled up his kit to send it home. Word came through the next day that both Butler and Robb were prisoners of war and unwounded. They had been forced to land by a bullet through the old motor. Probably Schaefer did bring down his bird, after all.

This squadron leader reported that, as the result of the second double raid, ninety-eight bombs, containing an even ton of "hot stuff," had been dropped on the Flying Uhlan's doorstep, and that four of his hangars had been reduced to ashes with incidental damages to his flying field and machine shops. The ground casualties inflicted by the raiders are not so easily determined, but they are believed to have been more than light.

In Richthofen's opinion, the only effect of bomb dropping at night was a moral one. He did not believe the material damage thus caused was worth the effort.

Bombing might be killing, but it was too impersonal to suit the intense spirit of Germany's leading ace. He was ever the hunter. He liked to see the man he was going to kill, he liked to mark him out for death, lay his plans to get him, and then get him.

He got one the following day. It was his thirty-seventh.

This victory celebrated his promotion on that day to the rank of captain. The orders had come through that morning,

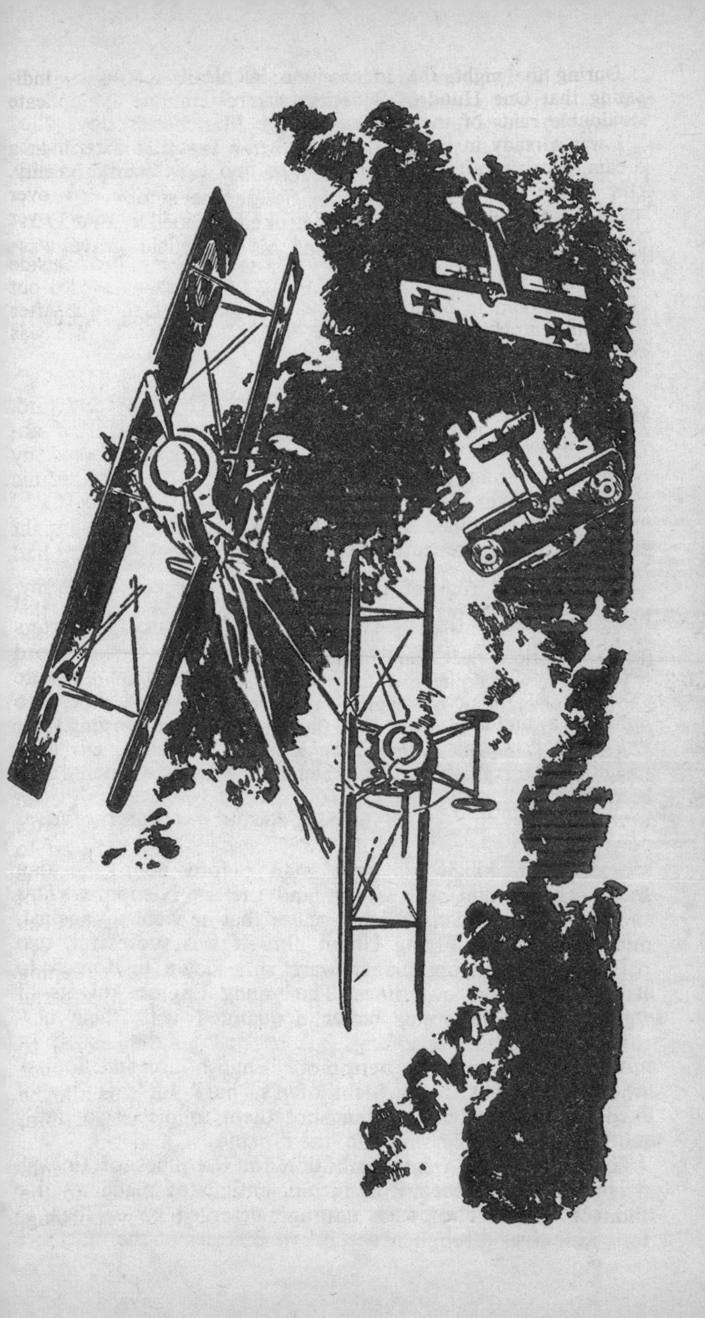

whereby the Freiherr Manfred von Richthofen would from now on carry the handle of "Rittmeister."

"No. 37" was a nineteen-year-old Manchester boy who had flown out from his airdrome after tea that afternoon. Three hours later, his charred remains were being buried by lantern light in a shell hole beside the smoking wreck of his Nieuport, and on the broken propeller that was placed as a cross at the head of his battlefield grave was scratched the inscription:

Second Lt. G. O. Smart, R.F.C. Killed in action, April 7, 1917.

Richthofen's account of the fight is brief:

Requesting Acknowledgment of My 37th Victory

Date: April 7, 1917.
Time: 5:45 P.M.
Place: Mercatel, other side of our lines.
Plane: Nieuport one-seater, English, details not at hand.

Together with four of my gentlemen I attacked an enemy squad of six Nieuport machines south of Arras and behind the enemy lines. The plane I had singled out tried to escape six times by various tricks and manœuvres.

When he was doing this for the seventh time, I managed to hit him, whereupon his engine began to smoke and burn, and the plane itself went down head first, twisting and twisting.

At first I thought it might be another manœuvre, but then I saw the plane plunge without catching itself to the ground near Mercatel.

(Signed) BARON VON RICHTHOFEN.

Richthofen killed his next man before noon the day following his fight with Smart and the six Nieuports. This time it was a new Sopwith two-seater that he went up against, and although the Flying Uhlan himself was successful, two of his accompanying planes were shot down or forced to land behind their own lines. The young English knights of the air were becoming better acquainted with their new models.

"No. 39" represents two more English "second louies" whose lives went to fill Richthofen's "bag" for that day of April 8th. The Flying Uhlan shot them to pieces so badly that he never could find out their names.

Richthofen had great admiration for the pluck of English flyers who risked their lives in old, antiquated machines. He thought that men of such courage deserved better than to lose their lives through structural weaknesses of the machines they flew. He was quick to report any such weakness in any of his own machines, and frequently was unsparing in his criticism of errors in German design or manufacture.

The German ace well appreciated the value of his flyers having confidence in the machines they flew. The danger of diving any great distance in a plane which might collapse under the strain of coming out of the dive was enough to prevent many flyers from adopting this most effective method of sudden attack. Richthofen felt that, while the Albatross D triplane was superior to the British planes he was then encountering, it had certain weaknesses which left it far from perfect.

Among the chief properties of a good pursuit plane [he wrote in a secret opinion to the technical staff] are the following: A good plane must not lose altitude even when curving and after flying and turning several times on its back, provided, of course, the motor is doing full speed.

It would be ideal if a plane could even gain in altitude while performing these manœuvres, but this is not the case with the Albatross D 111, and that is its chief drawback. When moving the side or altitude rudders, even the slightest change must effect a big movement. With the Albatross, the ailerons are not quite sufficient, and this is a most important factor with a pursuit plane.

Great speed and great altitude are both necessary. To be able to fly slowly by regulating the motor is very essential.

A pursuit plane must be able to stand the strain of diving down 3,000 feet. The Albatross does not do this always.

The English flyers, handicapped in their old machines, had learned this weakness during April and were frequently able to escape the Albatross by descending to three or four hundred feet above the ground, at which low altitude the Albatross pilots did not like to risk diving on them. It was too close to the ground for the speedy machines.

But, in spite of these weaknesses, the Albatross flyers continued to exact terrific toll from the English every day. On the day Richthofen gave the above opinion, which was April 11th, eighteen English planes were shot down. It was a loss the Royal Flying Corps could ill afford in the height of the battle of Arras, which then had been waging for three days.

The German ace contributed one of the victories that made up the eighteen planes. It was another old B. E. "flying piano," and although it did not reach the ground whole, its occupants escaped with wounds, and by reason of their landing behind the English lines, do not figure in the list of prisoners of war.

Eleven days of "Bloody April" had passed, and the

Flying Uhlan had added eight more victories to his record, but this last combat was one of particular significance to him.

With his fortieth conquest, he had at last equalled the record of the dead Boelcke, the man who had taught him to fly. From now on, he would reflect, with the pride that was strong within his Junker heart, that no German living or dead had killed more men in the air than he.

Chapter VIII

As a marksman requires a target to shoot at, Richthofen demanded records to break. Having brought his score of air victories up to the high level established by the great Boelcke, he now sought to exceed the accomplishments of his master and reach a new goal which would bear his name.

He did it two days afterward.

It was April 13, 1917. In three flights, morning, noon, and afternoon, he shot down three planes and killed four men in the space of ten hours. These combats brought him the much-desired credit for his forty-first, his forty-second, and forty-third victories, any one of which was sufficient to establish a new record in German air fighting.

Amongst his comrades in the flying corps and at German headquarters, particular significance had been placed on that number "41." It had proved fatal to Boelcke. He had met his death as he dived to shoot down his forty-first victim.

Already Richthofen's superior officers were beginning to fear the loss of the new super-ace. They could ill afford to be without such an individual killing force as the man who had made his red fighting plane known as the terror of the skies. The death of Richthofen would also be a blow to home morale.

The ace was told that he would have to go on a leave of absence after his forty-first victory. That number was designated in consideration of Richthofen's unspoken but well-understood zeal to make his record surpass all others. This desire was so keen in him that he wanted to veil it from his millions of German admirers. It would require the effort of no great psychologist to penetrate the intended obscurity which Richthofen expressed as follows:

> As a matter of fact, I had been allowed to bag only forty-one. Anyone will be able to guess why the number was fixed at forty-one. Just for that reason, I wanted to avoid that figure.

I am not out for breaking records. Besides, generally speaking, we of the flying service do not think of records at all. We merely think of our duty.

Boelcke might have shot down a hundred airplanes but for his accident, and many others of my dear dead comrades might have vastly increased their bag but for their sudden death.

Records and trophies were as precious to Richthofen as they are to any pot hunter of the links or the traps, or, for that matter, to any human in whom there is the combination of the competitive and the combative. The Flying Uhlan referred to the day of his forty-first victory as "My record day."

This referred to another record. It was the first time that he had "shot a triple," which was his manner of describing the day's "bag of game."

The ace took great pride in the feat because it was accomplished under the keen eyes of a high-ranking and probably a noble officer of the German High Command. Four men paid with their lives for this gladiatorial exhibition of the skies, which the visitor from headquarters followed closely with his eyes glued to a telescope. It seemed strange to Richthofen that this prominent spectator was not unduly thrilled by the sight of burning planes and their human freight plunging earthward from fearful heights.

The day began well [the ace later wrote]. We had scarcely gone to an altitude of six thousand feet when an English patrol of five machines was seen coming our way. We attacked them with a rush, as if we were cavalry, and the hostile squadron lay destroyed on the ground. None of our men was even wounded. Of our enemies, three had plunged to the ground and two had come down in flames.

The spectator down below who was watching us through the telescope told us later that the affair had surprised him much because it did not seem as fierce as he had imagined. He had thought that it would be far more dramatic and look quite different.

He thought the whole encounter had looked quite harmless until suddenly some machines came plunging down like flaming rockets. I myself have gradually become accustomed to seeing machines falling down, but I must say that it impressed me very deeply when I saw my first Englishman fall, and I have often seen the event again and again in my dreams.

It was verily a day of records. That evening, it was possible for Richthofen to report proudly that six planes of his Staffel had destroyed thirteen enemy planes in the air. The Flying Uhlan reflected his satisfaction in this accomplishment when he wrote:

Boelcke's squadron had only once been able to make a somewhat similar report. At that time, it had shot down eight planes in one day. But to-day one of us had brought low four of his opponents. The hero was Lieutenant Wolff, a delicate-looking little fellow in whom no one could have suspected so redoubtable a hero. My brother had destroyed two, Schaefer two, Festner two, and I had destroyed three.

Captain Jimmie Stuart, an Irishman from Colraine, and Lieutenant M. H. Wood, a rollicking youngster from Essex, were the two victims of the Flying Uhlan's first combat on his record day. Flying an old R. E. 8 as an escort to photography planes, together with other planes of the British Fifty-ninth Squadron, they bumped into the jolly Baron's red birds about nine o'clock in the morning and found out, at the cost of their lives, that their Vickers and Lewis guns were no match for the sputtering two Spandaus that snorted death from the nostrils of the Flying Uhlan's sky charger.

After a late breakfast, the baron went aloft again for his noonday flight, but it is doubtful whether the officer at the telescope on the ground at the airdrome was able to follow the combat, because this fight occurred over the British lines, and it would appear from the British casualty records that Richthofen's victims escaped, not only with their lives, but without wounds, because the English reports carry no account of the affair.

Richthofen's flying comrades confirmed his report of the fight, and the all-necessary credit was granted.

There was always uncertainty about planes that were shot down behind their own lines, and the German, as well as the English and French and later the American flying services, demanded ample verification of these affairs before the pilots-claimant were credited with victories. The fact that most of the fighting occurred behind the German lines was a double advantage for Richthofen.

In the first place, in case of a forced landing or a slight wound, or in the event that he was shot down behind his own lines and survived, it did not mean the end of his fighting career, as would have been the case if the downfall had occurred behind the English lines. In the second place, it was easier to substantiate his victories when the planes he attacked came to earth behind the German lines.

There was ample substantiation for his forty-third victory, the third that went to his credit on April 13, 1917. He killed both of the occupants of the plane which he shot down over the village of Noyelle-Godault, just behind his own lines.

Second Lieutenant Allan Harold Bates and Sergeant William Alfred Barnes were the two unfortunates that paid the price and together with Stuart and Wood went to make up the quartette of deaths representing the results of Richthofen's record day.

That night, at the Douai airdrome, the fighting pilots of Jagdstaffel 11 toasted their leader for the first time as the ace of all German aces. His forty-third victory had established a new mark in the annals of the German Flying Corps.

Richthofen returned the toast and the plaudits of his comrades, congratulated little Wolff of his feat in bringing down four machines that day, and thanked the flyers of the squadron as a whole for hanging up the new record of thirteen enemy planes down in one day.

Some of the occupants of the thirteen enemy machines had survived the day as prisoners, and several of these had been brought to the squadron's mess. The flyers were always at odds with the army command on this question of entertaining captured aviators. The army insisted that air prisoners, like any others, should be turned over immediately to the intelligence section for examination and then sent off immediately to the prison camps.

Whenever possible, the war birds, whether they were English or German, "recaptured" their own prisoners, and on various pretenses transported them to the airdrome for a meal, drinks, and a general discussion of the business of killing one another in the air.

Men who had flown at one another during the day high above the clouds and emptied their machine guns at one another frequently sat facing one another over a mess table that same night.

The captor would drink to the health of his prisoner, compliment him on the fight he had put up, and, to take the salt out of the prison prospect, would remind him that at least he was safe for the rest of the war.

The prisoner would lift his glass to the man who shot him down, declare with a smile that it had been a real pleasure on his part to fight so capable an adversary, and end with a sporting announcement that the best man had won.

With this exchange of compliments, the evening would progress as merrily and as late as the supply of liquor permitted. Usually, it permitted.

Richthofen's four victims of the day were dead, but he took delight in exchanging views with the living victims of his Staffel. One of these must have made a quick analysis of the Flying Uhlan's disposition and lack of humour, because it appears that he took advantage of it to the extent of pulling the German ace's leg.

Of course the prisoner inquired after my red airplane [Richthofen wrote concerning the evening]. It is not unknown even amongst troops in the trenches and is called by them "le diable rouge." In the squadron to which the prisoner belonged, there was a rumour that the red machine was occupied by a girl—a kind of a Jeanne d'Arc. He was intensely surprised when I assured him that the supposed girl was standing in front of him. He did not intend to make a joke. He was actually convinced that only a girl could sit in my extravagantly painted machine.

The English version of this incident was told many times amongst the Royal Flying Corps men in German prison camps and contributed not a few hearty laughs to the life of confinement. Richthofen was a stranger to English humour.

The German communiqué of the following day called particular attention to the achievements of Richthofen's squadron on his record day. Every man in the unit took individual pride in the official statement, "Six German machines have destroyed thirteen hostile airplanes."

It was good stuff to start the new day on. It contributed something to the flying and fighting by which the Staffel knocked down eight more planes before nightfall. Of this eight, Richthofen received credit for one.

The two victims of the Flying Uhlan's next victory, his forty-fifth, landed behind the British lines. The motor went clear through one of them, and the other one woke up five weeks later with wounds which kept him in the hospital for more than a year and a half.

They were Lieutenants Willie Green and C. E. Wilson. When they dug the motor out of the ground, they found what remained of Wilson under it and buried him there.

The Flying Uhlan's next prey, representing his sixteenth victory for the month, escaped with wounds following the fight which sent them to the ground near Laignicourt behind their own lines.

Lieutenant W. F. Fletcher, piloting the machine, which was returning from a photography reconnaissance, was badly wounded about the head and arm in the landing crash, and his observer, Lieutenant W. Franklin, carried away one of Richthofen's bullets in his left leg.

The telephone messages from English front-line observers who watched the combat coincide in detail with the report written by Richthofen.

Nineteen-year-old Sergeant Alfred Tollervey with Second Lieutenant E. A. Welch, was shot down and killed by Richthofen on April 23d in an air fight which added another victory to the Flying Uhlan's well-filled game bag. British infantry saw Welch and Tollervey attacked by a red scout plane, saw one wing fold back on the hard-pressed English plane, and then turned their backs as the remnants fell to earth.

Richthofen thought his victims fell behind his own lines, but he didn't take into consideration the fact that the second battle of the Scarpe was in full swing that day, and the front lines were by no means stationary.

In the following five days, Richthofen made daily flights at the head of his Jagdstaffel and engaged in several combats, but results were not forthcoming, and he was still two units removed from the goal he had set before he would go on leave.

But with the opening of the week beginning April 27th and ending May 3d, the business of killing in the air took a brisk spurt which attracted new repute to the fighting Jagdstaffel.

In those seven days, twenty-six British machines were shot down behind the German lines. Richthofen and his fighting pilots accounted for twenty-three of them, and the rest of the victims were divided amongst the other Jagdstaffels. Jagdstaffel 11 figured it out on paper that it had accomplished more than seven times as much as all the rest of the German Flying Corps put together. It was a boast worth writing home about.

Of those twenty-three successful combats, Richthofen came off victor in five and he only worked two days at it. The first of the quintette, his forty-eighth conquest, occurred on the morning of April 28th.

The German ace liked a good gallery. He knew he was "the goods" in the air, and it gave him great enjoyment to put up a good show for interested spectators on the ground. The presence of a grandstand inspired him to greater exertion of the power and will that had brought him such success and fame in the air.

Under the eyes of a special guest from headquarters, he had shot down three planes and killed four men on the thirteenth of the month. To-day, he would even break this record, because there was someone on the ground watching him with eyes that reflected mixed emotions of pride, love, and fear.

The witness of this day's carnival of death with which the young Uhlan closed his flying for the month of April was none other than his father. Richthofen was still young enough to enjoy exhibiting his prowess before the father whose ability as a hunter and as a marksman and whose love for the antlered and feathered trophies of the chase had been the boyish inspiration of the German ace.

He could remember the many days in the old home down in Schweidnitz, when his eyes would stray from his lesson books to the walls of the large drawing room, on which were mounted several hundred bleached white skulls and horns that had once been living sprites of the forest before they had fallen under the gun of the head of the family. He well recalled and still loved the dusty glass cases in which stuffed eagles, falcons, hawks, and buzzards, all victims of his father's marksmanship, looked down on him with what life a German taxidermist could put into their glass eyes.

He reflected now that the walls of his rooms were hung with human scalps in the form of strips of fabric bearing the numbers of the planes he had brought to earth and there on his desk was the ever-increasing collection of little silver cups of death, which kept pace with his conquests in the air. Showing the old man how he did it was a joy.

There was another development that also piqued his pride that day. It had been reported to him through the intelligence department that his name and fame and that of his squadron had become so well known behind the enemy lines that the British had organized an "anti-Richthofen" squadron for the special purpose of driving him from the air.

It is true that the first man Richthofen killed on this day, April 29th, was in the air with two others for the express purpose of dealing with the German ace. These three English air knights who flew on that special mission, Richthofen and two of his comrades shot down, killing two and taking one prisoner.

We flew to the lines, hoping to find our enemy [Richthofen explained]. After about twenty minutes, the first arrived and attacked us. This had not happened to us for some time. The English had abandoned their celebrated offensive tactics to some extent, having found them somewhat too expensive.

Our aggressors were three Spads, one-seater machines. Their occupants considered themselves quite superior to us on account of the excellence of their apparatus. Wolff, my brother, and I were flying together. We were three against three. That was as it ought to be.

Almost from the beginning of the encounter, the aggressive became defensive. Our superiority became clear. I tackled my opponent and could see how my brother and Wolff each handled his adversary. The usual waltzing began.

We were circling around one another. A favourable wind came to our aid. It drove the fighting away from the front and farther behind the German lines.

My man was the first to fall. I suppose I smashed up his engine. At any rate, he made up his mind to land. I no longer give pardon to anyone. Therefore, I attacked him a second time, and the consequences were that his whole plane went to pieces.

His wings dropped off like pieces of paper, and the body of

the machine fell like a stone, burning fiercely. It dropped into a swamp. It was impossible to dig it out, and I have never discovered the name of my opponent. He had disappeared. Only the end of the plane's tail was visible and marked the place where he had dug his own grave.

Simultaneously with me, Wolff and my brother had attacked their opponents and forced them to the ground not far from my victim. We were very happy, and flew home, and hoped that the Anti-Richthofen Squadron would often return to the fray.

Richthofen's three opponents in the combat related above were Major H. D. Harvey-Kelly, D.S.O., Second Lieutenant R. Applin, and Second Lieutenant W. N. Hamilton, all from the Nineteenth Squadron. Richthofen killed Applin, Wolff killed Harvey-Kelly, and Lothar took for himself the credit for forcing Hamilton to land as a prisoner.

Lothar's account of the fight, which, in the light of the story of the only living survivor, is inaccurate in a number of details, follows:

The warm April morning is beautiful. We are standing near our birds, waiting for orders. The telephone rings. Enemy planes south of Arras! A short command to the N. C. O. of the start service, the alarm bells ring, and suddenly everything comes to life. The engineers come hurrying to the machines and test them. The pilots rush along. Which shall be the commanding plane? My brother's!—Start.

We arrive above and south of Arras at about three thousand metres. No enemy planes! Yes, there are three Englishmen, and now we have something to wonder about. The three of them attack us, dropping down on us from a great height.

My brother takes the first in hand, Wolff the second, and I myself deal with the third. As long as the Englishman towers above me, he shoots incessantly. I have to wait until he is on my level, otherwise I cannot shoot. Now he is quite near me. I am just preparing myself to shoot when he suddenly drops down, down, down. I am thinking: "What *you* can do, *I* can do also!" Down I go.

Now my opponent is flying straight onward. I take my machine in hand and follow him. As soon as he notices me, he starts wild curves. As we have west wind, the fight will gradually slip farther to our side. I follow my adversary. As soon as he tries to fly straight, I shoot to scare him. Finally, I grow tired of it. I try to hit him whilst he is flying curves. I shoot and shoot.

In the meantime, we tower in about five hundred metres' altitude. I force my opponent to continue his curves. When doing curves, one's plane is forced, gradually, lower down and lower down, until one has to either land or try to fly home in a straight line. My opponent decides to try the latter manœuvre.

"Your hour has come, my poor friend!" I manage to think, and then I approach him. I start to press the trigger of my gun in about fifty metres' distance, but, damn it, no shot can be heard. Damn! My gun is jammed! And so near victory as I was at that moment! I have a look at my gun. Confound it! I had discharged all my shots, 1,000 cartridges. Never before had I used such a lot.

"You must not let him get off!" is my idea. To have fought for 15 minutes with a red plane, and to manage to get away unhurt would be too much of a triumph for my opponent. I approach him nearer and nearer. I calculate: 10 metres, five metres, three, now only two metres!

Finally, I think of a rather desperate measure: shall I knock off his rudder with the help of my propeller? Then he is done for, but with me it would be the same.

Another theory: If I turn off the engine the moment I touch him with my plane, what then? In this moment, my Englishman turns and looks in a horrified way at me. Then he stops his engine and goes down, landing somewhere near our third line. On the ground, I can see his engine still running.

If one has the misfortune to land behind the enemy's trenches, one always tries to destroy and burn one's machine. In order to prevent this, it is the duty of the pursuing pilot to shoot round about the landed machine so as to drive the inmates away. That is exactly what I did, and when the Englishman heard my bullets tearing through the air, he skipped out of his plane, waved to me, and surrendered to the infantry. [But he had no cartridges.]

As I found out some time later, investigating a similar event, I should most certainly have been killed if I had tried to touch the Englishman with my propeller. For his sake, I must say he had no idea that *my cartridges had run out.*

One single cartridge would have done with him, so near as he was to me at the moment. If he had turned it would have been I who would have been compelled to flee. He had only discharged some fifty cartridges, whereas I, run out of ammunition, was utterly helpless.

But I had succeeded, and that was the chief thing. The next day I went by plane to the squadron that had salvaged the Englishman's plane, a then very good Spad, and had a good look at my captured treasure. But look as I might, I found no evidence of having hit the machine. And I had discharged 1,000 shots! I asked whether my opponent had been wounded, but I was informed that this was not the case. Not one hit in a thousand. A fine performance! I had to laugh. The Englishman had gone down simply because I had scared him!

In my book of victories I inscribed: "On April 29, 1917, in the morning, near Izel, one Spad, inmate an English officer." I never had a chance to speak to my victim, our camp being too far from where he came down. Thus, most probably, he will never have heard that I had no cartridges left and that he had gone down from sheer terror. When I came home to camp that day, I said to myself: "Surely, you cannot tell this story, no hit in a thousand!"

My brother and Wolff had brought their enemy planes to the ground. I don't think I told anybody anything of my wonderful shooting. By the way, it is interesting to hear how many shots are required to bring down an Englishman. When flying for the first time with my brother, I noticed that he really began to shoot when his adversary was more or less falling. Up till then, he had mostly not used more than twenty bullets.

But this is by no means the rule. When attacking English planes, it is best to do so from backward. If the English plane is then flying straight on, a good shooter will hit him fatally after the first shots. But if the adversary starts to making curves so that one cannot get him right in front of the gun, only a chance hit will bring him down.

The fact that two men quite frequently, if not most frequently, give different accounts after witnessing the same incident, is not considered sufficient to condemn either for a falsehood, and Lothar's account differs in many essentials from that told by Lieutenant Hamilton.

Lothar, however, contradicts himself in his own story when he says that all of his ammunition was expended in the air, and later, forgetting this statement, writes that he fired his machine gun around Hamilton's plane on the ground to prevent the latter from burning it. It would seem that Lothar was not averse to making a good story at the expense of facts which he might not have considered important in view of the propaganda purposes his story might serve at that time.

Hamilton was one of those men honest enough to admit that he has experienced fear, but Lothar was mistaken when he wrote that he had bluffed or scared Hamilton to land. Why the English pilot was forced to earth is revealed in the account by himself.

Hamilton, as a young branch manager of a leather factory in India, went back to England in 1915 to fight. He enlisted and gained his commission in 1916. Attached to a battalion of the Northumberland Fusiliers he went through the first battle of the Somme and then transferred to the Flying Corps. His story follows:

"I was sent to England to train as a pilot, and after a two weeks' theoretical course at Oxford, was posted to an airdrome near Edinburgh to learn to fly.

"In February of '17, after completing my air training, I went to France and was attached to the Nineteenth Squadron (Spads). I had been in C Flight, which, in common with the other flights at that time, had been divided into two groups of three machines each.

"This we had permission to do, as we found that, if we patrolled in sixes, the enemy kept very clear of us and we had nothing to do. Our particular beat at that time was from 18,000 feet upward with the baby Nieuports and Sop pups patrolling below us.

"Even when reduced to groups, we had little or no excitement, an occasional enemy machine taking photographs being our only 'bag'; so that, after considerable application, we were given a roving commission.

"The morning of April 29, 1917, broke very thick. I was on the early patrol, and took my machines up, but, as at 10,000 feet we were lost in a thick bank of clouds, it was no use continuing, so I washed out the patrol and returned to the airdrome.

"In addition to being group leader, I was squadron machine-gun officer, so that, after a second breakfast, instead of returning to bed for a few hours, as my next patrol was not until 2 P.M., I returned to the hangars and pottered about with the guns.

"The whole squadron was fitted with Vickers, one to each machine, and no Lewis guns were carried. It is necessary to explain that each plane's gun was fixed along the port side of the engine and was synchronized to fire through the blades of the air screw, the gearing used being peculiar to the Spad, as the gun was built into the engine and the tripper bar tripped direct from the port cam shaft which operated over the feedblock cover. A double feed or any jam occurring in the feedblock necessitated a partial dismantling of the engine before the feedblock could be freed. This, of course, could not be done in the air.

"We used a continuous metal belt made up of sections, each section being attached to the next by the cartridge case, so that, as each cartridge was extracted from the belt, that section of the belt was allowed to fall away from the machine. At first, the belt was carried wound on a drum under the gun.

"In practice, we found that, after a burst of say twenty rounds, the drum having got up a bit of speed, there was a possibility of it forcing the belt on even after the gun had ceased firing, and this would cause a double feed. In order to overcome this fault, I was at that time fitting all our machines with boxes instead of drums. In fact, the change had been completed except for my own bus.

"While I was in the hangar attending to the guns, Harvey-Kelly came to me and said that the wing commander was 'hot-airing' about Richthofen's circus having been seen over Douai and he wanted three Spads to go up and deal with them. Owing to the fact that the machines of the other flights were either away on patrol or not ready, I was ordered to send up three from C Flight.

"In the ordinary course of events, the other group should have taken the job as mine had already done one patrol that day, but, as the matter was urgent, I agreed to take my pilots up again. At the last moment, Harvey-Kelly insisted that he himself would go instead of me, but, as I declined to be left behind, I detailed one of my pilots, Harding, to remain behind and to let Major Harvey-Kelly have his machine.

"Harvey-Kelly and myself got off the ground together and hung around for a spell waiting for Applin, but, as he appeared to be making no attempt to follow us, we presumed something had gone wrong, so we started off by ourselves. We were not on any particular patrol, but cruised about looking for Richthofen and his circus.

"We had been in the air about two hours when a third Spad joined us and, judging from the markings, I concluded Applin had eventually got off the ground and found us.

"This was particularly praiseworthy as Applin had had very little experience over the lines, and it required considerable pluck for a more or less raw pilot to hunt for us by himself forty miles behind the German lines. He took up a position on my right rear as we always flew that way, in V formation, with No. 1 plane leading and No. 2 slightly higher than No. 1, and No. 3 slightly higher than No. 2. In this formation it was the duty of No. 3 to protect Nos. 1 and 2 from attack from behind.

"Soon after Applin joined us, we sighted the circus about a thousand feet below us. There were eighteen planes flying more or less on a line ahead, slightly échelon.

"As we were only 4,000 feet up, I did not expect Harvey-Kelly would attack, but at the same moment we noticed six triplanes, Royal Navy Air Service, flying toward us. Harvey-Kelly immediately gave the signal to attack the enemy, but the triplanes sheered off and left me to it.

"Harvey-Kelly had already turned and dived at the tail Hun, and I was turning to attack the centre machine, so as to break up the formation and prevent the leading machine getting above us.

"Applin was following me, when I saw him stall on his tail and go down in a spin and then burst into flames.

"I looked up and saw that Richthofen in his all-red plane had been cruising about two thousand feet above his circus, which incidentally was his usual position, and had evidently shot Applin down as he swooped away immediately afterward.

"I carried out my original plan of attacking the centre machine, noticing, as I did so, that Harvey-Kelly had apparently accounted for two Huns and was pretty busy with four or five more.

"I joined battle a second or two later, our position at that time being somewhere over Epincy. I didn't see Harvey-Kelley again, as I was fully occupied with my little bunch and carried on a running fight until, over Douai, my gun jammed.

"I made a rapid examination and found my cursed drum had forced a double feed, so that there was nothing to be done except get away.

"I 'splitassed' to get toward our lines, when they managed to hole my main tank, which, being under my feet, was force-fed into the engine. Of course, the moment the pressure was released, my engine stopped, and as it stopped on the turn, I stalled and spun.

"I got her out of the spin almost immediately, switched on to my gravity tank, and dived to pick up my engine, but in doing so I naturally lost a bit of height and cooled my engine to such an extent that she wouldn't give me full revolutions, so that I was now much slower than my opponents, in addition to being below them.

"I held my bus down to keep up speed and steered for our lines, but very soon had four of the enemy on my tail—at least, one was on my tail, one above, and one on each side behind.

"They made pretty good shooting and managed to shoot away all my instruments and most of my struts and flying wires, so that, before long, I was practically flying a monoplane, as my bottom plane was flapping. Had I been flying any machine other than a Spad, it would have crumpled up, but as a Spad has no dihedral, the main spar of the top plane was solid right through, which no doubt saved my life.

"I was now down to about three hundred feet off the ground, when they holed my gravity tank, and my engine stopped for good. I made a good landing just behind Oppy wood about a kilo short of the line, and while the Huns on the ground were running up to secure me, I endeavoured to fire my bus. During this time, however, the four Huns in the air (one of them was Richthofen's brother flying a red-nosed Albatross) continued firing at me. Owing to my having no petrol left, I was unsuccessful in firing my bus but I saw her hit by our own guns soon after, so that she was completely destroyed.

"I heard later that Applin was dead and that Harvey-Kelley died in a hospital three days later from head wounds. I also understand, but could never get authentic confirmation, that Harvey-Kelley and myself accounted for five of the Huns before we were shot down. Applin, of course, was killed before he could fire a shot."

The father of the German ace was waiting by the hangars of the Douai airdrome when his two sons returned from the fight with the three English Spads. He had seen Applin go down burning, and he had seen the other two English machines forced to earth.

Lothar jumped out of his plane first and, running over to the bearded head of the family, who stood there erect in his major's uniform of field gray, saluted militarily and said:

"Good-morning, Father. I have just shot down an Englishman."

This greeting, sounding curiously cold to Anglo-Saxon ears, is good form according to the code of the Prussian military family.

Richthofen himself followed his brother, standing before his father. He clicked his heels and said:

"Good-morning, Father. I have just shot down an Englishman."

Describing that curious meeting between father and sons, Richthofen wrote:

> The old man felt very happy, and he was delighted with our reports. That was obvious. He is not one of those fathers who have fears for their sons. I think he would have liked very much to get into a machine and help us with our shooting. We all had a meal together.

The family reunion at table was interrupted by an air combat taking place immediately over the airdrome. The persistent, dogged Englishmen were at it again. The three Richthofens watched the fight from the ground.

Suddenly, from out the *mêlée* above them, a German machine came plunging down in uncontrolled curves. It turned over and over, but finally righted itself, to the relief of the tense spectators on the airdrome. It reached the flying ground safely, but made a rough landing and turned over.

The elder Richthofen walked hurriedly across the ground to the wreck. The disabled plane was a two-seater. The machine gunner in the rear seat was dead with an English bullet through his head. The pilot was slightly injured in the landing.

Richthofen, senior, was seriously silent as he walked back across the field behind the group that carried the body of the dead observer. The incident actually amounted to a prevision of what was to happen months later to his eldest son. This part of the exhibition was not on the programme and was something that Richthofen would have preferred to remain hidden from his father's eyes. Grimness replaced the previous heartiness when the interrupted meal was resumed.

Several hours later, the German ace shot down and killed two English airmen, both of whom were under twenty years of age. They constituted his much-desired fiftieth victory, the record which he had wanted his father to see him make. Unfortunately for his plans, the fight took place beyond the range of the telescope with which the father scanned the sky from his post of observation on the Douai flying field.

On the front below, where the battle of Arleux was now forty hours under way, the day was beginning to fade, but up aloft there was still light, and Richthofen was yet to knock down two more planes before sunset.

Number fifty-one—his start on the second "half century" —was an English artillery plane, but neither Richthofen nor the English casualty reports are able to reveal the identity of the airmen, because the wrecked plane, while burning on the ground, was blown to bits by shell fire. Five other English planes of the same type were shot down that afternoon, so that it is not possible in this case to specify which one was Richthofen's victim.

The Flying Uhlan had spotted two artillery flyers who appeared to be without escort. By wiggling the wings of his plane, he signalled to Lothar to attack with him. The two brothers flew toward their prey with increased speed. Each brother knew the flying and fighting capacity of the other. They knew that their red-nosed Albatross machines were superior to those of their intended victims. There was confidence in their dual attack.

Before opening fire, both Richthofens looked carefully around to see whether any escorting planes were in sight. These two victims looked almost too good to be true—so good, in fact, that the ace had the fleeting suspicion they were bait in a trap set for him. But the sky appeared clear above him. The wasps were alone with the butterflies.

It took several minutes' manœuvring to get into the favourable position under the tail of the two-seater—then a short burst of machine-gun lead, and the old English plane collapsed in the air. The German ace said later that he had never had a more rapid success.

Lothar had engaged the other enemy plane, and the fight was going on hardly five hundred feet away from the elder brother's moving position. He watched every development of the engagement.

I had time to study the struggle [he related afterward], and must say that I myself could not have done any better. He had rushed his man, and both were turning round each other. Suddenly, the enemy machine reared.

This is a certain indication of a hit. Probably the pilot received a bullet in the head. The wings collapsed and the plane fell. It fell quite close to my victim.

I flew toward my brother, and we congratulated each other by waving. We were highly satisfied with our performance and flew off. It is a splendid thing when one can fly with one's brother like that and do so well.

Not fifteen minutes later, Richthofen found himself attacked by a speedy pursuit plane of a new model and much more worthy of his attention than the slow artillery plane.

It was a new Nieuport from Squadron Forty, and the twenty-two-year-old youngster, Captain Frederick Leycester Barwell, who handled the stick was looking for trouble. He picked Richthofen out from all the rest of his planes and dove on him.

Richthofen was able to avoid Barwell's first dive. He escaped the shower of lead that spurted from the Englishman's Vickers gun as the speedy little Nieuport darted down from above. That miss cost Barwell his life.

The dive carried him below Richthofen, who from then on maintained the superior position above. It was the proud boast of the German ace that anything that was beneath him in the air, especially a pursuit plane that could not shoot to the rear, was lost.

Barwell's machine was good and speedy. He did not concentrate his attention on Richthofen, but let fly at any black-crossed plane that he could get within range of. At one time, he was flying right in the midst of Richthofen's formation, but through it all the German ace hung tenaciously to his position on the tail of the Nieuport. The fight between the two swung eastward over Lens, with the rest of the Jagdstaffel hovering on both sides between the lone Englishman and his lines. Richthofen resorted to a trick to deprive the Englishman of the advantage of his speedy plane.

He began firing his machine gun, although he realized he was not within range. The sound of the double Spandaus coming from behind had the effect of making the English pilot immediately relinquish the straight line he was flying in. The Nieuport began flying a zigzag, curving course, hoping to prevent his pursuer from hitting him.

This was what Richthofen wanted. The zigzag course reduced the speed of the Nieuport just sufficiently to permit the red Albatross to approach within range.

When within fifty yards of the Nieuport's tail, Richthofen steadied his plane and sent his eyes down the sights of the

Spandaus. He aimed carefully and pulled the triggers.

The aim was true. There was a slight hissing sound just audible as the pressure escaped from a punctured petrol tank. Then a fine white vapour ribbon trailed from the Nieuport's tail. The terrible nature of the end that followed just a second later loses none of its terror in Richthofen's own words:

> Then I saw a bright flame, and my lord disappeared below.

The Flying Uhlan never learned Barwell's name. He was too busy that night celebrating with his father the great day that he had had in the air.

Not only was fifty-two an unheard-of number of victories at that time, but the downing of four enemy planes in one day was a feat he had never achieved before. Lothar having downed two, the brothers could say that, between them, they had wiped out one complete English flight.

Richthofen, senior, joined in the big dinner and glowed with pride and undoubtedly with some happiness owing to the fact that he knew that his son was scheduled to go on leave from the front the next day. There was to be a rest from the killing and a recess from the danger of going the way of his many victims.

At eight o'clock, in the course of the dinner, the ace was called to the extension telephone in the mess hall. He found himself in communication with the grand headquarters of the High Command, the Holy of Holies of the All Highest War Lord.

The following message was read to him:

> I have just received the message that to-day you have been for the fiftieth time victor in an air battle.
>
> I heartily congratulate you upon this marvellous success with my full acknowledgment.
>
> The Fatherland looks with thankfulness upon its brave flyer. May God further preserve you.
>
> WILHELM I. R.

At the close of "Bloody April," when he went home from the front on leave, this was the balance of Richthofen's books of death:

SUMMARY THROUGH APRIL 29, 1917

NUMBER OF PLANES SHOT DOWN IN APRIL, 1917 . . .	21
PREVIOUSLY REPORTED	31
TOTAL PLANES SHOT DOWN	52

KILLED IN APRIL, 1917	23
PREVIOUSLY REPORTED	32
TOTAL KILLED	55
WOUNDED OR PRISONERS OF WAR IN APRIL, 1917 . . .	13
PREVIOUSLY REPORTED	13
TOTAL WOUNDED OR PRISONERS OF WAR . .	26

Chapter IX

It was May 1, 1917, when Richthofen said good-bye to his flying mates at Douai and retired from the front on a leave of absence that the High Command had insisted that he take. His superiors had even ordered that he confine himself to the ground during his vacation away from the battle lines, but this did not prevent the Red Knight of Germany from making the trip by air.

The cheers and congratulations of his pilots and mechanics rang in his ears as he flew away, this time a passenger in a two-seater observation plane, much slower and safer than the speedy little red Albatross in which he had sent so many men to their death.

With the unprecedented "bag" of fifty-two victorious combats on his record, the German ace of aces went back to receive the plaudits and worship of the Fatherland's millions, who breathed his name with praise and prayer. Prince and peasant acclaimed him as Germany's young war god. The Kaiser, the War Lord himself, extended himself to shower new honours on this keen-eyed blond Prussian youth who had served his country so well.

Girls with fluttering hearts and reddened cheeks caressed him with their warmest smiles and glances everywhere he went. Their presence frequently embarrassed him. He would find himself surrounded by bevies of them, and every time he sought escape from the charming but somewhat terrifying circle, he looked into glowing eyes all carrying the same avowal of adoration.

Boys followed him in the street or clung about him in swarms whenever he stopped. They would walk ahead of him, with faces turned back over their shoulders to look up into the features of the great champion. His walk, his manner, his smile, his uniform—no detail escaped these young male eyes who saw in their hero the man who had killed half a hundred men. He was their ideal of courage and bravery, of power and strength, of right and might. He could fly, shoot, fight, and kill, and do it better than any one.

The Flying Uhlan's younger brother, Lothar, succeeded him to the command of Jagdstaffel II, although neither in rank nor number of victories was he the senior officer. The German public demanded the name of Richthofen in the air, and the High Command was not asleep to its propaganda benefits.

Richthofen wore only the oil-stained flying togs that comprised almost his entire wardrobe at the airdrome. Dressed just like him was Lieutenant Kreft, one of his pilots also on leave, who handled the stick in the two-seater. Toothbrushes carried in coat pockets constituted their only other baggage.

They left the thunder of the battle of Arras behind them, and soon the last of the German sausage balloons disappeared over the hazy rim of the flat horizon. Away from the zone of war, they flew over peaceful countrysides, over rivers, canals, and railroads, over wooded mounds that were the mountains of the Meuse.

The ace traced the route on the map, descending once through some clouds to identify Namur just beneath, and then on by way of Liége and Aix-la-Chapelle to Cologne, where the coming of the war hero had been flashed by wire.

The airdrome was jammed with people whose cheering drowned the blare of the band. Every "*blatt*" in Germany on the previous day had carried the news of the fifty-second victory, and every one of their millions of readers was anxious to get a look at the new D'Artagnan of the air.

The ranking officers who received him as he stepped from the airplane were succeeded by a delegation of Cologne fräuleins who presented him with bunches of freshly cut flowers. The rewards of war-won glory were the same in Cologne as they were in Paris, London, New York, or What Cheer, Iowa.

Richthofen was self-conscious and shy in the presence of these girls, who received their war thrill from the knowledge that by their presence they alone could bring blushes to the cheeks of a man who had faced death so often without a change in complexion. He smiled boyishly and mumbled his thanks clumsily. He felt intensely uncomfortable with the bunches of flowers in his hands and with warm glances seeking his eyes everywhere he looked. He was not a "ladies' man."

Pleading a headache due to his three-hour flight from Douai, the ace escaped from the cheering mass packed round the flying field and gained the security of an officer's quarters, where he immediately went to bed for the midday nap that had become his habit and nerve stimulant. In an hour, he and Kreft returned to the refuelled plane and sailed away amid cheers that they could hear above the roar of their motor.

They flew low over the Rhine and late in the afternoon reached the German army headquarters at Kreuznach, where they reported to General Heppner, in command of German aviation. The ace spent the night quietly with old comrades who were attached to headquarters and whom he quite openly pitied as poor "ink spillers" whose duties, far away from the fight, deprived them of "half the fun of war."

The next morning, he waited first in the anteroom of General Field Marshal von Hindenburg. The headquarters hummed with activity. Numbers of high-ranking civilians and soldiers went in and came out of huge doors guarding the private office. Here was the German brain centre of the war.

Richthofen was warmly received by the marshal, whose attitude was as much fatherly as military. Only commonplace greetings and salutations passed between them, but Hindenburg notified him that His Majesty the Emperor had learned that to-day, May 2d, was Richthofen's twenty-fifth birthday, and that he was commanded to lunch with His Majesty.

In the antechamber of Von Ludendorff's office, Richthofen saw and met men high in the affairs of state and industry—men who had been only names to him before. In one corner sat Balin, the shipping magnate, in serious conversation with a general staff officer. Helfferich passed through the room at a quick walk. Bethmann, the Minister for Foreign Affairs, succeeded him in the private office. If anything, the scene was even busier than that in Hindenburg's office.

After an hour's wait, an officer called Richthofen from the dozen or more generals who were waiting and ushered him into Ludendorff's office. The marshal shook his hand and waved him into a chair.

"How's the air activity at Arras?" was the first question he shot at the ace. Richthofen at first liked the businesslike directness and the absence of any time-wasting congratulations or inquiries about his health. He answered as directly and endeavoured to keep himself strictly on the subject of Ludendorff's question. Frequently, however, when, in attempting to illustrate a point, he wandered off on to a personal anecdote that might not have been of military importance, Ludendorff would stop him suddenly with a wave of the hand and bring the conversation back to the original question.

In half an hour, the popular idol had been pumped dry

of all information of a military nature concerning the struggle in the air. The stern inquisitor then abruptly dismissed him. Richthofen left the office with relief. Ludendorff's trip-hammer questions and overpowering seriousness left him almost breathless.

At noon, he lunched with the Kaiser. Wilhelm the Second was playful and dignified by turns. With his keen eyes, he measured the ace from head to foot, missing no part of the well-worn Uhlan's tunic, riding breeches, and leather puttees, which seemed rather out of place in the midst of the well-pressed uniforms and brilliantly polished boots and leather accoutrements of the Emperor's household.

The monarch familiarly poked him in the ribs with his thumb and remarked that he was looking fat and gay. He congratulated him both upon his successes in the air and upon his twenty-fifth anniversary, at the same time expressing the hope that he would live to more than double both his birthdays and his air victories.

As they left the table two orderlies entered the room carrying a heavy bronze and marble bust of Germany's war lord in full martial array, from bristling moustaches to golden helmet. It was the birthday present from the monarch to Germany's greatest individual champion. It occupies a prominent corner in the drawing room of Mother Richthofen's home in Schweidnitz.

After the meal, the Kaiser talked with Richthofen for fully half an hour, the conversation being mostly on the subject of the latest developments in anti-aircraft artillery which the ace found to be rather a monotonous subject.

That night, the young Uhlan was the guest of honour at a dinner given by Hindenburg. He sat on the right of the marshal at a table around which were seated no less than eight knights wearing the star of the order Pour le Mérite. Richthofen had never seen so many notables of the order assembled before. Hindenburg impressed him as amiable and elderly. The marshal addressed his birthday felicitations to the ace in a warmly worded speech of praise and congratulation, and proposed his health and continued success.

"Now, tell me, Richthofen," the marshal asked, in his characteristic low voice, "have you ever been a cadet?"

"I was a cadet at Wahlstatt, sir," the ace replied, and in answer to further questions related that he had begun his military career in Room 6 in the barracks at that school.

Hindenburg smiled broadly and observed:

"Good, I also began my life playing soldiers in Room 6 at Wahlstatt and I have given a picture of myself to be hung on the wall of that room in token of my happy memories."

Ten years later, Hindenburg, as President of the German

Republic, was to stand bareheaded at the foot of a huge block of black marble as it was placed over Richthofen's final resting place in a cemetery in Berlin.

On the following day, the ace, piloted by Kreft, flew from Kreuznach to the country place where the Kaiserin was staying, not an hour's flight from General Headquarters. Her Majesty had commanded him to report to her, and her desire to see the new hero of the Fatherland was so keen that she waited for his arrival at the private airdrome on the estate.

Richthofen apologized for the old leather jacket he wore, but explained that it was part of the flying equipment that he had used in his air combats at the front.

The Empress examined the coat carefully and even passed her hand over the worn leather sleeves that had become somewhat thin at the elbows.

"A good old jacket," she said, "and just imagine that it has seen fifty-two victories."

She concluded her birthday congratulations by presenting him with a gold and white enamelled cigarette case inscribed with her name, and then insisted that the ace lunch with her that day. Richthofen liked her. She seemed like a dear old aunt or a grandmother, and he took delight in showing her how the motor of his plane was started.

Although all Germany was waiting to fête him, this first week of glory and celebration annoyed him as much as it impressed him. The attentions of the high rankers were oppressive. The wholesale compliments embarrassed. They left him speechless and feeling foolish.

It was all so different from the feeling of solitude and of individual power that one experienced soaring at a hundred and fifty miles an hour above the clouds. This world of compliments and neatly turned phrases was not his. He yearned for the heights and for the feel of triggers under his steady fingers.

He applied and obtained permission to go to a state hunting preserve at Freiburg and roam the forest in search of game. He declared that he needed it for his nerves, that his system required it just as other constitutions required the relief that was to be had in a week or two in the mountains or at the seashore.

In his forest retreat, with his dogs, guns, and red wet hunting bags, Richthofen did not know that Lothar was lying at that moment close to death in a hospital. The younger brother had been brought to earth by an English bullet as easily as the elder brother had been knocking down pheasants.

It must be remembered that rivalry, as well as love, existed between the two brothers. The younger brother was the taller. He always carried a riding crop, either tucked under the left armpit or grasped in the right hand, and used for smartly rapping the right boot leg. It was the mannerism of the mounted corps, and with Lothar it became an easy habit. Tapping his boot leg with the riding crop indicated interest additional to the smiling admiration with which he frankly looked on every attractive girl.

Girls could make Manfred blush with one tender look. Lothar made women feel not unpleasantly uncomfortable when he looked at them. Lothar was just as much of a killer as his elder brother, but he was a "lady-killer" also—something that Manfred decidedly was not.

Where Manfred was modestly retiring, not through an absence of pride, but on account of a great self-consciousness, his younger brother was socially forward, gay, debonair, always at ease, and ever as ready for a battle of the lighter emotions as he was for a death duel in the clouds.

He liked women, wine, and war, and was not backward in acknowledging his complete absorption in that ticklish triangle. He could drink, flirt, and fight, and did. He thought it was not only the best war he had ever been in, but the happiest period of his life. He was well aware that that life might come to an abrupt end at any minute in the air, but fräuleins and flagons were pleasant anodynes for such thoughts, and besides, he enjoyed the happy lenitive of superstition.

He always flew with a talisman. At first it was the riding crop that had been with him when he charged with the dragoons. He attached great importance to its being beside him in the plane. He believed that to fly without it increased the chances against him. Three times, when he had left it behind him, he had encountered additional difficulties in the air.

But when he left the bombing planes on which he first flew and became a fighting pilot in a small scout plane, the stick was too large to carry, and he had to discard it.

"When I went up alone for the first time," he explained, "it required all my courage and determination to leave that stick on the ground."

The incident was more than trivial. Lothar had a friend, Wintgrens, who also flew with a riding stick. Once he flew without it, and on that day he was killed. Lothar had to force himself to overcome the feeling of protection that he had in the company of his first talisman.

He held it to a degree responsible for carrying him safely through his first flying days and the dangerous work of night-bombing expeditions. He had heard the whine and thump of anti-aircraft shells as they exploded around him, and he was fully acquainted with the dangers of landing at night in land fogs. But, on the whole, he preferred night bombing.

Dropping nocturnal bombs gave him greater satisfaction because, under cover of darkness, he could approach his objectives closer and be more certain of a hit.

> At night the enemy could not see us [he wrote]; therefore it was easy to descend within 300 feet of the ground and release the bombs from there. The explosions would illuminate the surroundings in bright light.
>
> Bungalows filled with troops, provisions, or munitions could be seen splendidly. Once we succeeded in blowing up a whole munition dépôt. One single bomb did it. The explosion spread over the entire camp, which was about a square kilometre in size.
>
> Columns of fire leaped up 10,000 feet from the ground. One dump detonated its neighbour, and they exploded one after another. The next day, it was possible to see that the entire camp had been destroyed by fire.

Back in the airdrome, Lothar and his comrades would congratulate one another on the night's work, while they took on heat and new courage from steaming mugs of rum, hot water, and sugar. Sometimes the squadron would make as many as three separate raids or "deliveries" a night.

Graduating from the bombing service, Lothar attained the peak of his desires early in 1917, when, after his first solo flights, he became a member of his famous brother's fighting unit. He inherited one of Manfred's old well-tried-out planes—a bus in which the ace had gained ten victories.

As a new talisman to replace the old riding crop for which there was no space in the cockpit of the fighting plane, the fledgling received a pair of old fur gloves from his brother. Lothar was conscious of the fact that these gloves had transmitted the ace's finger pressure to the triggers in many a victorious air duel, and the knowledge brought him a confidence that carried him through his first ten combats in the air. After that tenth victory, the old bus and the gloves went to pieces, and the novice, now with new reliance in himself, advanced to a new plane and new equipment.

The younger brother's offerings upon the altar of chance were not unique in Richthofen's Jagdstaffel, or, for that matter, in any air service. Little Wolff always wore an old German nightcap under his flying helmet, and Voss would never fly a plane over the lines unless his special death-defying device of a black skull and crossbones was stencilled on its side.

One superstition general among the German flyers was that it was extremely bad luck to be photographed just before a duty flight. Boelcke had defied this fear and paid with his life. A friend had snapped him in front of his plane just before he took to the air. He never came back. Schaefer's death was preceded two hours by a personal photograph, and so was Manfred's. The camera fiend was not a welcome guest on the airdrome just before a flight.

It was noticeable, however, that the respect and importance given to charms was less prevalent among the flyers whose background was the discipline and training of the regular army. War was more a science to the trained professional, and chance, although admittedly ever present, was the minor consideration.

The war birds from civilian life flew with almost as much desperation as they did with hope. If luck was against them, they would be killed; if it was with them they would survive, was the way most of them accepted the proposition, and it was a feeling that contributed greatly to the daring and recklessness with which they wrote their names in the stirring annals of air fighting.

Manfred knew that his brother was in this class. Soldiering as a career was of no interest to Lothar, but war was a game and a gamble that he loved. Manfred prided himself that he killed through a sense of duty and for a purpose. He believed that Lothar shot down his enemies for the pure sport of it.

Manfred characterized Lothar a "butcher," not unkindly. He compared his brother with the "game hog" who prefers killing everything in sight to the careful, well-planned and executed stalking of one victim. His opinion, while adversely critical, was not without a big element of pride in the youngster's prowess, because there is a place in war for the game hog as well as for the war craftsman who excels in the technique of methodical killing.

The difference between the two types is great. Lothar killed when and where and as he could. Manfred figured each attack out beforehand and did it according to the book of regulations. Lothar depended upon his luck. Manfred depended upon his skill and his trained coördination of mind and muscle.

Good fortune flew at Lothar's side during the war, which he survived with a record that remained a source of pride to his organization. In four weeks after his arrival in Manfred's unit, he had downed twenty planes. His flying was reckless and daring, and this made him more popular with the officers and men of the squadron than his brother.

Manfred, with the will power and energy to command men, was a strict disciplinarian. Popularity was not one of the results he was looking for. He prided himself that he was a soldier who obeyed orders whether he liked them or not, and he insisted upon his subordinates obeying his orders whether they liked them or not. Lothar was a "good fellow."

It was on May 7th that Lothar received his first taste of some of the punishment he had been inflicting upon the enemy. His daring on that day netted him an almost fatal wound from a British bullet. He needed all the assistance that good fortunes reserves for the brave, for consciousness left him in the air from loss of blood, and only chance brought his plane safely to earth behind his own lines.

When Manfred, at his hunting camp, received the telegram that his brother had been wounded but not mortally, he obtained details of the affair by long-distance telephone and characterized Lothar's conduct as plain rashness.

Having succeeded the ace as leader of the Jagdstaffel, Lothar had selected Allmenröder to fly with him late on the afternoon of that day when the Battle of Bullecourt raged on the ground beneath them.

From an altitude of 6,000 feet, young Richthofen dove down to attack an English flyer who, from an altitude of 3,000 feet, was making frequent dives upon the German infantry and spraying them with machine-gun lead. The British infantry flyer accepted combat with the fast German fighting plane, and Lothar found that he was up against an opponent who was ready to hold his ground. Every time he approached the infantry flyer from the rear, the English observer sent forth a stream of lead from his rear machine gun. Attacks from the front were met with equally warm receptions.

Allmenröder went down and joined his fellow officer, down came the rest of the red Albatross unit, and then there came another descent of English planes from above. Bait had piled up on bait, and in less than five minutes a general dog-fight was on at an unusually low altitude. The sudden burst of air fury almost stopped the battle on the ground.

At times, the battle swung back of Vimy Ridge, now in the hands of the English, and again it was carried on the wind back of the German lines. Planes went down on both sides—some like dead flies, some like falling firebrands.

Lothar and Lady Luck were hard pressed. He found himself with a particularly speedy Englishman hanging close on his tail and literally blistering it with hot lead. He failed to recognize the terrain below him, and for the moment did not know whether he was behind his own lines or not.

Twist and swerve as he might the Englishman hung on and pumped lead. Lothar saw the splash of bullets on the motor in front of him and saw splinters fly up from the woodwork of the instrument board. Then came a sharp pain through the hip and a stream of warm liquid flowing down his right leg.

Below was a meadow. He headed for it. He looked down at his leg, saw his own blood, and fainted. This is recognized as a psychological condition entirely removed from the question of moral courage. There are brave men to whom the sight of their own blood is a paralyzing shock. The red Albatross, speeding at more than a hundred miles an hour and hardly a thousand feet in the air, plunged earthward with its unconscious pilot strapped in the seat.

Lothar's lucky star landed the machine safely. How, the wounded man never knew, because everything remained a blank until he woke up in a field hospital with no other injury than the bullet-shattered hip.

As a result of the fight, he was given credit for his twenty-second victory, and the downed English plane designated as his particular victim was that of Captain Albert Ball, the leading British ace whose wonderful career in the air ended with his death in action on that day.

It is rather well substantiated that Ball was killed in the same general fight in which Lothar escaped with a wound, but there are serious grounds for doubting whether it was a bullet from the younger Richthofen's guns that passed through the head of the famous English ace and sent him crashing to earth.

The meagre German accounts of Ball's end all state that the Englishman was flying a triplane, which was not the fact. There is a strong probability that Ball received his death blow in the general air scrimmage instead of in a single duel, and that the German pilot who killed him lost his life in the same fight, with the result that no one claimed to have downed the English youth, and that credit for it was given to the disabled Richthofen.

Ball was the idol of the British flying service. Like the elder Richthofen, his victories had passed the half-century mark, and his country had acclaimed him the greatest flyer of the war and heaped him with honours. He wore the Victoria Cross, the medal of the Distinguished Service Order, and the Military Cross.

Marksmanship, airmanship, careful planning, and extreme bravery were the characteristics that contributed to the destructive capacity of the young English ace. Like Richthofen, he possessed the killing instinct. His flying comrades report that he would often follow his burning victims earthward, pouring streams of machine-gun lead into them.

In his public appearances at home, he had an engaging boyish smile that won the hearts of all who saw him, but in the air or on the airdrome in France, he was reticent to the degree of being almost unsocial. While members of his squadron idled an hour over "pegs" of whisky in the mess hall, Ball would be found alone in his quarters with his phonograph. He liked good music and flowers, and in the presence of these or under their influence would hatch out most of the plans and manœuvres that made him so successful in the air.

He would spend hours at the gun butts, ever improving his marksmanship. He carried empty paper boxes and tin cans up with him, and before returning to the airdrome from a flight over the lines would toss them out and expend his remaining ammunition upon these moving targets as they fell.

The men in his own squadron knew very little of him, except that they were all aware that he possessed one overpowering ambition, which was to kill as many Germans as he could. What was sport or duty to them was food and drink to the fire that raged within this strange youngster who hid his fighting instincts behind a mask of boyish smiles. Bashful, shy, retiring in the presence of others on the ground, he was a grim and fearless demon in the air—cold, calculating, and merciless. He believed in no quarter and expected none.

Ball preferred to fly alone. Surprise and sudden attack from as close as thirty feet were the secret of his tactics. He practised it on his own mates, frequently flying for miles under the tail of a British plane without the pilot being aware of his presence in that fatal position. From the attack at short range, Ball gained an added security which he employed when he made his famous lone attacks on superior numbers of the enemy. He could cling so close to his special victim that the other Germans would not dare fire on him for fear of hitting their own man.

At the time of his death, Ball preferred the fast French Nieuport scout plane to any of British make, and his squadron, the Sixtieth, was equipped with these in place of the Morane biplanes it had been using. With the machine-gun mounting employed on this plane, Ball was able to surprise his victims by varying his aim without changing the course of his plane.

Stalking his intended victims from above and behind, exactly as Richthofen did, he would dive, zoom upward beneath the selected German plane, and then, at a range of hardly ten yards, would spray the enemy machine with lead from nose to tail. He would accomplish this by the slightest oscillation of the control stick, and most frequently would heave

a hundred pounds into his victim before the latter was aware of his presence.

His delight was to hang on above the tail of a German formation of from seven to twelve planes, making sudden dives and shooting bursts of lead until one of them would leave its position in the flying V. The first German machine to leave its station would be pounced upon, and usually the deadly shooting and superior airmanship of the English ace would send it down in flames.

There is no English account of Ball's last fight. If any of his flying mates saw him go down, they did not recognize his plane. He was reported missing that night, and several days later the German dropped the following note, which seems, for once, at least, to have permitted a personal pride and exultation to replace the respect that was generally expressed for a fallen foe whose gallantry was acknowledged. The note read:

R. F. C. Captain Ball was brought down in a fight in the air on May 7, 1917, by a pilot who was of the same order as himself. He was buried at Annœulen.

This was apparently written after credit for Ball's death had been given to Lothar Richthofen. The Germans found in Ball's pocket a newspaper clipping which they sent to the hospital to Lothar, who placed it proudly among his trophies in the scrapbook that remains to-day in his mother's home. The clipping shows Ball with the casket which was presented to him by the City of Manchester when he was given the freedom of the city. On the day that the photo was taken, Ball and his mother and father had proudly posed for other pictures, which are the last photographs taken of him in England. Shortly afterward, he returned to France and to his death.

To both of the Richthofens and to their family and, for that matter, to all Germany, it was a source of pride that two brothers had each laid low an English champion of the air. All of the newspaper accounts accrediting Lothar with the killing of Ball recalled that Manfred had killed, as his eleventh victim in the previous year, the no less renowned and decorated British ace, Major Hawker.

Assured that his brother would recover from his wounds, the ace on leave continued his pursuit of small game, unmindful of the fact that conditions at the front were fast changing from what they had been when he left. While on the state hunting preserve, he received an invitation from the Prince of Pless to shoot bison on the latter's estate.

Richthofen was overjoyed at the prospect of matching his

wits and gun against one of these mighty monarchs of the forest which exist in Europe only at Pless and on the estate of the late Czar at Bialowicza. In the latter forests, the bison had almost been exterminated by hungry German and Russian soldiers. All that was Prussian and aristocratic in Richthofen resented the thought that game which he believed should have been reserved for the sport of a ruling monarch, or at least someone of title or lineage, had gone to fill the mess kit of a hungry common soldier.

These thoughts did not prevent him at Pless from rushing from the station to the estate keeper's lodge and demanding that they set off into the forest that very afternoon, because he was determined to bring down one of the rare animals on the first day of his visit. He got his kill.

Two hours' tramping through the woods, and they sighted the herd through the trees. A mighty bull charged toward them. Richthofen put three successive bullets into him, and on the third shot the ponderous, charging beast toppled over dead, fifty yards from the mound on which Richthofen stood and tingled with what he later described as one of his greatest hunting thrills.

The ace, with his own hands, assisted in the work of skinning the animal and cutting off the enormous head which he had properly mounted and placed on the wall over his bed in Schweidnitz.

Richthofen's sport in the forests of Pless was cut short by more ominous news from the front. The struggle in the air had become a struggle indeed. German air losses were increasing. The conditions that prevailed during the previous month of "Bloody April," when the Germans had destroyed four British planes to every one of their own brought down, had changed. The advantages of superior equipment, which had been responsible in no small degree for Richthofen's record bag of victories during that month, no longer existed. The spring model British planes had at last reached the lines.

The ace was needed back at the front. He received orders cancelling his extended leave, and on June 10th, he reported for duty at General Headquarters at Kreuznach. There followed two days of conferences and lunches with the Kaiser and the King of Bulgaria, who decorated him with the Bulgarian cross for bravery. He liked the seventy-six-year-old monarch for his lively interest in aviation, and he enjoyed the exchange of hunting stories with the old Prince of Pless, but uppermost in his mind was the thought that his presence was necessary at the front, and that his Jagdstaffel, which during his absence had suffered numerous losses, needed him to reorganize it and give it new inspiration for the fight.

In the week from June 1st to June 7th, during the operations preliminary to the battle of Messines, the British air force had actually wrested the air superiority from the Germans. Twenty-four German machines had been shot down, and many others driven down out of control. During the battle itself, which was in progress while Richthofen was at General Headquarters, the British airmen managed to drive the German fighting units away from the immediate battle zone, with the result that German guns lost the advantage of aërial observation, and English infantry advanced with less danger from annihilating enemy barrages.

New British machines and pilots began to arrive at the front in numbers, and the Germans began to hear that thousands of Americans were going through speedy courses of training for both the French and British air services. The new British models were the two-seater Bristol fighters, the S. E. 5 single-seater fighters and the D. H. 4 two-seater fighter-bombers. They began to prove themselves birds worthy of meeting the speedy Albatross and Halberstadt.

Richthofen reached the front on the fourteenth and resumed command of Jagdstaffel 11, which, in addition to that of his brother, had suffered losses. Surviving officers reported to him that things had changed in the air and that the British were stronger now than they had been since their last superiority on the Somme, a year earlier. The ace was warned that the new enemy planes were speedy, that it was unhealthy to attack the new two-seaters from behind and most difficult to approach them from beneath, and, furthermore, that the new crop of young British pilots were more reckless and daring than ever, and that the enemy still maintained its offensive policy of carrying the fight in the air to the German side of the line.

While the German units at the front had endeavoured to meet this new condition of affairs by combining into larger formations, air headquarters was working on plans for the perfection of new flying organizations on a larger scale than ever attempted before. These were to be the "Jagdsgeschwaders," or fighting squadrons, each composed of four Staffels and numbering about forty-eight planes in all.

These were the organizations that first earned the name of "Circuses" amongst the Allies, because they were moved from time to time to different parts of the line, where the locally stationed air forces needed reinforcement. They were manned by the best fighting pilots, and were led in the air by a special commanding officer. The organizations were not completed during June, and did not make their appearance on the front until about the middle of July.

Richthofen's return to the front was ill-omened. His first

official duty was to attend the funeral of his old friend and fellow airman Lieutenant Schaefer, himself an ace with thirty English planes to his credit. Schaefer had fallen in a dog-fight under the guns of Lieutenant Byhys-Davids, the English pilot who was later killed after his eighteenth conquest in the air.

Lothar owed his life to Schaefer. The younger Richthofen, engaged in a furious fight with a single English plane, found himself at a low altitude some miles behind the enemy lines. He was forced to withdraw from the combat and streak it for his own lines, when he was attacked from behind by another English plane. Lothar, with his guns pointing forward, was defenseless from the rear and could only resort to a zigzag flight and sharp curves to keep out of the pursuing Englishman's relentless fire.

Then the stream of lead and tracer bullets cut through several of the bracing wires on the German plane. The necessary tension was lost, and the wings trembled from the unequally distributed air pressure. Any sudden stress would result in the loss of a wing and destruction. Conscious of this new danger, as well as of the persistent Englishman hanging on to his tail, Lothar dared one last curve in an effort to get behind his enemy. His plane held together, but at that minute a streak of red dropped from the heavens, and the English plane burst into flame.

It was Schaefer, thank God [Lothar wrote after]. I could have laid any wager that within the next half minute I should have been shot to the ground or my wings would have crumpled up. Instead of me, my enemy went burning to the ground. Schaefer flew with me back to the airdrome, and I bought him the best bottle of champagne in the mess. Good that one could at least do that.

Manfred had spent one anxious night in March telephoning all along the front for trace of the ever-smiling Schaefer, who had failed to show up after a late afternoon patrol. The missing flyer had gone down to 600 feet to pick off an English infantry flyer, and had been shot down between the lines for his pains.

Schaefer jumped out of his machine and into a shell hole as the English infantry poured a murderous machine-gun fire into the disabled Albatross. He took a cautious observation and found himself uncomfortably close to the English first-line trenches. While bullets ripped at the rim of his shell crater and an occasional shell burst near by, the German pilot lighted a cigarette and waited for the approaching darkness.

As night fell, Schaefer, who was also an accomplished hunter and woodsman, heard a couple of partridges near by suddenly fly away with a frightened flutter of wings. Interpreting this as the approach of a hostile patrol, the German started crawling from one shell hole to another in the direction of his own lines.

Again noises in the darkness in front of him indicated the approach of another party. This time they proved to be Germans, who guided him back to the nearest command post in his own lines. It was two o'clock the following morning before he could report his escape by telephone to the anxious Richthofen.

And now Schaefer was dead—gone the way of the thirty or more men he had killed.

There were strange faces replacing the old ones in the Jagdstaffel. Richthofen wondered which of the remaining survivors would be next to go. There was a different feel in the air and a different tone in the morale of the unit as it took the air again under its old leader. Now the fighting was around Ypres and Dickebush and between the Nieuport canal and the sea, where the Flanders offensive of the English was starting on the red carnage that was to continue on until November.

Richthofen's first victim after his return to the front was not one of the British new spring model planes. It was another piece of the same "cold meat" that had boosted his string of victories so high in the month of April. The German ace had listened well to what had been told him of the performances of the new English machines, and his plans for successfully combating them were far from complete. But he knew how to handle the old planes, and he jumped the first one he spotted alone.

It happened to be an old R. E. 8 two-seater, slow, comfortable, and easy-going, and engaged at the time on a photographic reconnaissance behind the German lines. It was one of several of its type that failed to return on that day.

The first kill after his vacation brought some of the old-time thrill back to Richthofen, but not much consolation, and it did not succeed in overcoming the sombre thoughts of deaths and funerals, losses and wounds that had been ever present with him since his return.

It was good flying weather, these days of late June, with long, light evenings. Richthofen flew daily, but warily. It was not like the harvest time seven weeks earlier, when the sky was full of easy prey, and a man with a red Albatross would call it a bad day if he didn't return with anywhere from one to four fresh victories to his record.

The new enemy planes were marvels of speed and manœuvrability, and whereas the German pilots, least of all Richthofen, would not admit that they were superior to the Albatross biplanes and triplanes and the Halberstadt, none of them would deny that the old advantages of the German models had been greatly reduced, and that now, in a man-to-man duel, victory went to the best man, because the new machines were almost equal.

Having maintained their offensive policy over the German lines during the days of mechanical disadvantages, the British pilots now became more daring, and at the same time the German flyers concentrated on extending and perfecting flying in larger groups, to reap a new advantage from this quarter.

Combats and feints at combats occurred daily, while the ground battle waged across the torn-up plains of Flanders, but it was not until almost a week later that Richthofen could report another victory, and this a doubtful one.

Requesting Acknowledgment of My 54th Victory

Date: June 23, 1917.
Time: 9:30 P.M.
Place: North of Ypres.
Plane: Spad one-seater.

I attacked together with several of my gentlemen an enemy one-seater squad on the enemy's side of the line. During the fight, I fired some three hundred shots into a Spad from the shortest possible distance. My adversary did not start to curve and did nothing to evade my fire.

At first, the plane began to smoke, and then it fell, turning and turning, three kilometres north of Ypres, where it touched the ground without having caught itself.

(Signed) BARON VON RICHTHOFEN.

It is a curious thing that neither the British nor the French lost a Spad machine on that day. Several Nieuports and Sopwith machines were shot down, but none at so late an hour as 9:30. It is possible that the murkiness of the hour impaired or possibly prejudiced Richthofen's otherwise good vision. It is also possible that the plane he fired into may have landed unharmed behind its own lines, in which case it would not appear on the Allied casualty lists.

Similar vagueness casts a shadow over the report Richthofen made of another combat three days later when he claimed to have shot down an English De Haviland DD plane behind his own lines after nine o'clock at night. Again the otherwise impeccable English casualty lists reveal no loss of any plane of that type on that day. Richthofen's report reads:

Requesting Acknowledgment of My 56th Victory
[Recorded as his 55th victory]

Date: June 26, 1917.
Time: 9:10 P.M.
Place: Between Keibergmelen and Lichtensteinlager, this side of lines.
Plane: De Haviland D. D. one-seater.

With six machines of my Staffel, I attacked an enemy formation consisting of two reconnaissance planes and ten pursuit planes. Unimpeded by the enemy pursuit planes, I managed to break one of the reconnaissance planes in my fire.

The body of the plane fell with its two occupants into a hangar between Keibergmelen and Lichtensteinlager, this side of our lines. The plane burned when it crashed, and destroyed the hangar.

It would appear that the changed conditions in the air had their effect on the usual course of events on the ground because, in this particular instance, there is an absence of the available detail that marked Richthofen's previous reports on his victories. Undoubtedly, telephone communication between the ace's airdrome and the German hangar could have established the exact type of the plane and the names of its occupants, unless both planes and occupants were incinerated in the fire that destroyed the hangar.

On the day previous to this combat, Richthofen had reported downing another plane behind the German lines, but credit for it had been delayed, so that, on the German records, it carries the number fifty-six in the ace's list of victories.

It was a tough life for any of the English pilots who had to continue flying the old planes. The decrepit R. E.'s were duck soup to Richthofen. He seemed to concentrate on them, and seldom missed an opportunity to knock one down.

Not that he did not have his encounters with the speedier models. He did. But discretion sat beside him when he tackled these new birds of equal power, and if none of them show up among his victims at this period of his career, at least he did not figure among the victims that fell to them. And that, after all, was a matter not entirely devoid of personal satisfaction.

A week went by, and another R.E. fell under his guns.

The air activity along the front took on a new spurt and revealed for the first time the new German plans for bigger organization flying.

Captain H. L. Satchell and Lieutenant H. L. Jenks, leading an offensive patrol of old F.E.'s during the lunch hour in the vicinity of Comines, were attacked successively by five formations of German planes totalling about fifty Albatross scouts and two-seaters. The English planes were now equipped with two forward-firing guns and one protecting the rear. The fight took place at an altitude ranging from one to two miles above the earth, which was completely hidden by clouds.

> On occasions, the leader of the enemy aircraft fired a white light which burst into several stars [Satchell reported]. During the fight, which lasted on and off about an hour, we hit with both forward guns a red enemy plane which was very persistent. It fell out of control, emitting black smoke. Flames were seen on this machine by Pilot Joslyn and Observer Potter, Pilot Trevethan and Observer Hoy. The clouds beneath us prevented us from seeing whether it crashed or not.

There is no record that Richthofen suffered any serious difficulty on this day, so the presumption is that the red Albatross fired by Satchell was one of his squadron, and it is also presumed that it was Richthofen who led the formation and sent up the white signals.

The audacity of the old F.E.'s ploughing into big enemy formations of speedy scouts indicates the extent to which the British offensive policy was being carried over the German lines, and the development of air signals being given aloft to multiple flying units revealed the efforts of the Germans to gain new advantages of manœuvre by adapting naval methods to the air and handling enlarged formations as a fleet at sea is directed from a central command.

The struggle increased daily in bitterness, extent, and losses. Four days after his 57th victory, Richthofen himself went hurtling down from a fearful height with an English bullet wound in his head.

It was the first wound he had received in almost three years of war. He had had many narrow escapes, but this was the first time that the enemy had touched him.

The man who shot Richthofen down that 6th of July morning was Flight Commander Albert Edward Woodbridge, who was a Second Lieutenant at the time and was acting as observer for Pilot Captain D. C. Cunnell, commanding a wing of the Twentieth Squadron, R. F. C.

Cunnell was killed six days afterward, but Woodbridge survived the war to tell this story.

"Our Squadron No. 20 was quartered at Marie-Chapelle, not far from the road between St. Omer and Cassel. We didn't have the new machines yet. They had us still using the old F. E. 2 d's, pusher type, you know, with the motor behind and the observer sitting out in front in a sort of a front porch with a shape to it like the back end of a bathtub. The motor was behind the pilot and aimed to go right through his back in case of a nose crash. There was no covered-in fuselage built out to the tail like the planes of to-day, but the rudder and elevators were connected to the body by a trellis of openwork wooden spars like three or four ladders bound together in a horizontal pyramid sticking out behind. They were jolly dodo's!

"The motor, though, was reliable if not speedy, and being immediately in back of the pilot, it offered him some protection if we were attacked from behind, but such an attack usually either killed the engine or ignited the petrol tanks, and that was never for the best.

"The armament had been improved and tripled to meet the emergency condition developed by the Albatross scouts employing twin Spandaus firing through the propeller. That doubled the enemy's volume of fire from each plane. As we did not fire through the propeller, we did not employ the synchronizing mechanism.

"The principal weapon was manned by the observer. It was mounted on a movable pivot attached to the flooring of the front porch, and had a wide field of fire. This gun could fire forward and to both sides and slightly upward and downward in the same three directions. It could not, however, fire to the rear either above or below the plane.

"A second Lewis gun was fixed to the side of the forward cockpit and could be fired by a trigger on the pilot's controls, but it would only be aimed by pointing the entire plane. A third Lewis was fixed on another tall pivot rising from the observer's cockpit. With this one he could fire backward and upward above the rear plane.

"But, in order to fire this gun, he had to abandon the forward gun and elevate himself by standing up on the edges of his cockpit and facing the rear, a rather ticklish position in a moving plane two miles in the air. It was all makeshift, but it was the best we had, and we had to 'carry on.' We were 'cold meat,' and most of us knew it.

"And our job was offensive patrolling—in other words, we were supposed to go out and light into any enemy planes we could find. We knew the Albatrosses and Halberstadts could fly rings around us and shoot hell out of us from that blind spot under our tails. We were like butterflies sent out to insult eagles.

"It was a fine morning, that 6th of July, and the wind was in our favour. The six of us composing our flight buzzed off about ten o'clock and started for our patrol area, which was over Comines, Warneton, and Frelinghein, up between Ypres and Armentières. We had been on our way about half an hour and were well over the German lines at an altitude of about twelve hundred feet.

"Swinging down from the north, we spotted a formation

of eight speedy German planes. They wheeled around to the west of us and got between us and our own lines. I notice that the Baron calls this manœuvre a trick to cut off our retreat. That's pulling it rather long, because, you know, we did most of the fighting over the German lines—that's where it all took place—and according to orders we were there looking for it.

"As soon as they were behind us, we turned around and started for them to engage them. We had hardly got in contact with them when other enemy formations—larger ones—seemed to close in from all sides. Gad, I don't know where they all came from. My word, I never saw so many Huns in the air at one time in my life before. We estimated later that there must have been about forty Albatross scouts altogether in formations that seemed to number from eight to twenty.

"As Cunnell wrote in this report, 'A general engagement ensued.' That's formal verbiage for the damnedest scrimmage imaginable. I fired my fore and aft guns until they were both hot. I kept jumping from one to another. Cunnell handled the old F. E. for all she was worth, banking her from one side to the other, ducking dives from above and missing head-on collisions by bare margins of feet. The air was full of whizzing machines, and the noise from the full out motors and the crackling machine guns was more than deafening.

"The Jerries showed more spirit than usual. They went to it hammer and tongs. This enabled us to fire from the closest range and was really to our advantage. Cunnell and I fired into four of the Albatrosses from as close as thirty yards, and I saw my tracers go right into their bodies. Those four went down, and fortunately some of our flight saw them tumble, because we were given credit for them. Some of them were on fire—just balls of flame and smoke, you know—nasty sight to see, but no time to think about it at the moment."

"Two of them came at us head on, and I think the first one was Richthofen. I recall there wasn't a thing on that machine that wasn't red, and God, how he could fly! I opened fire with the front Lewis, and so did Cunnell with the side gun. Cunnell held the F.E. to her course, and so did the pilot of the all-red scout. Gad, with our combined speeds, we must have been approaching each other at somewhere around 250 miles an hour.

"Thank God, my Lewis didn't jam. I kept a steady stream of lead pouring into the nose of that machine. He was firing also. I could see my tracers splashing along the barrels of his Spandaus and I knew the pilot was sitting right behind them.

His lead came whistling past my head and ripping holes in the bathtub.

"Then something happened. We could hardly have been twenty yards apart when the Albatross pointed her nose down suddenly. Zip, and she passed under us. Cunnell banked and turned. We saw the all-red plane slip into a spin. It turned over and over and round and round. It was no manœuvre. He was completely out of control. His motor was going full on, so I figured I had at least wounded him. As his head was the only part of him that wasn't protected from my fire by his motor, I figured that's where he was hit.

"But I didn't see him crash—Gad, no—too busy for that. More Jerries dove in from all directions, and we just kept on pumping it into any of them that whizzed by or that we could dive on. Hell of it was that it never seemed to let up. I had been in short fights before, but this seemed like it was going to be an all-day affair. Fact is that it only lasted about forty minutes, but that's eternity in an air fight.

"My hands were burned and blistered and my throat aching dry when we finally pulled out with all of our ammunition expended. The Archies gave us hell as we streaked it back for the lines. Our flight had knocked down seven Huns, of which number Cunnell and I were given credit for four on the testimony of other pilots. Our credit did not include the all-red chap, who now appears to have been Richthofen, because I was not sure whether he could not have righted himself before crashing, but he certainly was out of control."

How close Woodbridge came to killing Richthofen is best shown by the helmet which the German ace was wearing when the English bullet turned off his lights. The missile struck the German ace on the left side of the head, a glancing blow which tore a bad hole in the helmet.

The gruesome relic hangs to-day in the Flying Uhlan's bedroom in Schweidnitz. Richthofen frequently looked at it and pondered over how closely death had missed him. He had the helmet with him during the days in the hospital, when he wrote the following thrilling account of his narrow escape:

On a very fine day, July 6, 1917, I was scouting with my gentlemen. We had flown for quite a while between Ypres and Armentières without getting into contact with the enemy.

Then I saw a formation on the other side and thought immediately, these fellows want to fly over. They approached the front, saw us, turned to one side, and I began to feel that they flew away, but in the meanwhile I watched the enemy's squadron closely.

Not long afterward, it approached our front again. We had an unfavourable wind—that is, it came from the east. I watched them fly some distance behind our lines. Then I cut off their retreat. They were again my dear friends, the Big Vickers. [Richthofen's name for F. E. planes.]

This English type has a body braced with cross-bar construction. The observer sits in front. It would have taken us some time to get contact with them, if we had not been above them and forced them down. After some time, we approached so close to the last plane that I began to consider a means of attacking him. Wolff was flying just below me. The hammering of a German machine gun indicated to me that he was fighting.

Then my opponent turned and accepted the fight, but at such a distance that one could hardly call it a real air fight. I had not even prepared my gun for firing, for there was lots of time before I could begin to fight. Then I saw that the enemy's observer, probably from sheer excitement, opened fire. I let him shoot, for, at a distance of 300 yards and more, the best marksmanship is helpless. One does not hit one's target at such a distance.

Now he flies toward me, and I hope that I will succeed in getting behind him and opening fire.

Suddenly, something strikes me in the head. For a moment, my whole body is paralyzed. My arms hang down limply beside me; my legs flop loosely beyond my control. The worst was that a nerve leading to my eyes had been paralyzed and I was completely blind.

I feel my machine tumbling down—falling. At the moment, the idea struck me, "This is how it feels when one is shot down to his death." Any moment, I wait for my wings to break off. I am alone in my bus. I don't lose my senses for a moment.

Soon I regain power over my arms and legs, so that I grip the wheel. Mechanically, I cut off the motor, but what good does that do? One can't fly without sight. I forced my eyes open—tore off my goggles—but even then I could not see the sun. I was completely blind. The seconds seemed like eternities. I noticed I was still falling.

From time to time, my machine had caught itself, but only to slip off again. At the beginning I had been at a height of 4,000 yards, and now I must have fallen at least two to three thousand yards. I concentrated all my energy and said to myself, "I must see—I must—I must see."

Whether my energy helped me in this case, I do not know. At any rate, suddenly I could discern black-and-white spots, and more and more I regained my eyesight. I looked into the sun—could stare straight into it without having the least pains. It seemed as though I was looking through thick black goggles.

First thing I did was to look at the altimeter. I had no idea where I was. Again I caught the machine and brought it into a normal position and continued gliding down. Nothing but shell holes was below me. A big block of forest came before my vision, and I recognized that I was within our lines.

If the Englishman had followed me, he could have brought me down without difficulty, but, thanks to God, my comrades protected me. At the beginning, they could not understand my fall.

First, I wanted to land immediately, for I didn't know how long I could keep up consciousness and my strength; therefore, I went down to fifty yards but could not find amongst the many shell holes a spot for a possible landing. Therefore, I again speeded up the motor and flew to the east at a low height. At this, the beginning, I got on splendidly, but, after a few seconds, I noticed that my strength was leaving me and that everything was turning black before my eyes. Now it was high time.

I landed my machine without any particular difficulties, tore down a few telephone wires, which, of course, I didn't mind at the moment. I even had enough strength left in me to get up and to try to get out of the plane. I tumbled out of the machine and could not rise again—I was weak.

Immediately, a few men ran to the spot. They had watched the whole fight and had recognized my red machine. The soldiers bound up my head with bandages. I have only a hazy idea of what happened later. I didn't lose my senses entirely, but I was only half conscious.

I only knew that I had fallen into some thorns and that I did not have the strength to roll away.

By a lucky chance, I had landed my machine beside a road. In a short time, a motor ambulance came, and I was packed into it and taken to the field hospital at Courtrai. The surgeons there were already prepared and began immediately with their work.

I had quite a good-sized hole—a wound of about ten centimetres in length. At one spot, as big as a dollar, the bare white skull bone lay exposed. My thick Richthofen skull had proved itself bullet proof.

For days I had a deadly headache. At home, it was reported that I was lying in a hospital with wounds in the head and the stomach. As I write, I wonder whether my brother or myself (both wounded now) will be able to board his plane first. My brother fears that it will be I, and I fear that it will be my brother.

Cablegrams and letters of sympathy reached the hospital at Courtrai from his family and from comrades at the front, but not from the general public, from whom the news of his wounding had been withheld. It would hardly have helped German morale at the time if it had become generally known that the enemy had put both of the famous Richthofens out of the fight at the same time. But it would have been "jolly good news" in the camps of the Royal Flying Corps on the other side of the lines. The English airmen admired the flying Baron and his brother but would have been completely satisfied to have them remain in the hospital for the rest of the war.

Sitting up in the bed, the ace read his correspondence

and communicated with his old jeweller in Berlin, from whom he ordered five more little silver death cups, inscribed as before, to commemorate the five victories which had been placed to his credit during the three weeks' fighting since his return from leave.

He smiled at the showing. It didn't give him the same exultation that it had when he closed his books at the end of "Bloody April." But, then, conditions had changed, and no one knew it better than Richthofen.

As an ambassador of the grim reaper, the Red Knight of Germany still ranked highest among the killers of the sky.

His victories numbered fifty-seven.

His killing totalled forty-seven identified and fourteen unidentified.

Since he had taken no new prisoners since April, his rating in that department of martial efficiency remained, as before, at twenty-six.

But the red days were not ended. He would recover. He would return to the front. He would fly again. He would kill more. He willed it with all the fire of his indomitable spirit.

His fine and carefully preserved physique responded to the command of his will. He had to get back into the fight before one of his industrious disciples took advantage of his absence and wrested from him the crown of the ace of German aces. The war took on a new and personal tone to Richthofen.

Chapter X

Richthofen was never the same after that English bullet dented his skull and sent him tumbling down two miles to earth.

Still another score of enemy planes and as many men were yet to fall under his blazing guns, but in the head of the Red Knight of Germany were a scar and a memory that might be overcome but could not be effaced.

Wounded veterans know this. . . .

Men at arms go to their baptism of fire either with courage and hope or with courage and despair. Those that advance with despair usually meet the fate they fear. Those that plunge with hope may get it the same way, but the little something that carries them through is the feeling that their time is not up yet, and that, no matter how many others are killed, they themselves will survive.

It is a God-sent hunch that contributes in no small way to that greatly misunderstood and frequently overestimated quality called bravery.

Untested men, fearful of being cowards, are really ignorant of their potential bravery. "Brave" men emerging from the rest are always conscious of their fears.

Along with courage, Richthofen had always flown and fought with hope and with a feeling of superiority over his enemies. This latter conviction, however, did not permit him to act with contempt for those with whom he fought.

He was convinced he had certain advantages over them, both in training and in equipment, and it was his common-sense game to take full advantage of their handicaps. Post-bellum slogan-slingers bromided these tactics in the recommendation, "Never let the sucker have an even break."

Supplementary to the above conviction, but deep-lying and powerful in its motivating force, was the little inside hunch of personal immunity. He had felt that "his number was not up yet."

After that bullet touched his skull, he was not so sure.

"Manfred was changed after he received his wounds," his mother said. "I noticed numerous differences in him. His fears for Lothar's safety increased, and he was no longer certain that victory would come to our side. He said that people in Germany did not realize the power of the Allies as well as did the men who had to face their forces at the front."

And then there was the one girl he loved. Her letters came to him in the hospital by every mail. He kept them under his pillow. Their marriage had been postponed until after the war. The culmination of their strange romance of self-denial seemed even more distant now. The war seemed endless. Here was America growing stronger in the ranks of the Allies. Would it ever end? Would he survive?

There was lots of time to think about these things while lying on a hospital cot. The thoughts were not pleasing. The more they possessed him, the more that little immunity-hunch weakened. To relieve his mind, he would ask his nurse, Katie Ottersdorf, to read him some of the fan mail that continued to arrive from admirers all over Germany. There was diversion, as well as vanity food, in this general correspondence. The capable Fräulein Ottersdorf, sitting beside the wounded ace's bed, enjoyed the letters thoroughly. Among the many feminine hearts that skipped beats at the thought of Richthofen was a girl in a convent high in the hills of the German Tyrol, not far from the village of Oberammergau.

She was a frequent writer to her hero of the air, and Manfred had been sufficiently touched by the simplicity and sincerity of her letters to answer several of them, but always in the vein that the hopes and desires of individuals had to be suppressed in times of war, and that he had forbidden himself to think of his heart as long as he flew.

She wrote that there were only two objects on the otherwise bare, whitewashed walls of her convent room. One was a crucifix and the other was a photograph of Manfred in uniform and flying helmet. The presence of a man's picture in the room was a violation of the convent rules, and the Mother Superior had ordered its removal.

The girl took the picture down, but with brush and oil paints she covered the flying helmet and uniform with the black and white headdrape of a nun and left the face of the fighting airman looking forth calmly from a frame of religious habiliments.

In this camouflaged form, the picture of her hero remained on the walls of her convent cell until Richthofen's death, when the girl sent it to the ace's mother and, according to the story believed in Schweidnitz, she herself then took the veil.

There were other diversions besides love notes in the hospital at Courtrai. The ace received the attentions of the best surgeons and doctors that Germany could supply. There were frequently painful episodes in which new splinters of bone were removed from his wound, and his scalp was sore for days from thorn points. These had been driven in when he had fallen head first out of his machine after bringing it safely to the ground. He had landed on his head in a briar bush, and the first-aid sergeant, who attended him had shaved the scalp. This operation had cut off the tops of the thorns but had left the fine, sharp points still imbedded in the torn scalp.

The enemy was also attentive. Courtrai's population of 7,000 spent most of its nights, during that month of July, sleeping in cellars or in the fields outside of the town. French and British bombing planes flew almost nightly over the town and dropped tons of more or less well-directed bombs on the railway communications, which were of great military importance to the German war machine.

Richthofen was told that there were many wealthy French and Belgian families native of the town and that they had begged permission of the military authorities to give him an ovation as the airman who had shot down so many of the bombers that were making life unbearable in Courtrai. The ovation never took place.

The ace's father, who was commanding a reserve battalion, was granted leave to visit his son and the two spent many hours sitting together in the garden of the hospital.

German artists, too old for the ranks, came to sketch them.

Things were moving on the front. The battle of Messines, with the English capture of Wytschaete had been succeeded by renewed activity in the Ypres sector as the British applied, or misapplied, more pressure on their costly Flanders offensive. Richthofen's rivals in the air were adding new victories to their grisly scores and although the ace felt his crown safe with his present credit of fifty-seven successful combats, he was anxious to escape both the tedium and pain of the hospital and to return to his command.

A week later, he was back with the squadron, bringing himself up to date on what had happened during his absence. His return to his command was the occasion for an ovation by his surviving comrades and the new replacements who had come in to fill the gaps.

Although his rank remained that of a captain, he was now a squadron commander, with four and sometimes five Jagdstaffels under his orders. The administrative work was handled by ground adjutants. Richthofen continued to fly with Jagdstaffel 11, but it was not the same unit as before.

From the surviving veterans in its ranks had been taken the commanders for the other Jagdstaffels, so that Richthofen missed the old teamwork. The newcomers were keen and eager and well trained, but he did not feel he could place the same dependence upon them in a pinch that he put upon his old comrades. German flying men have since pointed out that Richthofen's successes in the air were never so great after death and promotions had scattered the personnel of the old flying unit. It is also recalled that almost all of the old Jagdstaffel's eleven veterans were dead within six months after they were transferred to command other formations.

After several test flights and front patrols, the ace had his next combat on August 16th, when he and his flyers pounced on a Nieuport single-seater. His report on this fight is missing from the files in the Reichsarchiv but Manfred registered this, his fifty-eighth victory, with a silver death cup, engraved with the type of the plane and the date.

It was his first fight after being wounded, and he knew that he was not the man he had been. The combat made a greater call upon his force and energy. His caution had increased. He was so tired upon his return to the airdrome that he went to bed, from which he arose several hours later unrefreshed by the fitful naps that now took the place of his former sound slumber.

Although he flew on daily patrols in which he endeavoured to revive the old organization spirit among his new flyers, he did not engage in another combat until ten days later, when a lone-flying Spad single-seater fell as his prey. Manfred's report on the fight unconsciously reveals the pains he took to take every advantage of height, sun, numbers, and location before he delivered the death blow. The report reads:

Requesting Acknowledgment of My 59th Victory

Date: Aug. 26th, 1917.
Time: 7:30 A. M.
Place: Between Poelcapelle and Langemarck this side of our lines.
Plane: Spad one-seater. English.

When flying with four gentlemen of my Staffel 11, I detected below me at 9,000 feet, a single Spad flying above a close cover of clouds. The adversary was probably trying to find a low-flying Germany artillery plane.

When he came out of the sun, I attacked him. He tried to escape by diving, but at this moment I shot at him, and he disappeared through the clouds.

I followed him and saw him falling below the clouds, and then he exploded at a height of 1,500 feet.

The new very bad F. B. ammunition had done a lot of damage to my plane, and my pressure pipes, intake pipes, etc., were shot through. It would have been impossible for me to follow an only slightly wounded adversary, and I had to try to turn in as soon as possible.

(Signed) BARON VON RICHTHOFEN,
Captain and Squadron Commander.

The victim of this fight was Second Lieutenant C. P. William, a pilot of the Nineteenth Squadron, R. F. C., who was not looking for German artillery planes at the time, but was engaged as a single escort to another plane, which was performing a "special mission." His combat with Richthofen's Albatross was witnessed from afar by English observation planes. The Germans reported his death several days later.

Richthofen's head had spun and his stomach contracted as he watched Williams go down to his death. This feeling of "squeamishness" was something new that he had to fight against. He revealed his inner feelings two days later in his letter home:

LIEBE MAMMA:

I am glad to hear of Lothar's continuing improvement, but under no circumstances should he be allowed to return to the front before he is entirely fit again.

If he is permitted to do otherwise, he will suffer a relapse or he will be shot down.

I speak from experience.

I have only made two combat fights since my return.

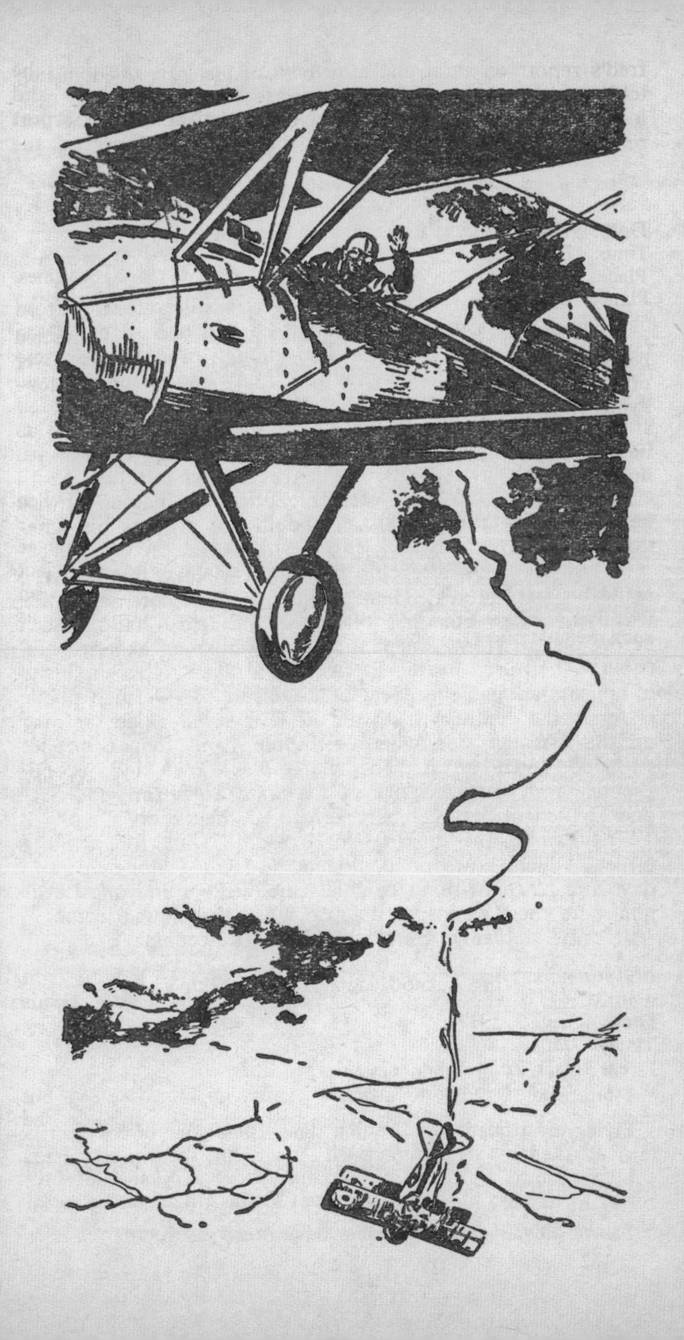

Both were successful, but after both of them I was completely exhausted. During the first one, I nearly became air sick.

My wound is healing very slowly: It is still as large as a five-mark piece. Yesterday they removed another splinter of the bone. I think it will be the last.

Some days ago, the Kaiser visited our section to review the troops. We had a rather long conversation. I am scheduled for leave and am looking forward to seeing you all together.

MANFRED.

It is quite apparent that the ace was still suffering from the effects of his wound. Although he had been back at the front just two weeks, he had had enough of it for the time being, at least, and longed for the safety and peace of leave in the homeland. This was not cowardice. His leave had been granted on the recommendation of the medical officers attached to his squadron. They affirmed that he was not yet in proper condition. With the leave assured but not yet in effect, he flew with even greater caution, so that an unwise engagement or surprise attack should not prevent his withdrawal.

It was six days after his fifty-ninth victory that the ace made his next attack. Then he jumped on a sure thing. He was flying a new Fokker triplane that the British had not seen before on this front, and that was not unlike an experimental triplane then used by the English naval flyers. This similarity in appearance had the effect of disguising the German plane.

Again the victim was an old R. E. bus, all alone far over on the German side when Richthofen and four comrades swooped down on it. The plane was flown by Second-Lieutenant J. B. C. Madge of the Sixth Squadron, and Second-Lieutenant W. Kember performed the observer's office.

They were not looking for "trouble" but for artillery targets, which, however, could not be located alone in those days and places without trouble. One Vickers and one Lewis gun were their means of defence when the trouble came.

It came suddenly. Here's Richthofen's account:

Requesting Acknowledgment of My 60th Victory

Date: Sept. 2, 1917.
Time: 7:50 A. M.
Place: Near Zonnebeke, this side the lines.
Plane: R. E. Two-seater. English.

Flying my triplane for the first time, I and four of my gentlemen attacked a very courageously flown English artillery plane.

I approached and fired twenty shots from a distance of fifty yards, whereupon the Englishman fell to the ground and crashed near Zonnebeke.

It is most probable that the English pilot mistook me for an English triplane, because the observer was standing upright in his plane and watched me approach without making use of his gun.

(Signed) BARON VON RICHTHOFEN,
Captain and Squadron Commander.

On the R.F.C. casualty lists, the finish of Madge's and Kember's air careers is a brief line:

Took off at 6.50 A. M. Machine attacked by E. A. (Enemy Aircraft) and came down in spin over Polygon Wood at 7.40 A. M.

Before returning to his airdrome, Richthofen flew back several miles to the cantonments of rest troops, where he knew his father had headquarters as a major commanding a battalion of reserves. Swooping low over the huts, the ace tossed out of his cockpit a small tin cylinder attached to a streamer of cloth. It fell in a company street and was taken to Major Richthofen, who opened the cylinder and removed a single piece of paper on which had been hastily scribbled:

My sixtieth.—MANFRED.

The performance of the new triplane pleased him. He had the chance to demonstrate his belief in his plane's superiority in a long and hard-fought combat early the next morning.

His account of the fight reads:

Requesting Acknowledgment of My 61st Victory

Date: Sept. 3, 1917.
Time: 7:35 A. M.
Place: South of Bousbecque, this side of the lines.
Type of Plane: Sopwith one-seater, No. B. 1795; 80 H. P. Le Rhone type "R" motor No. 35,123, carrying machine gun No. A 4723.
Occupant: Lieutenant A. F. Bird, made prisoner unwounded.
My Own Plane: Fokker F. I. 102—17 triplane.

Being engaged together with five planes of Staffel 11 in a fight with a Sopwith one-seater Spad, I attacked, at an altitude of 10,000 feet, one of the enemy's machines.

After considerable manœuvring, I succeeded in forcing it to the ground near Bousbecque. I was absolutely convinced that I had a very capable opponent, because he refused to surrender even after I had forced him down as low as fifty yards above the ground. Even then, he kept right on shooting.

Before he landed, he emptied his machine gun into a column of our infantry, and then, when on the ground, deliberately steered his plane into a tree and smashed it.

The Fokker Triplane, F. I. 102—17, was undoubtedly better and more reliable than the English machine.

(Signed) BARON VON RICHTHOFEN,
Captain and Squadron Commander.

Lieutenant Bird read Richthofen's report of the affair, but refused to add to it.

The report of Bird's capture is one of the best authenticated in Richthofen's collection, and serves as a sample of the method by which the claims of the German aces were presented to their superiors.

Attached to the report were seven affidavits of officers and men who had witnessed the fight.

Richthofen's report with the affidavits attached was forwarded by the ground adjutant of the ace's command to air headquarters, where it was considered and credit granted. The signed testimony and details accompanying the flyer's claims indicate the pains taken by the higher command to eliminate false claims. At times the job of deciding and giving the credit was an arduous one, as two or more flyers frequently claimed the same victims. These claims and counter claims were by no means confined to the German air service.

In the Allied air services the establishment of credit for German planes brought down was even more difficult, because, in the large majority of cases, the victims fell behind their own lines.

Richthofen now got a leave, and by special invitation of the government was allowed to hunt elk, which had become almost extinct, on a reservation in East Prussia. At the end of the expedition he wrote to his mother:

Gotha, Schloss Hotel,
Sept. 30, 1917.

LIEBE MAMMA:

I was extremely glad to hear of Lothar's sudden recovery. On my return from leave we can again go up together and show the English a few tricks. We will be in the same squadron.

My bag during the last fortnight has been far from bad—a large elk, three excellent stags, and a buck. I am rather proud of my record, because Papa has only shot three stags in all his life. I am leaving for Berlin to-day and will be with you in less than a week.

MANFRED.

Showing the English tricks in the air was becoming harder than ever, in spite of Richthofen's restored enthusiasm and healed nerves. Just a week before the above letter was written, the British themselves had been able to show a few new tricks in planes, pilots, and manœuvres that had cost the German Air Service one of its greatest pilots, the Reserve Lieutenant Werner Voss, an old friend of Richthofen and the flyer whose killings in the air closest approached the record of the first German ace. Voss had been shot down in an heroic struggle against odds.

Another ace whose career ended during that month of September when Richthofen was fortunate enough to be on leave was Captain Guynemer, the conqueror of fifty-five German planes and the idol of France. On September 11th, Guynemer, in the midst of a terrific air duel, went down between the blazing lines near Poelcapelle. The Germans recovered his body and placed it in a dugout that was later destroyed by artillery. The remains of the French ace have never been found, but in the hearts of the French people his place will always be that of the greatest hero of the air.

Richthofen spent a week in Berlin, where his every appearance caused excitement, and then a week with his mother at Schweidnitz. The farewell of the mother and son at the end of this visit was their last.

November found the ace and squadron commander back at the front in time to participate in the battle of Cambrai, which opened on the 20th with the tank attack by the British. These were the operations that brought the Allied offensive of 1917 to its bloody, futile close.

Richthofen's next victories, his sixty-second and sixty-third, were over Lieutenant A. Griggs and Captain P. T. Townsend, respectively. The exact fates of these men have never been learned. Their bodies were not found.

As cold weather gripped the fighting fronts, air activity lessened, and the ace turned his mind to thoughts of home and plans for spending his third Christmas in the Flying Corps. He wrote:

In the field, Dec. 11, 1917.

LIEBE MAMMA:

There is little doing here at present and things are consequently rather dull. I am leaving for Speyer to-day to look over an airplane plant.

Christmas I intend spending with my squadron, together with Papa and Lothar. My orderly has already sent a Christmas parcel to Bolko, and I trust I have succeeded in meeting a cadet's tastes.

MANFRED.

Another young Richthofen—Bolko—was taking his training for war.

The last year of the war, which was to be the year of his death, dawned happily for the Kaiser's deadliest ace. In January he went to Brest-Litovsk, and saw the revolutionary delegates of a beaten and disorganized Russia forced to accept the peace laid down to them by Germany.

He mingled and dined with the diplomats of Germany and her allies and met many of the Russian revolutionaries who believed they had found victory for their own cause in the defeat of their country. Some of them were women communists, and one in particular—a Madame Bicenko—interested Manfred deeply because of her vivid personality.

On the whole, however, diplomatic negotiations bored him, and, with permission from the commander in chief of the eastern front, he made a trip by sleigh to the forest of Bialowicza, there to hunt for bison and red stag in an old hunting preserve of the Romanoffs. He was accompanied by his brother Lothar, and hard-bitten by the snow, the cold, and the wind, the two brothers returned to Berlin January 20th, in high spirits. Before leaving the eastern front Manfred wrote:

January 15, 1918.

LIEBE MAMMA:

You will wonder why you have been so long without news from me, but that is always an indication that I am well. In this case, however, I have been seeing much. Lothar has already written you that we were in Brest-Litovsk. There we saw and were introduced to all the prominent diplomats. I should like very much to tell you all about it. As it is, I can only write you that peace was concluded along the lines laid down by Ludendorff. For a few days, we roamed through the forests around Bialowicza, where each of us shot a stag. The stay in the quiet forest has done us both a world of good. I will be in Berlin for a fortnight after the twentieth, when I hope to be able to see you.

MANFRED.

On the front, the situation in the air was changing. Russia's collapse had not only released German armies, but also German air squadrons, for duty in the west, where now, if ever, the Central Powers would have to force a decision before the arrival of America's full strength on the fighting line. Germany's intentions to break through to the Channel ports and separate the British and French armies were suspected. The Allies awaited the moment of the great enemy offensive with intense anxiety.

The British had profited by the costly lesson of April,

1917. Their terrific losses in the air had caused much inquiry and public questioning. An air board had been established, and new life had been injected into the air service to speed up the supply and distribution of material for the fighting airmen and at the same time to improve the equipment upon which they had to depend. Regular army "crocks" were booted out of the technical departments, and England's best brains were applied to the all-important work of aëronautical research.

Then the entire air service was reorganized by a fusion of the Royal Flying Corps with the separate Royal Naval Air Service, and this great third arm, called the Royal Air Force, was placed under the authority of a special secretary of state whose status was equal to that of the political heads of both the army and the navy departments.

In the training department, special attention was paid to marksmanship. It had been found costly to send expert flyers into the air if they couldn't use their machine guns effectively. A bad shot in the air represented wasted time and effort. He was "cold meat" for the enemy flyer who knew how to handle his triggers. In the air-training camps in France, special devices were rigged up in which pilots practised quick shooting.

To replace air mechanics who had been promoted to service in the air, English girls from homes and schools went eagerly into the grease and oil of the hangars and worked long hours on the repairing of planes. Other girls took the places of orderlies or motorcycle messengers, releasing these men for fighting service.

King George, Queen Mary, and the Prince of Wales began to honour the air service with attentions similar to those bestowed upon the senior services. They visited the airdromes in France, inspected damaged British planes, and talked with English, Canadian, and American flyers who had fought Richthofen and his circus.

At the same time, big improvements were made in the anti-aircraft artillery and ground defences that were required to keep German bombers and ground strafers a greater distance from the ground. The mechanical and administrative personnel of all airdromes in France were trained in anti-aircraft defence with all manner of improvised weapons. As the fighting reached higher altitudes, the use of oxygen tanks became necessary.

The effect of all of these new but delayed attentions to the air service began to show in the number of victories that these flyers were able to chalk up against the Germans.

At the beginning of the year, the British were equipped with Sopwith "Camels" or S. E. 5's which had a ceiling of 15,000 feet and could do 117 miles an hour at that height. There were Spads and Nieuports which could better this speed. The "Camel," upon improvement, developed into a type called the "Dolphin" and this was later succeeded by the "Snipe," which had still greater speed.

The Germans were using mostly the Fokker scout and triplane. Fokker and Junker monoplanes with 220 horse-power motors developed speeds of 150 miles an hour later in the year. The Albatross and Halberstadt models were considered the best fighting planes. The Germans suffered an increasing deficiency in essential materials, but never once gave up the race in the improvement of engines and the development of high-powered scout machines.

In spite of the best efforts of their engineering and efficiency experts and the endeavours of their combat leaders, German losses in the air increased throughout the spring. On March 8th and 9th, 44 German planes were shot down. On March 24th, 45 were destroyed and 22 driven down, as against 10 British planes. The English records claim 372 German planes destroyed and 205 driven down for the month of March. In the following month of April, the month of Richthofen's death, 172 enemy machines were destroyed and 75 driven down out of control.

German pilots driven down by non-fatal wounds behind their own lines or successful in making a landing there with disabled planes were not *hors de combat,* as most British and French pilots were under similar circumstances for the reason that the most of the fighting occurred over the German lines. A wounded German pilot landing successfully behind his own lines had immediate first-aid treatment and stood a good chance of being back in the fighting as soon as he recovered.

There is ample photographic evidence in the German archives to prove that many of the planes shot down suffered serious crashes, in which it is most probable that their pilots did not escape death.

It must not be believed, however, that the German air force always confined its activities to its own side of the line, because photographs in the British archives show many German planes that were brought down behind the British lines, over which they must have been fighting at the time.

The struggle in the air was inclining to the side of the Allies, and Manfred was not blind to it, those last days in Berlin when he received the acclaim of the crowds. He knew that the chances of death were piling up against him, and there is a prophetic note in the letter that he sent to his mother after his return to the front. He wrote:

At the Front, Feb. 11, 1918.

LIEBE MAMMA:

I am sorry that I was kept in Berlin so long that I could not come to Schweidnitz to say good-bye. It would have been so pleasant, and I was looking forward to it.

Now I think I will not come back to Germany for a long, long time.

Keep Lothar with you as long as possible. He is rather negligent with his ears and does nothing to cure them. He loses nothing here. Tell him from me, he should not leave before the first of March. Should things become more lively here, I will advise him by wire.

I am afraid Bolko is angry with me, but it was really impossible to make a landing in Wahlstadt. In the fall, with the crops off the field, I will do it surely.

MANFRED.

Toward the end of February and during the first days of March, aërial activity increased as the day of the great German offensive of 1918 approached. Lothar came to the front and joined his brother's squadron. On March 12th, Manfred shot down his next English plane and captured its two occupants, one of whom he had wounded in the air. The prisoners were Second Lieutenant L. C. F. Clutterbuck, a pilot of the Sixty-second Squadron, and his observer and gunner, Second Lieutenant H. J. Sparks, M. C. Manfred reported the capture as follows:

Requesting Acknowledgment of My 64th Victory

Date: March 12, 1918.
Time: Between 11:10 and 11:15 A. M.
Place: North of Nauroy, Square No. 2858.
Type of Enemy Plane, Bristol fighter, No. 1251; Motor, Rolls Royce 200 H. P. 12 Cyl. V-Shaped, No. 275.

Together with Lieutenant Lothar von Richthofen and Lieutenant Steinhäuser, both of Staffel 11, we attacked an enemy squadron between Caudry and Le Cateau at an altitude of 16,000 feet, far behind our lines.

The plane I attacked immediately dived down several thousand feet and tried to escape. The observer, who had fired only when high in the air, had then disappeared in his cockpit and only began firing again shortly before the machine landed.

During the fight, we had drifted off to Le Catelet. There I forced my adversary to land, and after doing this, both passengers left the plane.

(Signed) BARON VON RICHTHOFEN,
Captain and Squadron Commander.

The German ace never knew the names of these two

prisoners, and neither Clutterbuck nor Sparks was aware that their captor was Richthofen until the recent unearthing of the Flying Uhlan's report, which carried the number of the fallen English plane. Identification and location of the two English prisoners was possible through this number.

Clutterbuck wrote the following account of his last fight in the air:

It is nine years since the greatest incident in my life happened. It finished my career as a flying officer but, as a Hun officer remarked, "The war is finished for you," meaning that, being a prisoner of war, I should at least see the end of hostilities.

Until I saw the copy of Richthofen's own report, I believed that I had been brought down by one of the members of Richthofen's celebrated circus, and had no idea that it was the famous Baron himself whom I had tried to down and who succeeded in downing me and badly wounding my observer. Every detail of the scrap is as fresh in my mind as though it happened yesterday, but I can't begin telling it without paying my little tribute to Baron von Richthofen and the men who comprised what was known as his circus.

To my mind, they were undoubtedly the pick of the German airmen and although their methods of attack were different from our own, they were no mean adversaries, and certainly they were fine pilots, for which statement I can personally vouch. Richthofen handled his machine cleverly, was an excellent shot, and was entirely fearless.

It should be remembered that the German machines very seldom had the temerity to cross our lines, and when they did, it was usually at a great height, and consequently we seldom had the chance of a scrap on our side of the lines.

The squadron to which I belonged, namely 62, was equipped with the latest types of Bristol fighters. We flew over to France in January, 1918, having extensively trained together for several weeks in England, and I think I can say that we were quite an efficient body. After preliminary work in France, we were detailed to give our attention solely to fighting, and it was our job to patrol twenty to thirty miles inside the German lines and to knock down anything we encountered.

It was a delightful job; no red tape about reports when we got back, no bombs to carry, and no reconnaissance to make. Just scrapping, and, incidentally, we got it.

The day before I was brought down, the squadron had accounted for, and had had confirmed, fourteen machines of the circus, and we had lost no machines, nor had we had any casualties.

The fatal day for me, we set out nine strong, and after being over the lines for two hours at a height of 18,000 feet, we had not commenced operations, although the Germans had a decoy in the shape of a two-seater hovering below us, but the air had been rapidly filling with machines for some time.

My great friend Lieutenant G. Gibbons was flying on my left, and suddenly I saw him go down as though to attack the large two-seater. I followed him down, and my observer, Lieutenant Sparks, M. C., as usual tested his gun, but, curiously enough one empty cartridge case flew into my cockpit and lodged down between the tank and the joy stick, which rather curtailed my movements to climb. My friend in the meantime pulled out of the dive and climbed up again, while I continued to lose height until I managed to poke the cartridge case aside. By that time, my formation was some three thousand feet above me and a long way off.

A few minutes later, the three machines that had been in our vicinity for some time attacked me, and I had a little difficulty in placing my machine in a good position for my observer, owing to their coming out of the sun; that is, they kept the sun behind them and in a line with my machine—a position favoured by all experienced pilots.

My observer managed to get off a few bursts before he collapsed. I looked over into his cockpit and saw him huddled up, apparently dead. I quickly decided the combat was unequal and tried to withdraw. The Bristol fighters were excessively strong, and I had often dived them with the engine full on, and could always leave anything behind me in a dive.

I did so on this occasion until, glancing at my planes, I saw several of my bracing wires streaming aft. They had evidently been shot away in our little scrap. I pulled out of the dive at 4,000 feet and, to my astonishment, found I was much farther over the lines than I had thought at first. I now kept the machine's nose down and kept up a steady 140-mile streak for home, passing under numerous German machines.

Soon I discovered a machine gaining on me from above and behind. I unstrapped my belt and endeavoured to obtain my observer's gun, but, unfortunately, was unable to reach it; otherwise I could have continued my flight home and kept the enemy machine off my tail.

Gradually but surely, owing to his height, he gained on me—a sinister demon getting closer and closer every minute. I figured I should have to interrupt my flight home and try to send him down, so when I thought he was near enough, I turned and faced him. We were now approaching each other, nearer, nearer, at a terrific pace, neither giving way on direction and neither firing until quite close, when I believe we both opened fire simultaneously. My gun, after a few rounds, jammed—a number three stoppage, which usually took about three minutes to rectify in the air.

Now my gun was out of action and my adversary's guns were very busy. He had two of them firing through the propeller. For the moment I think I lost my head and decided to ram him head on, but he decided otherwise and passed below me a matter of a few feet.

He then tried to get on my tail or in a suitable position to hit me while I decided to ram him with my undercarriage, but always he would manage to pass a few feet under me, looking up into my face. I often wonder if he divined my intentions. During these dives he would get into a burst at me while flying in a vertical turn or from various weird angles. Although my machine was heavier than his single-seater, he seemed unable then to get above me or to sit on my tail, the fatal position.

After some trying minutes of these gyrations, my forward petrol tank either gave out or he put a shot through it, so I dived again and switched over to the other tank, and was now flying about one hundred feet up, but this time I was getting nearer to the lines, and in a few minutes I would be safe. Of course, I knew my adversary would continue to follow me down, which he did, and just sat on my tail pumping lead into me.

I suppose his machine was just a few miles faster than mine, because I could not gain on him, and all the time he kept firing bursts into me. I kept kicking the rudder to alter my direction and confuse his aim. This went on for a while, and I began to hope that he would run out of ammunition when, suddenly, my observer, whom I had taken for dead, got up to his gun and started firing.

It is hard to imagine my joy. I shouted and cheered the stout fellow. Half his arm was shot away, and he had been unconscious for some time and weak from loss of blood, but he had managed to crawl up to his gun and get off a burst. It was too much for him, however, for he sank back in a heap again.

My spirits dropped as quickly as they had risen, and a few moments later my adversary had punctured my petrol tank. It was a pressure-feed, and in spite of my efforts to pump up the pressure by hand, the engine gradually petered out, and before I knew what I was doing I was on the ground among shell holes. I pancaked from about five feet and stopped with my wheels in a shell hole.

By the time I had helped my observer out of the machine, the Germans rushed out of their dugouts and took great pleasure in telling us on which side of the lines we were, and so prevented us from firing the machine. Another minute in the air and I should have been on our side of the line, as it was only two miles away.

My observer was treated with great courtesy and kindness and his wounds dressed in a near-by dugout. We have nothing but praise for the manner in which we were treated near the line. We eventually arrived at a village a few miles away, where many troops were quartered and it amused us to see them turn out their band. When we inquired the reason, we were informed it was to celebrate our capture.

My observer and I eventually parted at Le Cateau, where he went to a hospital and I to a cell to be questioned by officers. We were generously offered a dish of likely looking horse and macaroni, but had it been *pâté de foie gras,* I am afraid we could not have eaten it at that moment. To the officer who looked after us, we tendered our best thanks for his kindness.

Lt. Sparks was a soldier before the war, having purchased his discharge from the Royal Marine Band, in 1913, after five years service. He reënlisted in the Black Watch in 1915, and received his commission as a lieutenant, April 1917, in the King's Royal Rifle Corps, where he won his military Cross.

Sparks transferred to the Flying Corps in August, 1917, and began flying in France in December of that year. After the war he became a government inspector of taxes at Sittingbourne. Here is his vivid recollection of the day Richthofen shot him on the wing:

There were eight of us Bristol fighters patrolling the line from Cambrai to Caudry or Le Cateau. Clutterbuck and I were flying in the machine on the extreme right at about 13,000 feet. We were due to leave the line at 11:05 A. M. At about 10:55, Clutterbuck drew my attention to three enemy machines hovering below. They had those noticeable fish tails, but otherwise, being highly coloured, they could not be detected as Huns. I quite anticipated a hot time, as I could hear machine-gun fire overhead, but, although I was equipped with glasses, I could see nothing on account of the dazzling sun.

About 11, our flight commander Captain Kennedy, M. C., fired a red Very light, which was the signal to prepare for action. I had been keeping my eyes on the three enemy planes below me. But no sooner had the action signal been given than we were pounced on from above by various types of Hun machines numbering about twenty. I could tell from the red under carriages that they were members of Richthofen's circus.

It seemed that it didn't matter which way my pilot turned, an iron-cross plane would appear. Clutterbuck immediately spun down. The last thing I noticed before he went into the spin was the flight commander's plane bursting into flames and the occupants falling out.

After our dive of about eighteen-hundred feet, we came in contact with the three machines that had been below us. . . . One after another, they attacked us. My pilot was busy placing me in position to fire, but it was difficult to take accurate aim, as new machines were always appearing above us. During these attacks, we came into very close range, and eventually I managed to get a good burst into a machine that was painted with black and white squares. I saw it go down entirely out of control. Clutterbuck and I both saw this machine on the ground afterwards while we were being led away as prisoners.

I was just getting into position to try my luck with the all-red machine which I presume was Richthofen's, but the baron got me before I got him. His first stream of lead went through my left shoulder and arm, rendering me entirely useless. The shock knocked me down into the cockpit.

But Clutterbuck never gave up. He put up an excellent fight with two Huns picking at him all the time. Our machine was completely riddled with bullets, and I will never understand why more of them did not hit us. I tried persistently to ring out a few shots, but I was too handicapped, and finally Clutterbuck was forced to land. Had I not been wounded so early in the fight, I believe I could have made it much more interesting for the baron. The time of the combat was about fifteen minutes, which is a long time for actually every minute fighting in the air. It seemed like fifteen weeks.

After landing, we were surrounded by German soldiers who seemed to spring from nowhere. They prevented us from destroying the plane. A German officer and his orderly, both on horseback, rode up, and the officer questioned us in broken English and finally led us away to a dressing station where my wounds were dressed.

We were taken to a battalion headquarters, I riding on the orderly's horse. I felt like Nelson the second or King Cole, riding in this manner through a big crowded village which I think was Caudry. We lunched with the German guard on coffee and black bread, after which we were taken in a motor car to Le Cateau and interviewed by some German general.

Clutterbuck and I would give no information concerning the number and whereabouts of our squadron, and refused to answer many other questions they put to us. . . . The general got rather annoyed and ordered us taken away. I was detained in the base hospital and Clutterbuck——I don't know where he vanished to, as I have never seen him since that moment.

During my second day in the hospital, a German flying officer came in and said he had been sent to see me by Baron von Richthofen, who wished me to accept half a dozen cigars with his compliments. I did, with thanks. The treatment received as a prisoner of war was nothing brilliant, and yet was not so bad under the circumstances. The worst time I experienced was the few months in the hospital.

Richthofen had followed his disabled opponents to the ground and frustrated their last attempts to regain their own lines and safety.

On the following day, March 13th, Lothar von Richthofen was shot down almost out of control behind the German lines, and crashed.

That smash kept Lothar in the hospital a number of weeks. It was the worst one he ever had during the war, which he survived with the rank of a first lieutenant and almost as many decorations as his brother. He was credited with bringing down forty British planes. In 1919, he married the Countess Doris von Keyserling, the daughter of an old privy counsellor to the Kaiser. There was a daughter by the marriage, but trouble followed the romance of the gallant war bird, and it ended in a separation.

Three years later, on July 4, 1922, Lothar and an American film actress, Fern Andra, and the latter's manager, were flying from Hamburg to Berlin in an old war-type plane. Motor trouble, a forced landing, another unseen electric wire, and a crash in which the war bird lost his life while his two passengers suffered serious injuries.

On that day of Lothar's almost fatal crash at the front, his famous brother fought, if possible, with even increased determination. He drove off the British planes that were in pursuit of his brother's disabled triplane and shot down one of the pursuing British pilots.

Although Richthofen flew daily during the next five days, during which there were numerous combats between large numbers of hostile planes, he did not succeed in bringing down his next plane, his sixty-sixth, until March 18th. The victim who survived without a wound but spent the rest of the war as a prisoner was William G. Ivamy.

I managed to survive at it until that day I came in contact with the jolly old Baron [Ivamy wrote]. It happened this way: A naval bombing squadron had been detailed to bomb the German airdrome at Molain on March 16th and 17th, and to do it without escort. On the next day, the 18th, the day of my last fight, the bombers were given an escort of ten S. E. 5's and nine Camels.

We crossed south of St. Quentin following the D. H. 4's, which carried the bombs. They were down around 9,000 feet and we were up around 12,000. I was deputy flight commander and brought up the rear of the last formation. After we were about 8 miles across, I could see the German planes getting into position to have a smash at us, they being about 3,000 feet above us and seeming to number between 50 and 60.

As we were following the bombers, the German planes were in position on four sides of us and above. Directly the D. H. 4's had dropped their bombs, they turned for home, and this evidently was the signal for the Germans to attack, and the lot of them came down on us with a bang.

Their plan of attack was to get anyone with streamers on. As deputy flight commander, I flew these streamers, and being in the rear of the flight and highest up, I got it first. I can't say that I had much of a fight with his highness the baron, as I was slightly handicapped from the start, having an explosive bullet in the petrol tank and the emergency tank being punctured.

I was saturated and blinded with petrol and sitting up there with a dead engine. There was nothing to do but descend, which I did in a veering nose dive. I have a faint recollection of the speed indicator going off the scale, but the old Sopwith hung together, and I made the best landing I ever made up the side of a hill among a bunch of German infantry who were training for the big push. They appeared none too friendly with their rifles. By the time I could get out of the bus, three German planes were buzzing around over it, and the scrap up above seemed to be over.

I looked up and saw that the S. E. 5's had pulled away a bit to the north, so we were rather in the soup. We lost five out of our nine: the flight leader, two deputy flight leaders, and two new fellows, three of them prisoners and two killed.

The S. E.'s lost two and the bombers one, and I don't know what the German casualties were. It was just two days after this that the big German push of March, 1918, began, and this accounts for the number of German machines that were in the air that morning. That was the end for me, as I was a guest of the Kaiser till the Armistice.

I am awfully curious about how Richthofen counted his victims. I have heard from various sources that the number of machines shot down by his entire circus was claimed by him personally and after the holy mix-up that morning, I should imagine it would be hard for anyone definitely to claim any one, especially a machine shot down at the beginning of the fight.

It appears from Richthofen's report that he, in command of three Staffels totalling thirty planes, must have been operating that morning in conjunction with another German squadron of equal strength, to comprise the sixty planes that Ivamy saw.

Individual man-to-man and plane-to-plane fighting that had won for the airmen their comparison with the knights of old was still the backbone of combat aloft, but the tendency to organization flying began to show itself more and more.

This factor, which begins at this period to make its appearance in the annals of all the fighting air services, is most significant, inasmuch as it probably marks the twilight of the days when knighthood ruled the air.

It was almost inevitable in the opinion of air experts that the war birds of future conflicts would have as much opportunity for individual combat as the infantryman of the Great War had for bayonet work. Control of the air would be decided, not by individual aces but by wings, flights, swarms, flocks, squadrons, fleets, clouds, and avalanches of highly specialized planes that would manœuvre under a central control. Team work would beat individual stardom in the air, as it does on land and sea.

Organized air fighting increased on both sides beyond all previous limits as the zero hour for the great German offensive of 1918 drew near. The onslaught opened early on the morning of March 21st, and Picardy, the ancient cockpit of Europe, was the scene over which the airmen flew to the aid and opposition of the conflicting ground forces.

The general fighting, which is known as the first battle of the Somme, 1918, opened with the battle for St. Quentin, which the Germans won decisively in three days' terrific struggle over the area bounded by the river Oise to Chauny, then the road to Guiscard, to Ham, to Péronne, to Bapaume, to Boyelles, and thence to the river Cojeul.

Again it was Richthofen's old stamping ground, and he knew it with the instinct of bird as well as man. He flew daily, but his new duties as commander of a bigger organization required that he stay aloft, observe and direct his fighting units rather than engage in personal combats that would have boosted his score of killings.

The German advance on the ground seemed overpowering. The British retreat had begun, and by March 24th, when the fighting extended all along the line of the Somme from Ham to Hem, it had become almost a débâcle. It might well have been, had it not been for the heroic services rendered on that day by the Allied air forces.

One English pilot who fought against Richthofen's circus broke all previous records by personally shooting down six of the forty-five German planes that were destroyed on, or above, the battlefield that day. His name is J. L. Trollope.

Richthofen commanded some of the planes Trollope downed that day. On the night before what both sides still call "The day of the great battle," Richthofen wrote a letter to his mother. It is the last one of these epistles that have been found to date.

He knew the plans for the morning and the uncertainty that went with them. He felt that it might be his last letter home, but he managed to keep this feeling out of the words he sent to the gray-haired woman who waited and prayed in the white house in Schweidnitz.

The letter read:

March 23, 1918,
In the Field.

LIEBE MAMMA:

You will have received my wire advising you of Lothar's fall. Thanks to God, he is doing nicely. I visit him daily. Please, Mother, don't worry about anything. He is really doing quite well.

His nose has already healed, only the jaw is still bad, but he will keep his teeth. Above his right eye he has a rather large hole, but the eye itself has not been damaged. Several blood vessels burst under his right knee and in the left calf.

The blood he spit out did not come from any internal injuries. He had merely swallowed some during his fall. He is in the hospital in Cambrai and hopes to be back at the front within a fortnight. His only regret is not to be able to be with us at the present moment.

MANFRED.

It was a busy five days that Richthofen started the following morning. In spite of speed and distance, the squadron commander, as the highest ranking officer in the air, had to keep in the closest possible communication with all of the planes under his control. Communication between planes at this time consisted principally of visual signals either by wing movements, streamers, or different-coloured pistol rockets. At the same time, the leader had to observe the approach of enemy units from all directions and not permit his own force to be taken unawares.

Nevertheless, in the five days that followed, he found time enough off from his executive duties in the air to engage in the actual fighting to the extent of downing one plane on each of the first two days, two on the third day, three on the fourth day, and one on the fifth day of the all-eventful period, which he concluded with his victory score boosted from sixty-six to seventy-four.

On the first day, March 24, Richthofen shot the wings from the plane of Second Lieutenant Wilson Porter, Jr., of Port Dover, Ontario; Wilson's body and the pieces of the plane fell to the earth.

In his reports Richthofen showed strict attention to facts, and particularly the fact of fire, as is shown in his report of the very next afternoon, when nineteen-year-old Second Lieutenant Donald Cameron went down in a wreath of flames and smoke, started by the twin streams of hot lead that the Flying Uhlan fired into him at a range of fifty yards. He reported:

Requesting Acknowledgment of My 68th Victory

Date: March 25, 1918.
Time: 3:55 P.M.
Place: Above Bapaume, Albert Road, near Contalmaison.
Plane: Sopwith one-seater. Burned. Englishman (beginner).

With five planes of Staffel 11, I attacked several English one-seaters northeast of Albert.

I approached to within fifty yards of one of the machines and shot it to flames.

The burning machine fell between Contalmaison and Albert and burned on the ground. Bombs that had apparently been in the plane exploded several minutes later.

(Signed) BARON VON RICHTHOFEN,
Captain and Squadron Commander.

The incendiary words "burn," "flames," and "explode" occur five times in the comparatively short report, and there is clear evidence that Richthofen was much more affected by those victories in which he sent his opponents down in flames than by any others.

Second Lieutenant W. Knox, a young Welshman from Cardiff and a fighting pilot of the Fifty-fourth Squadron, appears from an examination of all available material to have been the next living fuel for the fiery spirit of the air demon. On March 26th Knox was shot down in flames while on a patrol late in the afternoon. This was Richthofen's sixty-ninth victory.

Fifteen minutes after the death of Knox, Richthofen shot down in flames a British R. E. old type, two-seater.

There were two British R. E.'s missing that afternoon. The four men that flew in them were never heard of again. These obsolete machines, undoubtedly sent aloft as last straws to relieve the British emergency on the ground, were the easiest possible prey for the fast-flying Fokker triplanes.

Of the two daring ones who tried to fill the gap with their lives, it is most likely, from the available accounts, that Second Lieutenant Matt Leggat and his pilot, Second Lieutenant V. J. Reading, were the victims of Richthofer's seventieth. Armed with Lewis and Vickers guns, they had left the Fifteenth Squadron airdrome shortly after four o'clock in the afternoon to patrol the German line near Albert, and return, if possible, with a report of size and whereabouts of the German reserves then being brought forward. This would account for their flying at a low height (Richthofen's report says 2,000 feet) over so dangerous a part of the active front. They never came back.

The second R. E. that fell in the fighting that day and was most probably sent down by some of Richthofen's *"Herren"* was occupied by Lieutenant Observer C. E. Wharram and Second Lieutenant T. H. Buswell. They were engaged on an afternoon bombing expedition with other members of the Fifty-second Squadron.

Richthofen's aim and ammunition were proving particularly disastrous in the big push. Having set fire to two planes in the air on March 26th, he followed it the next day by firing three more, with similar fatal results.

Richthofen's seventy-first victim was H. W. Ransom, a twenty-one-year-old boy from Hertfordshire who had served in South Africa. Richthofen's report shows that he sent Ransom's plane down, in flames, into the "flooded part of the Ancre."

For his second victim of the day, the Flying Baron jumped on a low-flying two-seater plane of the Bristol fighter type.

Richthofen brought it down smoking and described it as burning, which was a mistake, because at least one of its occupants lived to tell the tale. Richthofen's report says that the fight took place at half past four near Foucancourt.

The English casualty records for that afternoon, hour, and place indicate that the occupants of Manfred's seventy-second were Captain K. R. Kirkham at the pilot's stick and Captain J. H. Hedley in the observer's coop. Nobody got hurt, and a delightful time was had by all, according to Hedley. Hedley said he and Kirkham were shot down from a low height but landed safely about twelve miles back of the German lines. He also said that they were brutally treated as prisoners. Hedley had previously had a remarkable experience while acting as an observer in the plane of a Canadian officer named Makepeace. They had been in an air fight when Hedley had been thrown into the air. He had fallen several hundred feet as the plane dove down almost vertically, and landed on the plane's tail. He had been brought safely to earth in that position. One wonders whether there is any thrill left for such a man to look forward to.

Five minutes after "his nibs, the Baron," as Hedley calls him, had shot Hedley and Kirkham down into the hands of the advancing German infantry, the Flying Uhlan put down in flames his third plane for the day and for this one the record on the English casualty list reads: "Never heard of again."

Much difficulty surrounded the identification of this victim, but the closest examination of the records indicates that he was Captain H. R. Child, a pilot of Squadron 11, who was flying a Bristol fighter two-seater on a special mission between Albert and the Somme. Child's civilian address was the Royal Air Force Club in London, but the records of the club show that he was never heard from again after that night when he lifted his last glass in the club smokeroom, said "cheerio" to his table mates, and returned to his squadron in France.

Three in one day was a pleasant reassurance to the Flying Uhlan that he was getting back into his old form, but it could not wipe out the fact that the total German air losses for the previous three days had been much larger than those of the British.

On the following day he shot down in flames an Armstrong two-seater flying homeward near Méricourt. It was his seventy-fourth victory and his last in March.

His victims were another team of nineteen-year-old second "looies"—Joseph Bertram Taylor and E. Betley. There is a noticeable absence of names and identifying numbers on Richthofen's reports during the days of the big German push, and this is quite understandable in view of the facts that the

Germans were advancing daily, that the ground they captured was battle torn and impossible for safe landing, and that communication between the rear and the advanced areas was almost impossible. Three English Armstrong planes were shot down that day, but two of them fell behind their own lines and were accounted for. The only unaccounted one was that occupied by Betley and Taylor, who were reported lost over the enemy line.

That day of his seventy-fourth victory marked the opening of the first battle of Arras, 1918, but it concluded Richthofen's string of successful combats for the month. While the fighting on the ground continued with intensity, there appears a lull of six days in the records of the German ace, during which he did not score again for death.

He resumed fighting on the third day of the next month, April, 1918—the last month of his life.

Chapter XI

The badge of the brave . . . the pay of the proud . . . another decoration was the reward granted to Richthofen on the first day of the last month of his life.

Three weeks later, his admiring and respectful enemies nailed still another one on his coffin. This was the thin plate of service duralumin on which were inscribed in English and German his name, age, date, and place of his death in action.

It was the Kaiser himself who signed the citation on April 1, 1918, by which the Red Knight of Germany added another, and the last, ribbon-hung bauble to the collection of gallant hardware that adorned the breast of his dress tunic.

This accumulation of highly prized and well-earned symbols of courage now assumed more the proportions of a bandolier than of a medal bar. It represented twenty-six special citations for bravery and service, and included among others the Pour le Mérite, the order of the Red Eagle, the Iron Cross of the First and Second Class, the order of the House of Hohenzollern, the Bulgarian Cross for Bravery, the German and Austrian Pilot Badges, the separate and highest orders of the states of Mecklenburg, Bavaria, Guttenberg, Coburg, Saxony, Hamburg, and Bremen, and three Turkish decorations, concerning the meaning and importance of which Manfred was more or less in the dark.

He had won all the martial distinction there was to win except that last and highest one that is conferred on Christian soldiers, not by kings or the high ranking, but by a simple burial detail. The French called this decoration the Croix de Bois. As the war birds used to say, it was not conferred with a kiss on the cheek, but the recipient of the honour was smacked in the face with a spade.

Manfred's last medal was granted to him in recognition of his seventieth victory—the late afternoon party of five days before, when he shot Leggat and Reading down in flames. The citation did not reach him until after he had added five more to his "bag."

That fifth one, his seventy-fifth, was paid for with the lives of nineteen-year-old Second Lieutenant E. D. Jones and Second Lieutenant R. F. Newton. It happened April 2d, the day after the Kaiser signed the citation.

Jones and his observer Newton, both of the Fifty-second Squadron, had left their airdrome at noon on April 2d in an old R. E. plane, engaged on a low-flying bombing expedition. They did not see Richthofen until he was within fifty yards of them. They went down in flames and their plane exploded on the ground.

Newton, the observer, was highly praised, not by name, but by reference, on the afternoon of his death, when Richthofen sat over a late lunch at the squadron's advance quarters and unofficially related the story of the killing for the benefit of an unexpected guest, Lieutenant Lampel.

The scene was an abandoned English hut of "elephant iron," in which it was just possible to stand. Light poured in through the open doors at either end. Richthofen and his officers sat on all four sides of the long table that occupied the centre and most of the room. The ace, himself, was seated on a wooden box at the head of the table.

He was wearing a heavy gray woollen sweater, which, being open in front, exposed a leather vest beneath. He wore a pair of yellowish-brown riding breeches and leather puttees. Other members of Staffel 11, including Lieutenants Weiss, Wolff, and Gussmann, were wearing the coats of their gray service uniforms. None of them was wearing decorations, and not one of the coats was buttoned. Some of the flyers still had smears of oil on their cheeks. They were all young, and tingling from the last flight over the line.

Lampel, the visitor, met the famous ace for the first time. Lampel was shy in his presence.

"Take a seat with us," Manfred invited, with a wave of the hand toward a vacant place at the table. "Orderly, another place and some lunch. It's not much, but you are welcome to the hospitality of our English bungalow. Our hosts left so suddenly, they forgot to leave a full larder."

Lampel asked what success the squadron had in the air that day.

"I have just brought down my seventy-fifth enemy plane," Richthofen replied simply.

While Lampel babbled congratulations, Richthofen was looking silently out of the door. The pictures of the burning planes were again in his mind, refreshed by the hour-old memory of Jones and Newton's plunge earthward in fire.

"Queer," he began slowly, "but the last ten I shot down all burned. The one I got to-day also burned. I saw it quite well. At the beginning, it was only quite a small flame under the pilot's seat, but when the machine dived, the tail stood up in the air and I could see that the seat had been burned through.

"The flames kept on showing as the machine dashed down. It crashed on the ground with a terrible explosion—worse than I have ever witnessed before. It was a two-seater but its occupants defended themselves well."

"You almost touched him in the air," Gussmann interrupted, almost in a tone of reproof. "We all saw you fly so close to him that it seemed a collision was inevitable. You scared me stiff."

"Yes, it was close," Richthofen replied with a smile. "I had to come up quite close. I believe that observer, whoever he was, was a tough party—a first-class fighting man. He was a devil for courage and energy. I flew within five yards of him, until he had enough, and that in spite of the fact that I believe I had hit him before. Even to the very last moment, he kept shooting at me. The slightest mistake, and I should have rammed him in the air."

The tale was interrupted by the appearance of a slim young officer in the doorway of the hut. He held a telegram in his hand. It was the announcement that the Emperor had conferred on Richthofen the third-class order of the Red Eagle with Crown. There were boisterous congratulations, and Richthofen urged his comrades to do their best.

Under the spur of their leader's parting remarks, the flyers of the circus took the air that afternoon and brought down three more English planes. Weiss shot down his fourteenth and Wolff his fourth which completed a credit of 250 planes to Manfred's old original Staffel 11. This record was the highest of any Staffel in the German air service at that time. The third victim fell to another Staffel under Manfred's command, making its total record 100 victories.

While the celebrations of these victories were being held in the Staffel messrooms that night, the ace spent the evening in his own hut reading. Manfred had a nerve control that enabled him to suppress the after-tingle of his strenuous air work and concentrate his attention on good novels or scientific works. He favoured geography and astronomy.

The leader's new decoration was both a source of pride

and a subject of conversation for the victorious celebrants that night. The Flying Uhlan was the German air hero *par excellence* and, as such, their idol. Lubbert, one of the new flyers of Staffel 11, pointed out that it would seem only natural if Manfred, with all his strenuous work and the honours he had gained, had no place in his heart for friends and comradeship.

He declared that he had found the exact opposite true. His leader, he held, was both a kind superior and at the same time a loyal comrade to all his fellow officers. When off duty, he played hockey with them or frequently took a hand at bridge after dinner. Lubbert had gone to him with questions and worries, and always found him sympathetic.

As a teacher, he had quickly gained the confidence of his pupils, but he demanded eagerness, enthusiasm, and application in return. He seldom lost his patience over stupid questions, and always had complete control of his temper. His strictness was directed principally in the selection of his pilots. He took all beginners under his close observation, and, if convinced that the applicant was not morally or technically qualified to fight in his squadron, he transferred him to some other unit. He judged his pilots upon their capabilities, and not according to his personal likes or dislikes.

Not only the officers but the enlisted men and mechanics of the squadron felt that these characteristics of their leader were responsible for making him the cool, capable, thinking killing machine he became in an air fight. They believed he had all the qualities necessary to an air fighter: to fly well, to shoot well, to see everything, to keep one's nerve and to be plucky. "Slow but sure" was the motto attributed to him, and he was quoted as saying, "Better shoot down one plane less than to be shot down one's self, because then one can be of no more use to one's country."

The battle of the Avre took place on April 4th in the area between the rivers Avre and Somme. Richthofen directed the air fighting of his Staffels on the 3d, 4th, and 5th, and engaged in several combats, but did not register another kill until the afternoon of the 6th.

From his report and all available records, it appears that the war bird he killed that day was Sydney Philip Smith, twenty-two years old, a captain and fighting pilot of the Forty-sixth Squadron, Royal Air Force, and a flyer whose skill and intrepidity were the pride of his squadron mates. As an airman, he had fought and bombed everything that the enemy had at the front, on the ground or in the air, and had missed only a personal encounter with the Red Knight of Germany. He had inflicted casualties to German observation, bombing, and fighting planes, had attacked supply trains and troop columns on the ground, and had sent German balloons down in flames and German ammunition dumps up in smoke. He was a young, soft-spoken, pleasant, smiling, fighting demon. He had flown almost daily in the fighting that preceded and accompanied the German ground offensive. A number of enemy planes, yet untotalled, were credited to him, and he had been cited for a D. S. O. He "got" his last man on April 2d, the same day that Manfred "got" Jones and Newton.

On April 6th Smith left his airdrome at 2:45 P. M., flying his Sopwith Camel single-seater with others to make another low patrol behind the enemy lines. The English air casualty lists on that day have inscribed behind his name "Last seen over Lamotte, shot down in flames." Richthofen's report and a letter to Smith's father from Lieutenant Donald G. Gold show that Smith was shot down in flames by Richthofen, who was leading five other members of Staffel 11—all using Fokker triplanes. Smith's body was never found.

The records indicate that Captain G. B. Moore, a six-foot-three Canadian who weighed more than two hundred pounds, followed Smith into Richthofen's list of victories on the very next day. Moore was one of the biggest men in the air service, and, curious to relate, he had had his greatest success in the smallest planes. He survived through all of the 1917 fighting by flying a small Nieuport with which his squadron, the First, was equipped at the time.

Although the German High Command acknowledged Richthofen's seventy-seventh victory, and his reports and the records indicate that the plane in question was piloted by Moore, the latter's friends who witnessed his death attribute the Canadian's end to a direct hit by an artillery shell.

Moore and his plane practically disappeared in the air at the moment, it would appear, when Richthofen was firing into him at the unusually long range of 200 yards. The plane was reduced in midair to such small parts that there was nothing left to salvage on the ground and nothing found of Moore to bury. One observer said the débris drifted downward almost like dust. Plane and pilot had disappeared in one sudden burst of smoke.

Careful analysis of Richthofen's report reveals no direct conflict with this theory of Moore's death. Although the ace claimed and received credit for the downing of this plane, he avoided the direct statement that it went down as a result of the fire he directed against it. It was Richthofen's method to deliver his death blows at much closer range, and he taught his disciples that long-range fire was a waste of ammunition.

In his next engagement, thirty-five minutes later, which was credited as his seventy-eighth victory, Richthofen again avoided stating that he had shot the plane down. He made the record truly as he saw the event—namely, that the plane "fell down" after he had obtained a favourable position in back of it several times. He specified that the machine was a Spad, and as there were no Spads among the English casualties that day, it is presumable that the occupant of the plane referred to escaped when it crashed to the ground behind the British lines.

Now came the calm before the storm—the last lull—the last gap in the killing record of the ace of German aces.

For thirteen days after his seventy-eighth credit, his balance with death was stationary. There was plenty of fighting, and he flew almost daily, but his new duties as squadron commander carried him to the highest altitudes, from which he could watch and direct the operations of his fighting Staffels below.

The battle of the Ancre, 1918, waged fiercely, with the Germans continuing their victorious advance on Villers-Bretonneux, in the direction of Amiens. The air fighting was intensive, and costly to the Germans. On April 12th, the English flyers succeeded in destroying forty German planes and driving twenty others down, as against the loss of twelve English planes.

Richthofen believed that the offensive was approaching a stall, during which he could go on leave. There were rumours that the High Command was going to order him back from the front and relieve him from combat flying. Manfred honestly did not want this, but he did cherish the idea of another hunting vacation, with his gun, on the trail of game in the peaceful forests of Germany, and, later, a visit to his mother. In the week before his death, he talked these matters over with his flying comrade Lieutenant Hans Joachin Wolff. Manfred wanted to shoot woodcock with him.

His final brace of human victories came in a hot three minutes of fighting on the late afternoon of the day before his death. In the first one, he killed Major R. Raymond Barker, M. C., and in the second and last, he captured Second Lieutenant D. E. Lewis. He shot down both of their planes in flames, and both of them landed behind the German lines.

A division in the German line in front of Villers-Bretonneux had called for protection from the low-flying English planes, which buzzed over it in swarms and peppered it with machine-gun fire. Richthofen and his squadron flew to its defence.

Major Barker, his first victim, was, like Richthofen, the commander of a fighting squadron composed of several flights. He had a long record in the air, where he had won his Military Cross. The German ace shot Major Barker down in flames during an engagement between six planes of Staffel 11 and a British squadron.

Manfred was in fine fettle, his speedy Fokker triplane, with red upper planes, red hood, red wheels, red tail, all red, responded to the controls like a thing of life. The fixed motor gave forth an even, throaty roar. The chambers of the twin Spandaus hungered for more of the feed belt.

Without following his first victim to the ground, he turned his guns on the nearest English plane and the result was that eighteen-year-old Second Lieutenant D. E. Lewis went down in flames as Richthofen's eightieth and last victim. Lewis survived the warm descent with blisters and bruises, and lived to describe the fight in which Richthofen shot down his last official victim.

On the evening of the 20th April, twelve of us left the airdrome on an offensive patrol led by Captain Douglas Bell of my flight (C flight) although the C. O. Major Raymond Barker was with us. The day had been a stormy one, with intermittent squalls, and there were still heavy clouds in the sky when we reached the German lines.

Knowing that the German anti-aircraft guns would have the range of the clouds, Bell thought it advisable to rise above them. In carrying this out, we lost touch, in the clouds, with the other flight, and continued the patrol six strong.

About four miles over the German lines, we met approximately fifteen German triplanes, which endeavoured to attack us from behind, but Bell frustrated this attempt by turning to meet them, so the fight started with the two patrols firing at each other head on. When the Germans came closer, we knew we had met Richthofen's circus—the machines of his squadron were always brilliantly coloured.

A few seconds after the fight began, Major Barker's petrol tank was hit by an incendiary bullet which caused the tank to explode and shatter his machine. Bits of his machine were still reaching the ground when I was shot down.

I was attacking a bright blue machine, which was on a level with me, and was just about to finish this adversary off when I heard the rat-tat-tat of machine guns coming from behind me and saw the splintering of struts just above my head.

I left my man and wheeled quickly to find that I was face to face with the renowned Richthofen. My machine was a Sopwith Camel (F.)—this before I forget. The baron always flew a bright red machine, that is how I knew it was he.

I twisted and turned in the endeavour to avoid his line of fire, but he was too experienced a fighter, and only once did I manage to have him at a disadvantage, and then only for a few seconds, but in those few ticks of a clock I shot a number of bullets into his machine and thought I would have the honour of bringing him down, but in a trice the positions were reversed and he had set my emergency petrol tank alight, and I was hurtling earthward in flames.

I hit the ground about four miles N. E. of Villers-Brettoneux at a speed of sixty miles an hour, was thrown clear of my machine and, except for minor burns, was unhurt.

About fifty yards from where I was, Major Barker's machine was burning fiercely, so I staggered over to him to see if it were possible to pull him out, but was beaten back by the flames.

From the seat to the tail of my plane, there was not a stitch of fabric left, it having been burned away.

The following articles were hit by Richthofen's bullets: the compass, which was directly in front of my face, my goggles where the elastic joined the frame of the glass—these went over the side—the elbow of my coat, and one bullet through the leg of my trousers.

The rest of my flight was saved from annihilation by the timely arrival of a squadron of S. E. 5's. Richthofen came down to within one hundred feet of the ground and waved to me.

Richthofen's jubilant wave of the hand to his last captive included also a column of German infantry, which cheered the well-known all-red triplane and its famous pilot. He returned to the flying field in a happy mood. Safely landed, he jumped spryly from the cockpit of *"le petit rouge"* without the assistance of the smiling riggers and mechanics who surrounded the machine.

"Gad—eighty—that is really a decent number," he said joyously, at the same time clapping his hands and rubbing them together in a gesture of complete self-satisfaction.

His comrades of the flight congratulated him. Wolff had missed the plane he had picked out for attack, but Weiss had sent one down in flames and raised his own score to eighteen. They clapped one another on the back with joy. Here was youth, daring youth, tingling with the joy of life and the wine of victory.

In the messroom, they lifted their cups and toasted their leader, their master and teacher, their idol and their comrade. Manfred's boyish, smiling eyes reflected the joy he felt, not only in the happiness about him, but in the pride of his accomplishment.

Yes—eighty was, in fact, a real number—a fat, well-rounded-out figure. It was emphatic and solid, ample and generous. It even sounded better than eighty-one, which had something accidental about it. Yes, eighty seemed like a goal that had been designated and gained. It was momentous, even, well balanced, and carried an air of finality. With this feeling of complacency, Manfred went to bed on the last night of his life.

On the morning of April 21, 1918, two young men rolled

out of their wartime bunks in France and took a look at the weather.

The two bunks were about twenty miles apart, but across that twenty miles thousands of men comprising battling units of two enormous military forces were engaged in death grips.

One of the young men was a Canadian. He was twenty-four years old and a war bird of the Royal Air Force. He awoke with a sick stomach and shattered nerves. He had been living for the past month mainly on brandy and milk and fighting in the air daily on that diet. He was almost all in.

His name was Roy Brown.

The other man was twenty-five-year-old Baron Manfred von Richthofen, the Red Knight of Germany and the Kaiser's deadliest ace.

His eyes were clear, his nerves were steady; he both ate and slept well. He felt fine. Brown and Richthofen had never met, or, if they had met, neither one of them knew it. Richthofen had never heard of Brown, but Brown had heard a lot about Richthofen.

Fate knew the life and record of both, and destiny had designated noon of that day for their fatal contact. Brown was due to kill Richthofen at midday over the little village of Sailly-le-Sec, in the valley of the Somme.

It seems there was a war on.

It had been going on for almost four years. It had yanked Richthofen out of his barracks in Silesia and sent him riding across the Russian frontier with his patrol of Uhlans, and later had put him into the air to kill, maim, and capture scores of his country's enemies.

It had carried Roy Brown from his home in Toronto at the age of twenty to the Wrights' flying school at Dayton, Ohio, there to study aviation at his own expense and risk. He wanted to fly and fight for his country, and he learned the first rudiments of how to do it in the United States of America, which at the time was not in the war.

With this American training, he gained his commission as a flight sub-lieutenant in the British Royal Navy on September 1, 1915, and in December of that year sailed from New York for England. He first felt the dangers of flying at Chingford, where, while undergoing combat training, he crashed to the ground and fractured a bone in his spine. It kept him in hospital until the beginning of 1917.

For the rest of that year and until the first of April, 1918, he flew with the Royal Navy Air Squadron No. 9, which was assigned to land duty in France. His unit patrolled the Belgian coast and escorted bombing raids far behind the

German lines. The squadron also did photographic and reconnaissance work and offensive patrols over the lines as far south as the British area extended.

Officially, he was credited with having shot down twelve German planes, but his flying comrades believed that this figure did not approach the actual number of enemy machines that were sent to destruction under his guns. He had won his Distinguished Service Cross in the air.

He was known for the modesty of the reports he made concerning his combats in the air. He had both disbelief in and dislike for the flyers who made victory claims after every engagement. He knew how difficult it was to obtain corroboration. He knew that many flyers actually discredited their good work by telling tall stories. Some of his successful engagements only reached his credit list because they were reported by other observers.

On the first day of the month in which he was to kill Richthofen, Brown was raised to the rank of captain and flight commander in the newly formed Royal Air Force, which combined the flying services of the army and the navy. With a number of other former navy pilots, he was assigned to Squadron 209.

His physical condition was bad. Fourteen months of the strain and uncertainty of constant air fighting—more than a year of hairbreadth and hair-raising escapes from death—long days and longer nights in the shell-torn war zone, with ears, eyes, and sensibilities shocked by recurrent concussions of high explosive—these, plus irregular hours and diet, exposure to inclement weather and the daily spectacle of death, suffering, and destruction had left an indelible stamp upon the brain, bone, and flesh of this war bird whose youth had been one of peace and tranquillity with never a thought of war.

His nervous system was disorganized, and his stomach was in revolt. He should have been in hospital or some convalescent rest camp back home in Canada.

No chance for leave for any Allied soldier, outside of an actual casualty, those hot days of April, 1918, with the German hordes still pushing down on Amiens. Everybody's shoulder was needed at the wheel—every active human body was needed to fill the gap—even sick men.

When Brown was not in the air, he was in bed, soothing the jumpy nerves, doping the rebellious stomach, and pegging himself with brandy and milk for nourishment. Then up again, twice a day, into the flying boots and togs, and into the air on the regular patrol.

Squadron 209 kept two dates every day with the Richthofen circus. Morning and afternoon, they bumped into the Flying Baron's aggregation of gaily decorated Fokker triplanes and Albatross scouts, numbering anywhere from twenty to fifty planes, and flying in various formations under a central command. Richthofen had developed mass manœuvres for the air, and the British had been forced once more to follow his lead.

The strategy of these manœuvres prevailed until the opposing air forces came into range of one another's weapons, after which the engagement became a rough-and-tumble affair in three dimensions. This was the "dog-fight" in which the man you got seldom saw you and you seldom saw the one who got you.

The fighting planes could be offensive only in the direction in which they flew; from every other angle they were vulnerable to attack. Shooting one's adversary in the back or from any undefended angle was perforce within the ethics of air fighting.

For several weeks previous to the morning of April 21st, Brown had been engaged in a couple of dog-fights a day with various units under Richthofen's command. He had singled out a Fokker triplane with a pale green fuselage and lavender wings, and each day he and this machine had emerged from the dog-fight together, each circling and whirling, trying to get on the other's tail. Brown's cherry-nosed Sopwith Camel and the unknown German pilots lavender-winged "tripe" spun out miles of tail chasing, without either opponent gaining the fatal position over the other.

One of Brown's comrades, the Canadian ace, Lieutenant Colonel W. A. Bishop, V. C., best described the whirl of the dog-fight in the following words: "You fly round and round in cyclonic circles, here a flash of the Hun machines, and then a flash of silver as my squadron commander would whizz by. All the time I would be in the same mix-up myself, every now and then finding a red machine in front of me and getting in a round or two of quick shots. There was no need to hesitate about firing when the right colour flitted by your nose. Firing one moment, you would have to concentrate all your mind and muscle the next in doing a quick turn to avoid a collision. Then your gun jams and you have to zoom up and fuss with it to put it right."

Brown's squadron, which was under the command of Major C. H. Butler, D. S. C., was located at Bertangles and was coöperating with the British Fourth Army on the Amiens front.

Richthofen's circus had its principal airdrome just east of the little village of Cappy. Manfred had slept there the night before, his ears tingling with the congratulations of his flyers upon his eightieth victory of the previous day.

In addition to this exultation, he felt particularly happy over the prospect of leave and game hunting in the Black Forest. This leave was to become effective on the 24th, and he and Lieutenant Hans Joachin Wolff had planned to spend it together. They hoped to be able to fly their machines back to Freiburg or to Speyer, but, in the event of bad weather, they had agreed to use the railroad and had purchased tickets for this purpose.

After a light breakfast, the German ace stepped out of his quarters, in front of which a regimental band was playing. It had been sent to the airdrome by a near-by division commander, who offered this serenade with his congratulations upon the eightieth victory.

Richthofen did not like the music. He said it was too loud. With Wolff, he walked away from the band, and together they went to the hangars where mechanics were putting the finishing touches on his plane.

The weather was cold, but there was just the touch of spring in the air. Richthofen noticed that the wind was from the east. This was not so good. German air tactics on the western front had long been devised to take advantage of their westerly winds which prevailed most of the time. It meant that a disabled German plane limping home had the advantage of the wind behind it. It constituted even a greater disadvantage to the British airmen, because, with most of the fighting over the German side, a disabled Britisher had to fight against the west wind when he started back for his own lines.

At the door of the hangar that housed his Fokker triplane, Richthofen stopped to play with a puppy. Someone with a camera recorded this act. It was the last photograph taken of him in life. In the air service, this snapshot has been sufficient to reinforce the superstition, long held among German flying men, that it is bad luck to be photographed just before departing for a fight.

A sergeant from among the mechanics came forward with a postcard addressed to his son back in Germany. He had asked Manfred to sign it for him.

"What's the matter? Do you think I won't return?" the ace inquired with a smile, as he signed his name for the last time.

Staffel 11 left the ground at about 11:30 A.M. German time, which corresponds with the English hour of 10:30. It flew in two groups of five planes each.

Manfred led the first group, which included his cousin Lieutenant von Richthofen, who, as a beginner, had been warned to take no chances but carefully to observe the tactics of the Staffel veterans and learn exactly how to kill without getting killed. Lieutenant Karjus, Lieutenant Wolff, and Sergeant Major Scholz made up the remainder of the group or chain. Staffel 5, also under Richthofen's command, had taken the air at the same time. They flew west toward the front.

Brown's squadron, composed of three flights of five planes each, had taken the air from Bertangles flying field at almost the same hour. The first flight flew in a close V-shaped formation, with Major Butler leading, two planes slightly behind him and at each side, and two others still farther apart and above and behind them.

Flanking the leading flight on the right, but in the same formation, was Captain Brown's flight, he being second in command. A similar unit of five planes flanked the Major's group on the left. This was the squadron's air formation for battle. It was out for trouble.

Up and down the front it flew, taking a methodical patrol beat over the lines which ran north and south. Flying in wide arcs, the squadron gradually gained an altitude of 15,000 feet. The visibility was fair, with few clouds, but Brown soon noticed that Major Butler and five planes of the leading flight were not in sight.

Upon this development, the young Canadian assumed command of the two remaining flights and signalled for the flight on the left to take up position behind and above him. With this formation, he headed eastward.

Two miles below Brown, a couple of slow-flying reconnaissance planes were taking photographs. They were old R. E. 8's, belonging to No. 3 Australian Squadron. They were flying at about seven-thousand feet, and their job was to train their cameras on the German lines around the village of Hamel.

A daring quartette of Australian youngsters manned these antiquated machines. S. G. Garrett, a former architect from Melbourne, handled the stick in one plane, with A. V. Barrow, a former salesman, operating the cameras. T. L. Simpson, an electrical engineer from Hamilton, Australia, flew the second machine, with E. C. Hanks, a Sydney surveyor, manning the rear machine gun. They were all lieutenants, but Simpson's expert faculty with the flying controls had won for him the Distinguished Flying Cross.

These were the essential human elements of the impending battle—Richthofen flying west—Brown flying east—the Australians' observation planes flying two miles lower, and all of them converging approximately over the village of Hamel.

The engagement opened when four Fokker triplanes started down to get the "cold meat" represented by the old R. E.'s. Simpson and Banks were first in their path.

Banks jumped from his camera sights and got into action with the rear machine gun. Simpson gave the old R. E. her full throttle and manœuvred for the best defensive position. While the rear Lewis gun was spitting out the last of two hundred rounds of lead, Simpson drove the machine into a cloud, seeking cover.

The Fokker "tripes" continued their swoop, training their Spandaus now on Garrett and Barrow. While Garrett dived and wheeled the R. E. to avoid the direct lines of fire from the attackers, Barrow kept a steady stream of lead from the after cockpit. The fight was uneven. The two old-fashioned observation planes were no match for the fast German scouts.

Suddenly, the English anti-aircraft artillery came to bat with a call for help. "Archie" shells bursting below him called Brown's attention to the plight of the Australian observation planes. Looking down, he saw them being savagely engaged by the three or four "tripes."

A kick on the rudder turned Brown's Camel on its side and brought to his vision for the first time that morning, the sight of the enemy he was out to kill. Richthofen's swarm of Fokkers was diving on the same planes. Brown saw the hard-pressed Australians giving the best possible account of themselves, but he realized that they could hold out but a few minutes against the superior numbers and fighting strength then descending upon them like an avalanche.

While he watched the fight more than two miles below—he estimated the engagement to be at 3,000 feet altitude—his mind, trained to the mathematical formula of flying formations, quickly reviewed the situation.

His first duty was to get enemy planes, but equally important was the requirement that he exercise every precaution to get his men back safely. Up to this time, both of his records in these directions were clear. He had shot down more than his share of planes, and he had never lost a member of his flight in enemy territory. He wanted to keep the record.

If he went to the assistance of the two Australian planes, he would be throwing his own formation into an uneven engagement, in which he was outnumbered more than two to one by the enemy organization that was the pick of the German air force. Brown knew Richthofen, his flyers, and his methods well enough to appreciate their fighting worth. If he did not go down into the *mêlée,* the observation planes would be lost.

His consideration of the problem was only momentary. He waggled the wings of his plane, the signal for the others to follow him. The next second, he pushed forward on the stick, stood the Camel on her nose, and dove straight for the combat, his plane splitting the air with the combined speed of a full-out motor and the acceleration of gravity.

Seven cherry-nosed Camels followed on the two-mile descent. Neither opportunity nor necessity for orders to the others. All knew they were to drive the attacking Fokkers off the flanks of the hard-pressed R. E.'s, who were still holding out by skill and luck. After that, it was to get as many of the enemy as possible and then get home.

This final objective was definite and specific. British air losses had been so severe that conservative orders had been issued to hold the remainder of the fighting air strength in being until new flyers could be trained.

Especially had these orders been given that day to one of Brown's men, who, like Richthofen's cousin in the opposing force, was a beginner. He was Lieutenant W. R. May of Melbourne, Australia. This was the morning of his baptism of fire in the air. He operated under instructions that forbade him under any circumstances to enter a general dog-fight. Without the experience of those that flew with him, he would have been "easy meat" for an enemy plane, if not a collision menace to his comrades.

He had been told to keep out of the *mêlée,* to pick out a single isolated plane and put it down if he could; if not, then to play with it until he could break away, and then to streak for home. Pilots on their maiden flights had had the habit of trying to do too much, and too many had been lost.

With the wind screaming through every strut and bracing wire, Brown pulled his phalanx out of the dive a bare thousand feet above the Fokker R. E. engagement. The R. E.'s were still aloft, but now additional Fokkers and Albatrosses appeared, giving the planes of the Maltese cross a hurriedly estimated strength of twenty-two.

With guns roaring and motors wide open, the eight Camels plunged into the *mêlée.* There was no order of battle—only thirty racing engines of destruction rolling, diving, turning, circling, banking, and firing bursts of bullets each time an opponent flashed across the sights of their guns.

The R. E.'s were saved—diving with all speed, they pulled out of the fight, leaving their assailants to deal with the new and more competent forces that now attacked them. In the *mêlée* that followed, all of the planes lost height and position, and, in the grip of the east wind, the combat swung slowly back toward the actual ground-battle line, the contestants getting lower and lower each minute.

Infantrymen in both the British and German front-line

trenches lifted their mud-stained, helmet-framed faces toward the sky to watch this battle royal of the clouds.

On the great natural grand stand of the Morlancourt ridge, Australian "diggers" and gunners stood in their pits and watched the ferocious, quarterless tourney of death taking place hardly a thousand feet above their heads. So close were the planes together, so swiftly did the individual units of this flying cloud of human gnats dart in and out on trails of fire, that friend or foe could not always be distinguished from the ground.

Manfred von Richthofen was in the midst of the fight, and it was to be his last. He had led his Staffel to the attack over Hamel as soon as he had sighted the descent of Brown's cerise-nosed Camels on the assailants of the struggling R. E.'s.

Apart from us five, there was Staffel No. 5, not far from us over Sailly-le-Sec [Lieutenant Wolff explained three days later in a letter to Lothar von Richthofen]. Above us were more Sopwith Camels, seven in all, but they partly attacked No. 5 Staffel, and some remained high in the air.

One or two, however, came down on us. We started to fight immediately. During the fight, I saw the captain several times not far off but as yet I had seen him bring down no plane.

Of our special group, only Lieutenant Karjus was with me. Scholz was fighting somewhere over Sailly-le-Sec, and Lieutenant von Richthofen was, as a beginner, not quite up to the affair.

While I and Karjus are fighting two or three Camels, I see that the captain's red machine is engaging a Camel which, apparently hit, drops down and then retreats to the west. This took place on the other side of Hamel.

We had a violent east wind, and most probably the captain had forgotten this fact. As soon as I had more freedom in the fight, I took good aim and brought down my Camel. While it was dashing down, I looked for the captain and spotted him in a very low height somewhere over the Somme and not far from Corbie. He was still pursuing the Camel.

I shook my head involuntarily and wondered why the captain was following a machine so far behind the enemy lines. Just as I am looking to see where my victim is going to crash on the ground, I hear machine-gun fire behind me. A new Camel is attacking me. He puts twenty holes into my plane.

After getting rid of him, I look for the captain, but the only one I can see is Karjus. It was then I felt the first forebodings of disaster, because I ought to have seen him, provided all had gone well. We flew in circles, were attacked once by an Englishman whom we chased as far as Corbie, but of the captain we saw nothing whatever. We returned, anxious and nervous.

Somewhere, indefinitely, in the dog-fight, Roy Brown had

spent the speediest and most exciting ten minutes of his life. Flying automatically, he concentrated on the triple problem of avoiding collision, putting his own bullets where they would count, and at the same time protecting himself and his plane from opponents equally intent upon doing the same thing to him. The synchronized Spandaus and Vickers spat twin streams of lead at one another every time a target whizzed by the speeding gun sights.

Brown's men were also units in the dizzy whirl of the fight. Lieutenant Taylor sent an Albatross down in flames. Lieutenant Mackenzie knocked down a triplane out of control. A triplane with a blue tail took the death dive earthward after receiving a full burst of lead from the guns of Lieutenant F. J. W. Mellersh.

Two more "tripes" fastened themselves on the tail of Mellersh's Camel, and, to save himself from disaster, he spun down to within fifty feet of the ground, where he made a forced landing, happily within his own lines.

May, the baby of the squadron, had been in the jam also. He had picked out his lone plane on the edge of the *mêlée*, and it had gone down in flames. Then he remembered his other orders, and started a long dive for home.

Brown, coming out of a death waltz with two Fokkers, saw May's departure. He wished him luck and turned his attention to his other planes, planning to stay with them, unless May got into trouble.

Trouble lit on young Mr. May immediately. It came out of the sky from above and behind. It came with terrific speed in the form of an all-red Fokker triplane.

In the single cockpit sat a young man who in three years of war had earned the title of death's ablest ambassador. It was his proud boast that any flyer that got below and in front of him was a goner. That was the way he had killed one of England's greatest aces. That was the way he had shot down eighty planes: that was the way he had sent scores of men to death.

Richthofen was flying on May's tail. He had selected him for his next victim. It will never be known whether the Flying Uhlan recognized his selected prey as a beginner or not, but that is beside the case. In his string of victories, amateur victims counted just as much as a fallen master of the air. In the business of war one destroys as one can.

The nose of the all-red Fokker was within thirty yards of the fleeing Camel. May, looking over his shoulder, saw the approach of death. He saw the openwork air-cooling casings of the two Spandau barrels pointing down on him from above. Between the butt ends of the machine guns, the top of a leather helmeted head was just visible, down as far as a pair of dark glass goggles. This he could see through the blur of the invisible propeller. The eyes of Germany's deadliest marksman in the air peered through the glasses.

They were the eyes of a hunter—cool—calculating—nerveless—deep—true of sight. They were eyes that had sent countless men and beasts to destruction. They were eyes that knew how to direct death—eagle eyes, trained specially for the job. They were eyes that men feared and women loved.

The open cockpit of May's Camel came within the wire-crossed circle of Richthofen's sights. The pressure of a steady finger on the trigger—two jets of lead—short burst—spouted from the gun barrels. Bullets snapped through the air close by May's ears. Splinters flew from the struts before him.

He was defenseless from the rear. He could only shoot forward. Richthofen kept behind him. The young Australian resorted to every stunt he knew to get out of that deadly line of fire. He darted to one side—darted back—went into a zig-zag course, but his pursuer seemed able to foresee his every manœuvre. Richthofen kept the nose of the red Fokker trained on the body of the fuselage. The short bursts continued to rip out from the Spandaus.

May pulled on the stick—kicked over the rudder—pulled up hard—looped—side-slipped, and turned in the opposite direction. He came out of the evolution only to find the sputtering red-nosed Fokker still bearing down on him.

The speed of the pair was terrific. They were going down the wind with full motors and depressed planes. May was flying for life against an agent of death who seldom failed.

Roy Brown, from the height of 1,000 feet, had seen the frantic efforts of his fledgling to extricate himself from the talons of the pursuing eagle. He nosed the Camel down again at full speed toward the whirling duellists, who were now not more than two hundred feet off the ground.

Directly in front and beneath the pair were the trench positions and gun pits of the Thirty-third Australian Field Battery of the Fifth Division. They were located near the crest of the ridge, and the waiting gunners watched with bated breath the two whirling, twisting forms of Richthofen and his harassed quarry.

May, still zig-zagging, made for the crest of the ridge in a last desperate effort to land before those two streams of lead reached him. One bullet had already traversed his right arm. The pain was forgotten in the excitement of the moment.

The Australian gunners saw that the leading machine was British and that the one behind it was an all-red Fokker.

The machine gunner on the nearer flank of the battery aimed forward and upward at the writhing on-coming pair, but so close was Richthofen upon May's tail that the gunner dared not fire. The two planes were almost in line. Another Lewis gunner beyond the ridge sprayed a stream of lead upward. His range was 100 yards. He saw splinters flying from the woodwork of the German plane.

But Brown had arrived at the end of his dive. He came out of it slightly above and to the right of the darting Fokker. His last drum of ammunition was in place. His sights came to bear on the red machine. He pressed the trigger, and the ready Vickers spoke in deadly unison.

He watched the tracer bullets going to the red triplane from the right side. They hit the tail first. A slight pull on the stick —a fractional elevation of the Camel's nose, and the Canadian's line of fire started to tuck a seam up the body of the Fokker.

Richthofen, with his spurting Spandaus still trained on May, was unaware of this new attack from the rear.

Brown saw his tracers penetrate the side of the Fokker cockpit.

The Fokker wavered in midair—faltered—glided earthward.

The Red Knight of Germany went down.

Mellersh, from the Australian line beyond which he had landed, had witnessed the escape of May, and now he heard the roar of Brown's motor as it swooped overhead less than a hundred feet off the ground.

The red Fokker hit the uneven ground, but rolled on an even keel. It lost one undercarriage wheel and came to a stop right side up in a shell hole not fifty yards from where Mellersh stood. It was on the outskirts of the ruined village of Sailly-le-Sec, not far from Corbie.

The terrain on which the triplane rested was open and exposed to fire from the German side. The Australians in the near-by shell holes and gun pits waited for the occupant of the plane to emerge. Telescopes in the German position a quarter of a mile away also trained on the machine for the same purpose. But the occupant made no effort to get out.

An Australian with a rope wriggled forward across the field, taking advantage of the protection of every shell hole. Bullets from indirect machine-gun fire flipped mud from the lips of the craters. He reached the machine, attached the line to the undercarriage and returned to his gun pit by the same route.

Then, carefully, so as not to overturn the machine, it was drawn back to the shelter of a small rise in the ground. Mellersh and the gunners looked into the cockpit.

The German pilot was sitting bolt upright in his seat, strapped to the back. His hands still held the control stick between his knees. There was blood on that part of the face which shows below the strapped helmet and the broken goggles.

Blood came from the mouth, and the lower jaw sagged. The man was dead.

The form was unstrapped from the seat and laid on the ground. From the pockets of the unknown were removed a gold watch and some papers carrying the name and rank of the bearer.

"My God, it's Richthofen!" exclaimed Mellersh.

"Christ, they got the bloody baron!" an Australian in the group shouted over to the next trench. Men crawled forward to take a look at the body of the terror of the air.

"Gawd, wot a scrapper he was. Young, too—just a blooming nipper," said a corporal. "Here, give us a hand. Shall we take him into the dugout, sir? There'll be all hell dropping round here in a few minutes."

Under Lieutenant Mellersh's instruction, the body was carried with awed reverence to the closest underground shelter, where a medical officer unfastened the bloodstained leather jacket and opened the red-wet blue silk pajama coat found underneath. There was a bullet hole in both the right and the left breast.

The news travelled almost like electricity through the trenches along the front. Men in advanced position heard it and, like all rumours heard in the army, disbelieved it but passed it.

"Hey, digger, the Fifty-third, machine gunners say they have killed the circus master himself. And also, did you hear that they signed the Armistice last month?" ran the comment among the men.

Back over the signal wires went the official information to army and air headquarters. Brown and May landed at Bertangles, the former with only half of his cylinders working and fifty bullet holes in his plane. May's bullet-torn arm didn't prevent him from heartily thanking the man who had saved him from the all-red Fokker. Neither one of them knew that the pilot of the downed plane was Richthofen.

In a highly nervous state, Brown wrote the following report:

Date: April 21, 1918.
Time: 10:45 A.M.
Place: 62 D.". 2. (Map designation.)
Duty: High Offensive Patrol.
Altitude: 5,000 feet.
Engagement with red triplane.
Locality: Vaux sur Somme.
Fokker triplane, pure red wings with small black crosses.
Time: About 11 A.M.

(1) at 10:35 A.M. I observed two Albatrosses burst into flames and crash.

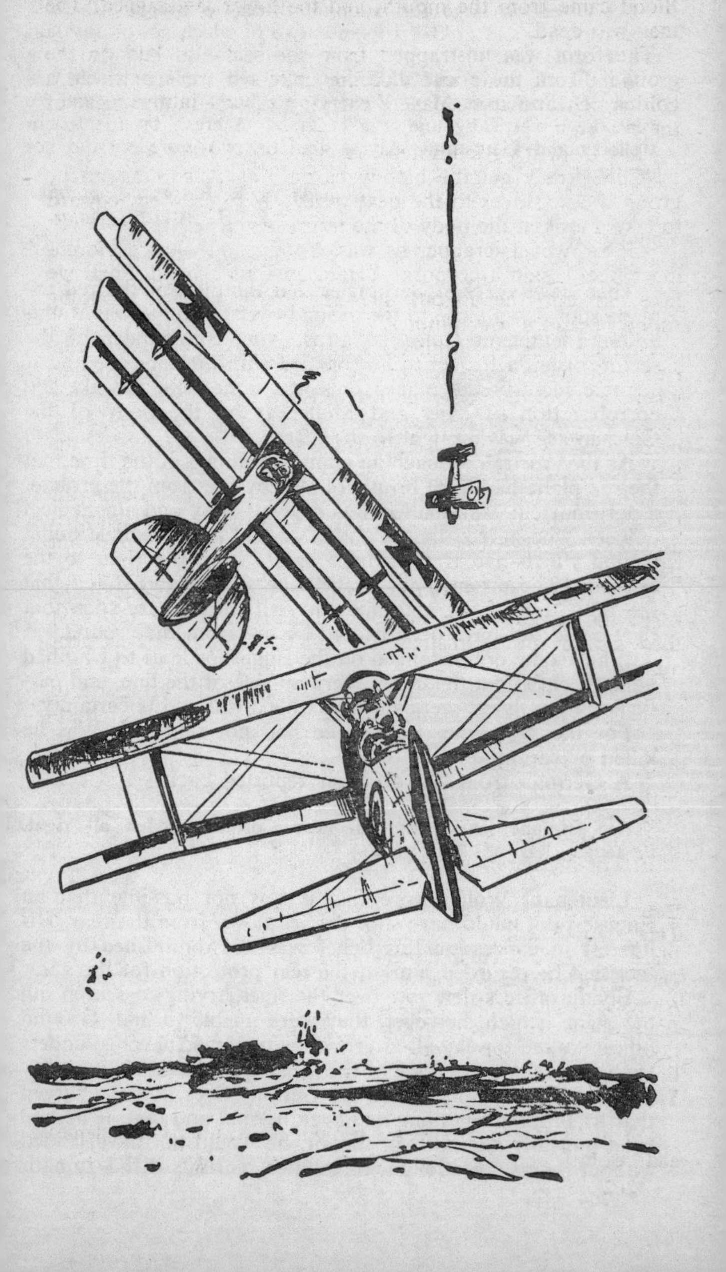

(2) Dived on large formation of fifteen to twenty Albatross scouts, D. 5's, and Fokker triplanes, two of which got on my tail, and I came out.

Went back again and dived on pure red triplane which was firing on Lieutenant May. I got a long burst into him, and he went down vertically and was observed to crash by Lieutenant Mellersh and Lieutenant May. I fired on two more but did not get them.

(Signed) A. R. Brown, *Captain.*
C. H. Butler, *Major.*

209 R. A. F.

Then news reached Bertangles that the pilot of the red triplane shot down close to the ground over the ridge was Richthofen. Lieutenant Colonel Cairns, wing commander of the sector, ordered Brown to go forward with him at once and if possible identify the plane. This was done with the aid and corroboration of May and Mellersh and the body of the German ace was brought to the rear.

As the Australian machine gunners claimed at the time that the red plane had been brought down by fire from the ground, a post-mortem examination was held by army and air medical officers, who agreed that Richthofen died from a single bullet wound which had traversed his breast from the right to the left side. The air medicos probed the wound and stated that the "situation of the entrance and exit wounds are such that they could not have been caused by fire from the ground."

While some doubt ranged on the English side as to who had killed Richthofen, the entire German side of the line, and particularly the flyers, were stunned with dread and uncertainty.

For the first time, Richthofen had not returned. Was he killed or captured?

A German front-line observer reported back:

Red triplane landed on hill near Corbie. Landed all right. Passenger has not left plane.

Lieutenant Wolff swore that it was not possible that an English pilot could have shot the ace down from the rear. His interest in expressing this belief was not diminished by the fact that he regarded himself the rear protection for the ace.

Flying officers flew low over the lines, trying to search out the plane, which, however, they were unable to find. Ground officers raked the sky all afternoon with powerful range finders trying to sight some trace of the missing triplane.

Ugly rumours ran behind the German lines. It was charged that Richthofen's landing had been normal and that, if he had been mortally wounded in the air, he would not have landed without a crash. Staffel 11, threatened reprisals if this rumour of Richthofen being killed on the ground was substantiated.

To the credit of those of Richthofen's comrades who survived, it must be noted that none of them believed the story of his death on the ground, but the wish is ever father to the belief that he was supreme and invincible in the air. It is a belief typical of the closest admirers of all the great aces who were killed in the war.

The last German hope that Richthofen had survived as a prisoner expired on the night of the 21st, when his death was announced through British official channels. On the following day, a pilot of Staffel 11 flew under special orders to a landing field on the Flanders front and personally told the father of the dead ace.

"May my son's spirit continue with you," were the words with which the soldier father received the news. They were also his message to the comrades who survived. Richthofen senior knew what war was.

Gloom hung over the squadron's airdrome at Cappy, and the hotheads among the flyers got together. Lieutenant Lowenhardt of Staffel 10 placed a daring and most ambitious plan before his comrades.

He proposed that he and two others should fly over the spot where Manfred's body rested. From aloft, they would signal all sector artillery on the German side to lay down a box barrage that would completely isolate the spot, and even though it was behind the English lines, he proposed with two others to land there in two two-seater planes, take the body of the fallen ace, and fly back with it to Germany.

"Sheer madness" was the comment that this proposal brought forth from German army headquarters, which emphatically forbade any attempted execution of the idea.

Meanwhile, Richthofen's body lay in state in one of the English tent hangars at Bertangles the following day. All English airmen who could be present viewed the remains and paid their respects in silent admiration for a brave foe.

But little remained of the all-red Fokker when souvenir hunters got through with it. Superstitious airmen took bits of fabric from it to carry with them on their hazardous daily jobs aloft. An omen of good luck surrounded the equipment of the man whose long success in the air had blazoned his record around the world.

British pilots who had been fighting the circus daily for the past month closely examined the dismantled twin Spandau machine guns with which Richthofen had sent so many of their comrades to death.

Roy Brown kept away from the tent, the guns, and the wreckage. Comrades came to his quarters to tell him he had done a bully fine job. He preferred not to talk about it.

While the body of the man he had killed lay in the tent, Brown led his flight over the line once more, and there engaged newly embittered units of the old circus, out for blood to avenge their fallen leader.

He had no recollection of ever returning from the patrol, and, for that matter, recalled but little of what followed for the next few weeks. He landed his Camel safely, but collapsed in the pilot's seat. He was removed to a hospital near Amiens, listed as a critical case suffering from stomach trouble accentuated by nervous strain. For three weeks, he was delirious.

In six weeks, he resumed duty as a combat instructor in England, where the Prince of Wales pinned an additional bar on his D. S. C. Several months later, he fainted in his machine in the air and crashed to earth. When he was lifted from the wreckage, he was pronounced dead, but the physicians managed to fan back a spark of life, which survived a number of skull fractures.

Richthofen was buried with full military honours on the afternoon of the day after his death. From the tent hangar, a plain black-stained wooden box, containing the remains, was carried on the shoulders of six fighting pilots of the Royal Air Force, who acted as pallbearers.

The coffin was placed in an open army tender and covered with floral tributes that came from all near-by air squadrons. Preceded by a guard of Australian infantrymen, who carried their rifles reversed, the cortège proceeded slowly down the road beside the airdrome. To the left of the road, the hum and roar of motors told of the arrival and departure of fighting planes to and from the front. The war continued as usual, but the busy war traffic on the road slowed up for once to the pace of a solemn funeral.

The procession arrived at the cemetery on the outskirts of Bertangles. There, at the foot of a tall poplar tree, an open grave awaited. It had been dug with entrenching tools by men who had been spending months digging trenches.

The black box was placed beside the grave while the pallbearers stood bareheaded at the foot. At one side were stationed two files of Anzacs, standing rigidly with bowed heads and the muzzles of their rifles grounded.

French children and old civilians beyond the years of military service attended, while Australians from the ranks ranged themselves behind the hedge fence on the road.

From the east, the rumble of the guns continued, as the English chaplain in white surplice repeated the words of the burial service of the Church of England. He recited a prayer for the dead, and a murmured amen came from the silent assemblage.

The casket was gently lowered into the grave by the pallbearers. The quiet was broken by a sharp order from a lieutenant. The double rank of Australians snapped to attention. Another order, and they raised their rifles. Three volleys, a parting salute, were fired over the remains of a respected fallen foe. The grave was filled.

On the following day, a British pilot flew low over Richthofen's old airdrome at Cappy. He threw down a metal container attached to a streamer. It fell not far from the hangars in front of which the German ace had stopped to pet the puppy mascot three days before.

The container bore a photograph of the funeral party firing its parting salute over the grave in Bertangles cemetery, and the following message:

TO THE GERMAN FLYING CORPS

Rittmeister Baron Manfred von Richthofen was killed in aërial combat on April 21, 1918. He was buried with full military honours.

From the BRITISH ROYAL AIR FORCE.

All the German war correspondents wrote long obituaries of the fallen ace. Dr. Max Osborn, in the *B. Z. am Mittag,* called upon his readers to revere forever the memory of Richthofen. War Correspondent Scheuermann, in the *Tägliche Rundschau,* related the German account of the last air-fight. All Germany mourned its hero.

In the big white house in Schweidnitz, Lothar, convalescing from his last wounds, read the telegrams and letters of condolence to his gray-haired mother. One was from Hans Wolff, who flew with Manfred on the last flight. Another was from Von Hoeppner, the commanding general of the air forces. Another came from General von der Martwitz to the dead airman's father. All of the letters praised Manfred von Richthofen in the highest terms, both as a soldier and as a man.

Frau Richthofen, with hands folded in the lap of her severely plain black dress, sat through the reading of the letters without a word. Her grief was inward and concealed. She knew the Spartan stuff that Germany expected of the mothers of its fighting men.

Her gaze was out of the window on the wet branches of the young firs and pines in the front grounds of the house. Manfred had played under them when he was young. Yes, it had happened, they said on April 21st. Why, that was only twelve days before his next birthday. On May 2d, he would be—would have been—twenty-six.

Seven months more, and the war was over—lost for

Germany. Her son had died in a vain cause. Another year, and her husband, Major Baron von Richthofen, slipped into the beyond. Two years more, and Lothar left for the same destination, by way of a flying accident.

There remained Bolko, the youngster of the family, whose age had kept him from the front, and one married daughter. They were with her seven years later when she went to Berlin to attend the final burial of her son.

It was the 19th of November, 1925, that Richthofen's body came back to Germany. After the exhumation at Bertangles, the remains were placed on a private train, which, as soon as it touched the German frontier, became the object of veneration all along the road to the capital.

Draped with black bunting, it passed through Karlsruhe, Darmstadt, Frankfurt, Kehl, and Baden. It steamed slowly through the stations, between crowds of silent bareheaded Germans. It arrived at Potsdam at night, where it was met by a torchlight procession which escorted the casket on a gun carriage to the Berlin church in which the body lay in state for two days.

There were two guards of honour. The dead soldier's helmet and sabre reposed on the new oaken casket at the foot of which rested the simple black wooden cross that had marked the grave in France. In front of the casket were the decorations of the ace. Floral tributes were banked high in the chapel.

Princes and princesses of the old empire that is gone followed common citizens in the crush of humanity that came to pay homage at the bier.

And not only Germans, but Americans and Britons attended the services. One of the most significant tributes was a large floral airplane propeller, carried to the church and placed before the casket by two Allied airmen who were members of the forces that Richthofen fought so successfully. They were Lieutenant John Clayton, formerly of the United States Army aviation corps, and Lieutenant John Hays, a Canadian pilot in the old Royal Air Force.

At the state funeral ceremonies on the second day, the casket was placed in front of the altar and at the foot of the Cross. Four of the old Spandau machine guns with which Richthofen had shot down so many of his victims were superimposed on the bier, at the foot of which a broken propeller projected through an enormous wreath.

Eighteen silent flying men, sombre knights of the air, in black leather helmets and jackets, stood the final guard. They were survivors and comrades of the Red Knight's war days. The church was packed with notables of the German state and army.

After the ceremony, the casket was carried by eight pall-bearers, all wearing the cross of the Pour le Mérite order, and placed on a gun carriage. Frau Richthofen left the church accompanied by Bolko.

Through long, stiff ranks of silent troops, a military band with muffled drums led the funeral cortège through the streets of Berlin to the cemetery. Throughout Germany, flags of the Republic hung at half mast and in many places, the old Imperial flag was flown. Pacifist organizations called the funeral a monarchist demonstration, but it could not be denied that it was the most largely attended funeral that had ever been held in the capital.

Before the horse-drawn gun carriage on which rested the casket, a steel-helmeted soldier carried a cushion bearing his decorations. It was a service similar to that which Richthofen himself had performed at the funeral of his old master and air-fight instructor, Boelcke. The most prominent fighting men of the old German Army, all wearers of the highest decorations for bravery, carried the floral pieces and flanked the gun carriage.

Frau Richthofen, in deep mourning but with the veil thrown back over her black bonnet, exposing a lined face that told the story of her sorrows, followed the casket on the arm of her son, and immediately behind her marched the old Field Marshal von Hindenburg, then President of the German Republic.

In Mercy cemetery, the body was lowered into the grave, while the military stood at the salute, civilians bared their heads, and the colours were dipped. All heads save those covered by the steel casques of the military were bared during the final prayer, and Hindenburg concluded the impressive rites by tossing the first handful of earth into the grave.

In October, 1926 Mother Richthofen stood again at the foot of her son's tomb in the presence of a number of German dignitaries, gathered this last time to unveil the stone that marks the final resting place of Germany's greatest war hero. The old war song of the Empire, *"Deutschland über alles,"* rose from five hundred intensely sincere German throats to the accompaniment of martial music. The simple ceremony ended with the firing of a volley across the grave. The mother took one last look at the heavy marble slab and returned to the old home in Silesia.

She lived there, a woman of dreams and hopes—a mother who had suffered and who could understand French, English, and American mothers who had suffered as she had. Her home is a museum of the relics of the life, the battles, and the death of the Red Knight of Germany—these and her memories were the treasures that remained.

Of all the honours and eulogies, praise and tributes that

Manfred earned in his remarkable war career, there is one she preferred above all the rest. She copied it in English in her quaint penmanship in her diary.

It was published in London, three days after Manfred's death, in the British aviation review, *Aëroplane*, a publication widely supported by British flying men. It reads:

Richthofen is dead.

All airmen will be pleased to hear that he has been put out of action, but there will be no one amongst them who will not regret the death of such a courageous nobleman.

Several days ago, a banquet was held in honour of one of our "aces." In answering the speech made in his honour, he toasted Richthofen, and there was no one who refused to join. Thus Englishmen honoured a brave enemy.

Both airmen are now dead; our celebrated pilot had expressed the hope that he and Richthofen would survive the war so as to exchange experiences in times of peace.

Anybody would have been proud to have killed Richthofen in action, but every member of the Royal Flying Corps would also have been proud to shake his hand had he fallen into captivity alive.

It is not true to say that Richthofen personally was credited with *all* planes shot down by his squadron. The German numbers are mostly exact and are, perhaps, sometimes exaggerated when strategic necessities make this advisable. It must be mentioned, however, that the Germans include army blimps [balloons] in the number of brought-down planes, but even so, Richthofen's victories would amount to seventy planes.

Richthofen was a brave man, a decent adversary, and a true nobleman.

May he rest in peace!

Beloved by his people, honoured by his foes, admired by the brave, the Red Knight of Germany, whose indomitable spirit made him the greatest individual killing force in the ranks of his country's fighters, earned well the epitaph that will be ever his in the hearts of his people.

He was a soldier.

Table of Richthofen's Victories and Final Defeat

1. Sept. 17, 1916, near Cambrai; Vickers 2 (i. e., two-seater); Second Lieutenant L. B. F. Morris, pilot, and Lieutenant T. Rees, observer, both died of wounds.
2. Sept. 23, 1916, on the Somme; Martinsyde 1 (i. e., one-seater); unidentified occupant*.
3. Sept. 30, 1916, on the Somme; Vickers 2; two unidentified occupants shot down in flames, killed*.
4. Date unknown, on the Somme; D. D. 2; two unidentified occupants*.
5. Oct. 16, 1916, on the Somme; B. E. 1; unidentified occupant*.
6. Oct. 16, 1916, on the Somme; B. E. 1; unidentified occupant*.
7. Nov. 2, 1916, on the Somme; Vickers 2; two unidentified occupants*.
8. Nov. 9, 1916, near Laignicourt; B. E. 2; Second Lieutenant J. G. Cameron, observer, died of wounds, Lieutenant G. F. Knight, pilot, made prisoner.
9. Nov. 20, 1916, on the Somme; Vickers 2; two unidentified occupants*.
10. Nov. 20, 1916, on the Somme; B. E. 1; unidentified occupant*.
11. Nov. 23, 1916, between Bapaume and Albert; Vickers 1; Major Lanoe George Hawker, killed.
12. Dec. 11, 1916, on the Somme; Vickers 1; unidentified occupant*.
13. Dec. 20, 1916, on the Somme; Vickers 1; unidentified occupant*.
14. Dec. 20, 1916, on the Somme; Vickers 1; unidentified occupant*.
15. Dec. 27, 1916, on the Somme; F. E. 2; two unidentified occupants*.
16. Jan. 4, 1917, on the Somme; Sopwith 2; two unidentified occupants*.
17. Jan. 23, 1917; S. W. of Lens; F. E. 1; Second Lieutenant John Hay, killed.

---

*Of Richthofen's 19 unidentified victims during this period, September 17, 1916, through January 4, 1917, 12 were killed and seven wounded or made prisoners of war.

18. Jan. 24, 1917, W. of Vimy; F. E. 2; Captain O. Grieg, pilot, and Second Lieutenant J. E. MacLenan, observer, both wounded and made prisoners.
19. Feb. 1, 1917, S. W. of Thelus; B. E. 2; Lieutenant P. W. Murray, pilot, and Lieutenant T. D. McRae, observer, both died of wounds on Feb. 2.
20. Feb. 14, 1917, Lens-Hulluck road, W. of Loos; B. E. 2; Lieutenant C. D. Bennet, pilot, wounded and made prisoner, and Second Lieutenant H. H. Croft, observer, killed.
21. Feb. 14, 1917, S. W. of Mazingarbe; B. E. 2; two unidentified occupants probably escaped uninjured behind the British lines.
22. Mar. 4, 1917, Acheville; Sopwith 2; Lieutenant H. J. Green, pilot, and Lieutenant William Reid, observer, both killed.
23. Mar. 4, 1917, N. of Loos; B. E. 2; Pilot Sergeant R. J. Moody, and Second Lieutenant E. E. Horn, observer, both killed.
24. Mar. 3 or 6, 1917, Souchez; B. E. 2; mistake: no English casualty records.
25. Mar. 9, 1917, between Roclincourt and Bailleul; De Haviland 1; Lieutenant A. J. Pearson, killed.
26. Mar. 11, 1917, S. of La Folie Forest, near Vimy; B. E. 2; Lieutenant E. Byrne, observer, and Second Lieutenant John Smith, pilot, both killed.
27. Mar. 17, 1917, Oppy; Vickers 2; Lieutenant A. E. Boultbee, pilot, and Air Mechanic F. King, observer, both killed.
28. Mar. 17, 1917, W. of Vimy; B. E. 2; Second Lieutenant G. M. Watt, pilot, and Sergeant F. A. Howlett, observer, both killed.
29. Mar. 21, 1917, N. of Neuville; B. E. 2; Pilot Sergeant S. H. Quicke, pilot, and Second Lieutenant W. S. Lindsay, observer, both killed.
30. Mar. 24, 1917, Givenchy; Spad 1; Lieutenant R. P. Baker, wounded and made prisoner.
31. Mar. 25, 1917, Tilley; Nieuport 1; Second Lieutenant C. G. Gilbert, made prisoner.
32. April 2, 1917, Farbus; B. E. 2; Lieutenant J. C. Powell, pilot, and Air Gunner P. Bunner, both killed.
33. April 2, 1917, Givenchy; Sopwith 2; Lieutenant Peter Warren, pilot, made prisoner, and Sergeant R. Dunn, observer, killed.
34. April 3, 1917, between Lens and Liévin; Vickers 2; Second Lieutenant D. P. McDonald, pilot, made prisoner, and Second Lieutenant J. I. M. O'Beirne, observer killed.
35. April 5, 1917, Lewards, S. W. of Douai; Bristol 2; Lieutenant A. M. Leckler, pilot, made prisoner, and Lieutenant H. D. K. George, gunner, killed.
36. April 5, 1917, Quincy; Bristol 2; Lieutenant H. T. Adams, pilot, and observer Lieutenant D. J. Stewart, gunner, both made prisoners.

37. April 7, 1917, Mercatel; Nieuport 1; Second Lieutenant G. O. Smart, killed.
38. April 8, 1917, near Farbus; Sopwith 2; Lieutenant J. S. Heagerty, pilot, wounded and made prisoner, and Lieutenant L. Health-Cantle, killed.
39. April 8, 1917, Vimy; B. E. 2; Second Lieutenant Kenneth L. Mackenzie, pilot, and Second Lieutenant George Everingham, observer, both killed.
40. April 11, 1917, Willerval; B. E. 2; Lieutenant E. C. E. Derwin and Air Mechanic H. Pierson, both wounded and escaped behind the British line.
41. April 13, 1917, between Vitry and Brebières; D. D. 2 or R. E. 2 (?); Captain James Stuart and Lieutenant M. H. Wood, both killed.
42. April 13, 1917, between Monchy and Feuchy; Vickers 2; two occupants and their fate unknown, downed behind the British lines.
43. April 13, 1917, Noyelle-Godault near Henin-Liétard; Vickers 2 or F. E. 2b (?); Second Lieutenant A. H. Bates, pilot, and Sergeant W. A. Barnes, observer, both killed.
44. April 14, 1917, S. of Bois Bernard; Nieuport 1; Lieutenant W. O. Russell, made prisoner.
45. April 16, 1917, between Bailleul and Cavrelle; B. E. 2; Lieutenant W. Green, pilot, wounded but escaped behind British lines, and Lieutenant C. E. Wilson, observer, killed.
46. April 22, 1917, near Laignicourt; Vickers 2; Lieutenant W. F. Fletcher, pilot, and Lieutenant W. Franklin, observer, both wounded but escaped behind the British lines.
47. April 23, 1917, Méricourt; B. E. 2; Sergeant Alfred Tollervey and Second Lieutenant E. A. Welch, both killed.
48. April 28, 1917, E. of Pelves; B. E. 2; Second Lieutenant F. J. Kirkham, observer, wounded and made prisoner, and Lieutenant Follett, pilot, killed.
49. April 29, 1917, swamps near Lecluse; Spad 1; Second Lieutenant R. Applin, killed.
50. April 29, 1917, S. W. of Inchy, Hill 90, near Pariville; F. E. 2b or Vickers 2 (?); Sergeant G. Stead and Air Mechanic Corporal Alfred Beebe, both killed.
51. April 29, 1917, near Roeux; B.E.D.D. 2; two unidentified occupants, both killed.
52. April 29, 1917, between Billy-Montigny and Sellaumines; Nieuport 1; Captain F. L. Barwell, killed.
53. June 18, 1917, Struywe House; R. E. 8. 2; Lieutenant R. W. Ellis, pilot, and Lieutenant H. C. Barlow, observer, both killed.
54. June 23, 1917, N. of Ypres; Spad 1; no Allied report of this.
55. June 26, 1917, between Keibergmelen and Lichtensteinlager; De Haviland D. D. 1; no Allied report of this.

56. June 25, 1917, near Le Bizet; R. E. 2; Lieutenant L. S. Bowman and Second Lieutenant J. E. Power Clutterbuck, both killed.
57. July 2, 1917, Deulemont; R. E. 2; Sergeant H. A. Whatley and Second Lieutenant F. G. B. Pascoe, both killed.
58. Aug. 16, 1917, place unknown; Nieuport 1; name and fate of occupant unknown.
59. Aug. 26, 1917, between Poelcapelle and Langemarck; Spad 1; Second Lieutenant C. P. William, killed.
60. Sept. 2, 1917, near Zonnebeke; R. E. 2; Second Lieutenant J. B. C. Madge, pilot, wounded and made prisoner, and Second Lieutenant W. Kember, killed.
61. Sept. 3, 1917, S. of Bousbecque; Sopwith 1; Lieutenant A. F. Bird, made prisoner.
62. Nov. 23, 1917, S. E. corner of Boulon Wood; D. H. 5. 1; Lieutenant A. Griggs, killed.
63. Nov. 30, 1917, near Moevres; S. E. 5. 1; Captain P. T. Townsend, killed.
64. Mar. 12, 1918, N. of Nauroy; Bristol Fighter 2; Second Lieutenant L. C. F. Clutterbuck, pilot, made prisoner, and Second Lieutenant H. J. Sparks, observer, wounded and made prisoner.
65. Mar. 13, 1918, between Gonnelieu and Banteux; Sopwith Camel 1; Second Lieutenant J. M. L. Millett, killed.
66. Mar. 18, 1918, above the Molain-Vaux road and near Audigny; Sopwith Camel 1; deputy flight commander W. G. Ivamy, made prisoner.
67. Mar. 24, 1918, Combles; S. E. 5. 1; Second Lieutenant Wilson Porter, Jr., killed.
68. Mar. 15, 1918, above Bapaume—Albert Road, near Contalmaison; Sopwith 1; Second Lieutenant Donald Cameron, killed.
69. Mar. 26, 1918, S. of Contalmaison; Sopwith 1; Second Lieutenant W. Knox, killed.
70. Mar. 26, 1918, N. E. of Albert; R. E. 2; Second Lieutenant Mat Leggat, observer, and Second Lieutenant V. J. Reading, pilot, both killed.
71. Mar. 27, 1918, River Ancre, N. E. of Aveleux; Sopwith 1; H. W. Ransom (officer), killed.
72. Mar. 27, 1918, near Foucaucourt; Bristol Fighter 2; Captain K. R. Kirkham, pilot, and Captain J. H. Hedley, observer, both made prisoners.
73. Mar. 27, 1918, N. of Chuignolles, S. of Bray-sur-Somme; Bristol Fighter 2; Captain H. R. Child, pilot, alone, killed.
74. Mar. 28, 1918, near Méricourt; Armstrong 2; Second Lieutenant J. B. Taylor and Second Lieutenant E. Betley, both killed.

75. April 2, 1918, N. E. of Moreiul; R. E. 2; Second Lieutenant E. D. Jones, pilot, and Second Lieutenant R. F. Newton, observer, both killed.
76. April 6, 1918, N. E. of Villers-Bretonneux, near Bois de Hamel; Sopwith Camel 1; Captain S. P. Smith, killed.
77. April 7, 1918, near Haugard; S. E. 5. 1, or Nieuport 1 (?); Captain G. B. Moore, killed.
78. April 7, 1918, N. of Villers-Bretonneux; Spad; no English record of this.
79. April 20, 1918, S. W. of Bois de Hamel; Sopwith Camel 1; Major R. R. Barker, killed.
80. April 20, 1918, N. E. of Villers-Bretonneux; Sopwith Camel 1; Second Lieutenant D. E. Lewis, made prisoner.

April 21, 1918, Sailly-le-Sec; Fokker triplane; Captain Baron Manfred von Richthofen, killed, by Captain Roy Brown in a Camel 1.